The Feng Shui Diaries

A Year in the Life of a Feng Shui Man

or

Which Way is Up?

Being the meanderings of a Feng Shui Man
in the Year of the Wood Rooster

BY

RICHARD ASHWORTH

Winchester, UK
Washington, USA)

First published by O Books, 2007
O Books is an imprint of John Hunt Publishing Ltd.,
The Bothy, Deershot Lodge, Park Lane, Ropley, Hants, SO24 0BE, UK
office1@o-books.net
www.o-books.net

Distribution in:

UK and Europe
Orca Book Services
orders@orcabookservices.co.uk
Tel: 01202 665432 Fax: 01202 666219 Int. code (44)

USA and Canada
NBN
custserv@nbnbooks.com
Tel: 1 800 462 6420 Fax: 1 800 338 4550

Australia and New Zealand
Brumby Books
sales@brumbybooks.com.au
Tel: 61 3 9761 5535 Fax: 61 3 9761 7095

Far East (offices in Singapore, Thailand, Hong Kong, Taiwan)
Pansing Distribution Pte Ltd
kemal@pansing.com
Tel: 65 6319 9939 Fax: 65 6462 5761

South Africa
Alternative Books
altbook@peterhyde.co.za
Tel: 021 447 5300 Fax: 021 447 1430

Text copyright Richard Ashworth 2007

Design: Stuart Davies

ISBN-13: 978 1 846940 17 0
ISBN-10: 1 846940 17 6

A CIP catalogue record for this book is available from the British Library.

Printed in the UK by Ashford Colour Press Ltd., Gosport, Hants.

The Feng Shui Diaries

A Year in the Life of a Feng Shui Man

or

Which Way is Up?

Being the meanderings of a Feng Shui Man
in the Year of the Wood Rooster

BY

RICHARD ASHWORTH

BOOKS

Winchester, UK
Washington, USA

DEDICATIONS

FIRST AND MOST IMPORTANTLY:

To my wife Sheila without whose endorsement I would never have embarked on this project and without whose love, encouragement and bottomless wisdom it would never have been worthwhile.

To my son Jaime for hints, encouragement and bons mots above and beyond the call of duty.

My children, Alex, Thom, Jess, Hen and Joey, my daughter-in-law Tracey and my grandchildren Gaby and Levi James for help and support and for containing my monomania.

TO THOSE WHO DID NOT MAKE IT THIS FAR:

Ruby, Rosemary, my father Bob Ashworth and my mother Barbara, Maurice and Pat Ellicott, Maria McKnight, Alan Butler, Timothy Tosswill and Doreen Tulloch.

OTHERS WITHOUT WHOM THIS MIGHT NEVER HAVE SEEN THE LIGHT OF DAY:

Janet Ashworth, Linda Lamb (and wee Georgie), Carlo-Amedeo Reyneri di Lagnasco, Derek Walters, April Crabtree, Cynthia GN Paige, Angie & Alan Briggs, Chuck & Lency Spezzano, Joe Gandolfo, Master Chan Kun Wah, Annie Waterhouse, Amelia Chow, Sasha Nathanson, Ron Smothermon, Helen McCreadie, Robert D'Aubigny, Adam Fronteras, Arielle Essex, Suzanne Corbie, Ann Marie Woodall, Michael Breen, Jeff Martin, Vernon Scannell, Geoff Helliwell, Jill Clark, Elisabeth Silvey, Ursula Monn, Peter Dunne, Michele Knight, Lillian Too, Johnni Javier, Clive Woods, Alvin Jordan, Nancy, Abe & Lily Furlong.

Illustrations by Jessica Ashworth.

CONTENTS

"Change the house, you change the person"

Before we start:
Explanation of obscure terms
for beginners

Real men of course don't read instructions and the true princess is disinclined to attempt anything too hard. So these ideas are all further clarified in the text. Meanwhile.....

Just what is feng shui exactly?

This is not a self-help book. At the end of it you will not effortlessly be able to create harmony within your own environment and I hope you will have more sense than to try. I trust this news is not too depressing.

Let me explain; most people know that mastery of any of the Oriental arts is a life study. No one unsectioned believes that they can become a merciless kung fu killing machine over a weekend. Feng shui is no different. Its principles and procedure have been passed down over millennia and they are complex. When I took to studying formally with a Master I was startled to realize just how demanding it was. After years of New Age workshops I had become used to simply sitting in the lotus posture and "receiving." As it turned out my feng shui studies were the most rigorous I had undertaken since university. Though paradoxically its roots are in the Tao which is almost impossible to comprehend via the mind, authentic feng shui is essentially an intellectual study with fixed principles and formulae.

These principles and formulae have been passed down in two

forms. One is a series of books: the *Classic of Burial*, the *Water Dragon Classic* and so on. The other is transmission by word of mouth from teacher to pupil down lineages. The Communist party has retrospectively legislated that lineages never existed but they are simply wrong. My own teacher's was at least several hundred years old. Totalitarians, whether they are Nazis or Church Fathers often believe they can demand changes in history because history does not fight back. But although the Communist party has bullied, tortured, killed and imprisoned practitioners of "superstition," it could no more order feng shui into non-existence than the Pope could order Galileo's conclusions unsound. Recently it appears to have given up trying.

I digress; my point is that feng shui is real and powerful and that to confuse it with a branch of flower-arranging to be mastered over a cup of tea is unrealistic. That is not to say that we are not all able to do all sorts of things intuitively, including balance energies. I know many people who do exactly this and their work is real and worthwhile.

My Chinese feng shui teacher was dismissive of intuition although he was a profoundly intuitive man himself. This rejection was based on his own apparent definition of intuition, which was something like: "fluffy thinking that flies in the face of the facts". You and I know that true intuition is the facility to *know for no good reason*. And it is quite reliable. But what he would say is that intuitive work is not feng shui.

When I came to feng shui in the early 90s I had already been in the world of woo-woo™ for more than a decade. I could easily believe two mutually inconsistent philosophies before breakfast. I was already able to feel what was *so* for a person or an environment.

As a long-time student of transformation, I had worked in the development of many ideas that have joined the body of knowledge known as Neuro Linguistic Programming and I had attended workshops and/or studied over a spectrum from Scientology to Guru Maharaji. In short I had been working this coal-face a long time.

There are many people who continue along these lines and make huge positive differences. But this I could do already. What I wanted was to master a physical, intellectual system. This involved rules, formulae and facts. Only once I had mastered what it actually was could I reinterpret it my way.

Which brings us finally to what was advertised: what exactly feng shui is.

Feng shui is the ancient Chinese art of chi (or energy) management. Generally it is thought of as a way to optimise the home environment but there is much more to it than this. About half of my work is surveying people's homes and offices to help bring their lives into line with their dreams. The other half includes drafting and interpreting ba zis (or personal feng shui) as well as calculating auspicious dates, compatibility and so on. I am happy to call all of the above feng shui.

For me feng shui is simply what it takes to make people happier than they were before I arrived. To this end and in line with ancient Chinese principles, I change décor and move furniture and I set up water features and all sorts of symbolic arrangements. I re-angle doors and I fiddle with mirrors. I place stones and insist on the demolition of walls. And I listen very closely to people. Because the main reason I move things is that they have meaning. Everything we see hear, touch and so on has meaning. I try to arrange things in such a way that an unhelpful meaning is replaced with a helpful one. Although different people attach different meaning to different things, feng shui provides me with a body of established meanings going back thousands of years. But paradoxically feng shui involves purely physical stuff that can be done to buildings to assist the people within them. And not all of it is symbolic in any recognisable way.

An example is *Grandmaster Yang's Double Mountain Upwards Strategy for the Relief of the Poor* which is some twelve hundred years old. This procedure which I use regularly, basically says that if you control the direction of the nearest and most powerful live water source, the fortune of the house changes. There are several accounts in these diaries that are essentially just that procedure in action.

So feng shui is at once both subjective and objective. It is both intellectual and spiritual, physical and subtle. It is something and nothing because it is, as I said, drawn from the Tao. It is both about fixed meanings and individual interpretation. The power of individual choices of meaning is that they can catch us by surprise.

For example, I was once fourth in a queue for a roadside café. At the front were two nuns placing their order. All at once the woman between me and them started shivering and muttering. She was clearly upset.

"Are you alright?" I asked and in response she put an index finger to her lip and shook her head rapidly.

Once the nuns had left with their bacon sandwiches and tea to go, she said: "Bloody nuns, I hate them. Give me the creeps."

"Perhaps you were burned at the stake in a previous incarnation?" I suggested.

"Perhaps *they* were," she said emphatically.

So what is chi exactly?

Chi is something like energy. Some say that chi has actual objective existence and certainly the trick is to treat it as if it did. I am not saying that it doesn't, simply that I aim to both respect feng shui as a model and act as if it were more than that. The key to paradox appears to be *not knowing,* which can be uncomfortable but seems to be a prerequisite for learning. How can we learn if we do not first admit ignorance? I'm sure I don't know.

Chi, whether it is there or not, is the building block of what I do. To quantify it is both crucial and impossible.

Some think of feng shui as a science and true Imperial feng shui is indeed very precise, involving minute measurement and orientation. But all schools of feng shui come up against the inevitability of imprecision which is why I am happy to call it art (rather than science) and make no claim to define anything "exactly" least of all the art itself.

When I am measuring the orientation of the back wall of a building to get a fix on its nature, neighbouring bricks will often be at different angles. Which of these defines the building? At times like this we go with our inner knowledge. But it remains important to be as precise as possible. Such a condition is commonly called paradox, a situation where two things can be true at once.

Here in the West we have been tyrannised for a century or so by *scientific* thinking. *Scientific* thinking insists that there are straight answers to every question. Paradox, being inexplicable, is inherently unscientific.

One of the fundamentals of scientific thinking is a medieval principle of formal logic called "The Law of Excluded Middle" which states that "Everything is itself and not another thing." This principle is very useful. If we are clear exactly what a thing is we can measure it, define it and make predictions about it. This is the thinking that has put men on the moon and brought us the microwave, the fridge freezer and the mobile phone. But the problem with the Law of Excluded Middle, in the words of Edmund Blackadder, is that it is bollocks. Everything is actually several things all at once.

This may seem a little tricky. How can a thing be more than itself? A good example may be the wooden African statuette that is on my window sill as I write. It is a lump of wood. But it is also an image of an African woman. It may too be a racist stereotype – she is statuesque and semi-clad and there are those who would find that offensive. And for all I know she may have some devotional significance. If all we count is what we can define, she is mere kindling.

When we concern ourselves with meaning, everything is clearly several things at once. The slogan "The future is Orange" is contentious only to competing telephone service providers except in Northern Ireland where it gains dangerous ambivalence. The penknife attached to your belt is a helpful tool on a campsite but at a football match it may land you with an Anti-Social Behaviour Order.

The process of drawing the appropriate meaning from circumstances is known as *divining* and on one level feng shui is simply divination. That is to say that a feng shui man can tell you a lot about yourself merely by looking at your house. Just as people are said to be like their dogs, so they are like their houses. There are those who can divine with tea leaves, Tarot Cards and runes or indeed with hair patterns. There is also the respected tradition of mían xiang which is divination by reading the face.

Where it differs from other forms of divination is that feng shui offers cures to correct whatever is wrong. If the part of the house that corresponds with the Eldest Daughter is weak we can shore it and her up. If the Youngest Daughter – who incidentally ought to be in the West – is missing we can reinstate her.

All over Britain and in some other regions of the world, I have observed rebalanced chi expressed as yin and yang, bring ease to homes that have been host to stuckness, discomfort, sadness and distress and indeed physical ailments. Equally I have assisted in the process of turning aspiration into success and abundance. I am not alone in this nor are my methods the only ones, I simply happen to be the author of these diaries.

Feng shui has, as I have said several times now, its roots in the Tao. What exactly is the Tao? Tao is a Chinese word meaning "way". The Tao is what we are referring to when we talk of "going with the flow" or "trusting the process" but Lao Tze who expressed this principle two and half thousand years ago was clear that "the Tao that can be named is not the Tao." We flounder generally when we attempt to pin it down. It may assist us to remember that the Tao is the grandfather of Zen, a term that is employed in the West to describe all sorts of whimsy. My own personal watchword is that I go with the flow unless I have a better idea – and *sometimes* I do. It's tricky stuff. The Tao is neither here nor there. And both.

So that's the Tao sorted, now what exactly are yin and yang?

Feng shui aims to manipulate chi for health, wealth and happiness. For this purpose, the feng shui master defines the chi itself as consisting of some combination of yin and yang. The nature of yin is darkness, damp, slower movement, cold, quiet, muted colours and subtlety; the essential female qualities. Yang is brighter, dry, more rapid, heat, noise, louder colours and clarity; the essential male qualities. Too much of either yin or yang is obviously not ideal. Too much heat makes for desert, too little for frozen waste. This heat can be metaphorical – standing for anger, loss or dry skin among other things. I am keen that people live neither in deserts nor refrigerators and helping them out of such jams seems worthwhile.

Yin and yang are further broken down into the *Five Elements*. These are fire, earth, metal, water and wood. Wood and Fire stand at the extreme of yang and earth and water at the extreme of yin but each has its yin and yang expression. Something that won't move is extremely earthy. A mountain is a good example. Something that won't stay put, like electricity, may be pretty much pure fire.

Generally we want neither to live on top of a mountain nor to be surrounded by pylons. Equally we don't want to be lonely but we don't want our homes to feel like Piccadilly Circus. These, though it may not be immediately obvious, are the same decisions.

Balancing these sorts of extreme is the task of the feng shui man. If I can balance their environment people are likely to be healthy, wealthy and wise. And if not, not.

Everything, it seems to me, is a choice. Some people are ill and some are unhappy. Using Chinese metaphors I present them with options; mostly better than what they've chosen to date. That is what I do and what these diaries are about. I hope it will all be clear by December.

THREE MORE THINGS

1. Some of the dialogue has been tidied up. My repartee is not invariably that snappy. But sometimes it reads better if I pretend it is. Indulge me.

2. No facts have been changed but sometimes chronology and emphasis have. Some cases have been joined up so what appears to be one person is in fact two while some single cases have been divided. In no case has clever editing been used to flatter me even when I have been tempted.

3. Because these diary entries cover the year 2004/2005, my comments about divining from the date *pillars* refer to that year. In the Chinese calendar, hours, days, months and years run in Cycles of 60. Consequently my comment on a month pillar is just as apposite (or not) when the same pillar governs a day or a year or an hour. So that aspect of these ramblings is valid at some point in any year, any month, or indeed any day. Watch out for them.

4. Most names have been changed to protect uh......me.

A WORD ABOUT THE ELEMENTS

It is hard to write at exactly the right level. Some will be confused already, others being told things for the *n*th time. I remember on the old *Rosanne* show, Rosanne Barr telling the very camp Martin Mull not to patronise her.

"I'm not patronising," he says, "I'm condescending."

On balance I'd sooner patronise than confuse. I hope that's alright.

The Five Elements

The Five Elements, wu xing, are only so-called because Europeans translating the Chinese texts found it convenient. In Europe we adopted this rendering largely because we were already using the term *element* for what the Greek natural philosophers believed were the ultimate components of the universe: earth, fire, wind and water. Blame Empedocles for this.

The Chinese Five Elements do not stand for the components of creation in the same way at all. They are more aptly called "movements" or "agents". Wood is not, according to classical feng shui, found in wooden furniture (which in the sense of it being low, square and brown is actually of the earth) but in the upward movement of plants. Yang wood is best exemplified by the upward thrust of tree trunks and yin wood by the relentless distribution of grass.

The real nature of the Chinese Five Elements is seen when they interact and in this sense they are best described as "agents". There are certain rules about this.

Rule One is *the cycle of production*: if a feng shui master finds too little wood in a location he can compensate for it with water which *produces* wood. This makes intuitive sense. No plant grows without water.

An example of too little wood is a dogmatic culture. A business with an autocratic management style is likely to be short of wood and can be helped with water. One manifestation of water is communication. In other words dialogue melts dogma. Which is pretty common-sense. What is not so straightforward perhaps is that we can literally paint a key piece of the environment blue (for water) and see the decision-making process change before our eyes. Physically, low levels of wood may coincide with bone weakness as well as premature ageing.

Similarly wood produces fire. Again this figures; fires are fuelled by wood.

Fire in turn produces earth in the sense that fire is the means by which nature turns everything back to dust.

Earth produces metal. Where else does metal ore originate but in the earth?

And finally metal produces water. That is to say that to make any use of metal we must melt and turn it into liquid.

As we have seen, when a space has too little wood the feng shui master may introduce more wood or he may introduce water to produce it. The same principle applies to each pair of elements but a shortage is only one of the imbalances the feng shui master is there to correct.

Excess of an element is another. Too much fire would tend to

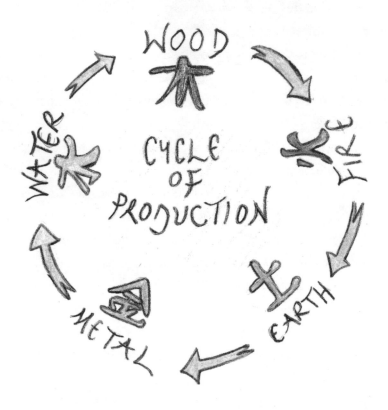

make for rash decisions and hurry. It might make for fire too!

Rule Two: a reverse procedure applies when we want to reduce an element. This is the *draining* cycle where one element reduces or weakens another.

Surplus earth often means stuckness, digestive, gynaecological and weight issues and inertia of all sorts and is relieved with metal which drains it. In a sense it drains by being produced. The same principle applies to the other elemental combinations; the draining cycle is simply the productive cycle reversed.

Rule Three concerns what is known as a *clash*. And yes, this does have something to do with Joe Strummer on which I will expand later. This is a distinct cycle in which wood clashes with earth, earth clashes with water, water with fire, fire with metal and metal with wood.

Each of these interactions are intuitively aggressive; wood invading earth, water putting out fire and so on.

What is the meaning of all this violence? It is very dynamic but not restful. Both elements are shaken up by it. But as a feng shui master said to me: "Nothing happens without a clash." It is the grit that produces the pearl, the shake up that brings change. And interestingly it is how the Chinese see the man/woman relationship.

A man clashes with a woman. And not the other way round. When a house is host to clashes there will be lot going on but it won't usually be comfortable.

So Produce, Drain, Clash, this is how the *agents* interact. Just as the whole of mathematics can be drawn from the eight theorems of Euclid so all that is truly feng shui can be derived from these rules. There are procedures that can with greater or lesser intention make big differences such as placing by an entrance a three toed toad loaded with Chinese coins and so on but such procedures are essentially Chinese folklore as opposed to feng shui. And yes I do use them; so go figure.

2005 THE YEAR OF THE WOODEN ROOSTER

Every year is overseen by one animal (known technically as a *branch*). By *overseen*, I mean that the nature of the year is reflected in that animal. The year covered by these diaries is a Rooster year. This means it is *metal*. Metal is precise and can be aggressive. At its heart is competition. Healthy metal speaks of healthy competition, unhealthy metal can be niggly, even warlike. These are the sort of words we can expect history to use to describe the events of this year.

Furthermore the Rooster is *yin* metal.

That the Rooster is yin (i.e broadly feminine) may come as a surprise since it is such a universal symbol of masculinity. Actually this goes some way to explaining the type of chi we associate with a Rooster year. The yang metal Monkey (of 2004) can be violent and the state of the world was consistent with that but it was violent in a straightforward way. The Rooster at its worst is more underhanded. Whether we can expect this sort of thing in 2005 or the Rooster at its best – fearlessly maintaining the highest standards and presiding over fair competition – depends largely on the *stem* attached to it.

Each *stem* belongs to one of the Five Elements which differentiates each animal from the other four variations. So the Rooster that relates to 2005 is a wood Rooster which is very different from the fire say, or metal rooster of 1957 and 1981 respectively. As I will elaborate, this is a volatile bird. Wood and metal are inherently conflicted as are fire and metal.

We join the Rooster year at its inception, dung gee or Midwinter, 21 December 2004. This the moment of maximum yin, is reckoned to be the beginning of the year by several schools of feng shui practice including my own.

The Rooster is a strutter, a universal symbol for a particular type of male pride. His demonstrations of power and ownership like any such demonstration are simply masks for insecurity. There is a Taoist principle that everything is its opposite, of which this is a good example. Who but the insecure need to trumpet their strength? What but the yin would be so yang?

Now I am not saying that anyone born in the years 1921,1933, 1945, 1957, 1969, 1981, 1993 and 2005 is a prig which would alienate around 8% of my readers. What I *am* saying is that those born in those years should recognise in themselves the sort of energy – or chi – I have described. So to some extent will anyone born in the month of the Rooster (September), the day of the Rooster (you'll need a Chinese calendar for this) or indeed the hour of the Rooster (late afternoon). What I am also saying is that this energy is prominent in the signature of the year. 2005 is not a modest or secure year.

Metal implies noise. One of the Rooster's jobs is to wake us up.* This year can be expected to feature warnings: concerning global warming, military over-confidence, famine or other extremes. They may be personal or general and they may or may not be heeded. This adds up to 2005 looking like a year of overreaching. Self-awareness will be at a premium.

---

* The Rooster that wakes the other Roosters incidentally is said to live on Taodu Mountain in the Southeast of China.

A note: My annual predictions are sent out in December each year; as of writing, 2005 is still available via my website.

The Month of the Fire Rat – bing tze – December 2004

The month we join 2005 is actually December 2004. Dung Gee or the Winter Solstice, is halfway through this month. Chinese months start around five days into ours – though this varies – because they are strictly solar while our own system is an odd hybrid of lunar and solar counting.

The Rat is broadly but not quite equivalent to December. Elementally the Rat is water and fire is attacked or *clashed* by water. So like the wood Rooster, the fire Rat is inherently conflicted. The Rat is said to have magical and prophetic powers so the Chinese are both suspicious and respectful of him although the character tze he borrows for the calendar is quite affectionate. It means something like "old boy".

The Rat character tze is at the beginnings of things and is used in certain sorts of ordering (as we might employ 'a' or a Roman 'I') often in conjunction with the wood stem chia.

Rat people are reckoned to be optimistic but illogical, cautious and contained, hospitable but not gregarious. They are plotters and planners and at their worst, manipulators.

A fire Rat then may be more sanguine and rather less cautious than other Rats. If you were born in a Rat year (1936, 1948, 1960, 1972, 1984 or 1996) the Rat month (December) the Rat Day or the Rat Hour (either side of midnight) some of this will resonate for you. But the important idea to take on is that it is the nature of this month.

For the purposes of prediction we treat the whole year as if its nature were decided on its first day. Together with the brashness of the wood Rooster, the fire Rat speaks of folly, a year of unnecessary risks.

The purpose of this sort of analysis is to set context so that we may make informed choices. Choice is the fundamental principle of reality. None of us are victims and we are as able to have a prosperous happy and useful year under a wooden Rooster even one initiated by a fire Rat, as any other year. Which is probably a good idea

Gung hei fat choi.

1.
SOLAR FORTNIGHT BEGINNING:
TUESDAY 21 DECEMBER 2004 20.33

Dung Gee: *Winter Solstice*

Month: bing tze **the Fire Rat**

Hour	Day	Month	Year
wood	wood	fire	wood
jia	jia	bing	yi
xu	xu	tze	yuw
dog	**dog**	**rat**	**rooster**

Dancer with Bruised Knees

I received a cheque from my old friend Hester last week.

In the '80s when I set out on this strange path, before I had even discovered Chinese metaphysics, I attended weekends and evenings with every new age teacher I could find. Not that there were many teachers out there in those days. Back then I always wanted to be the one telling instead of the one being told, not that I was unusual in that. I spent 1984-85 in an alternative community which had grown out of one of those seminars where they shouted at you and didn't let you out to the toilet. I learned a great deal there, some of which I had set out to learn. Frankly today I'd say that if you need to be locked in to achieve enlightenment you'd be better off waiting. But that was then and this is now.

Most of us who stuck at this path rather than taking a transfusion and returning to normality – which was always tempting – aspired to run our own trainings. We had learned something, we wanted to pass it on. Alert readers will detect a struggle with the ego here.

By the late 80s I saw that I was faced with a choice: be an absentee father/husband (it wouldn't be the first time) travel the world from hotel room to hotel room and gain rapid notoriety or stay home learning and growing and be present as my kids grew. I had by then five children, two of whom I had never neglected, and I had seen any number of other people's kids damaged by life with spiritually ambitious parents. I also incidentally had a relationship with a woman, my wife Sheila, to whom I would willingly trust my life

So the choice appeared to be: travel the world and get to be important or treat my wife and family as priority and trust that the process would take care of the rest. The bonus as it happened, was that in 1991 I discovered that the Chinese had the most powerful healing model I had ever encountered. So I could stop reinventing the wheel. A discovery I would probably not have made had I been on the road.

Meanwhile I watched my peers become legendary and I never regretted it. Nowadays I see their books in Barnes and Noble and their workshops in The Observer. Sometimes they use my material. Sometimes they acknowledge it. The deal was I could have whole children and a real relationship. Which is what I got. And that one way or another, what I did would make the world a better place whether anybody noticed or not. No contest really.

And of course we can always have it all but we may have to wait.

One of the teachers I observed was Dr Chuck Spezzano and it was on one of his workshops that I met Hester. Hester is a lady of a certain age; Jewish, a dancer with a ludicrously pliable body. She was and still is living with a well-known author who travels the world inspiring auditoriums of people.

Last week, as I said, she sent me a cheque which I had not been expecting.

In 2004 her Dad had died. It is pretty much a platitude to say that a woman has a complex relationship with her father but Hester was especially attached. His was a chequered story. A determined failure, whenever things were going right he'd cock it up. Good job; he'd cheek the boss. Wealth; he'd waste it on silliness. Adoring wife; he'd neglect her. But Hester worshipped him. Not that unusual: a woman either marries her father or she doesn't and some of the smartest people make some of the dumbest choices.

So when she rang I made time for her as soon as I could. She was stuck. She needed help. She was depressed, desperate, tired and ill. And she could not sell her father's flat. Which is a feng shui problem if ever I heard one.

So on a harsh December day, six months after his death, we went to the sheltered housing block in Finchley. The apartment was still full of his ornaments and furniture. It was still and cold in there, his bathmat was still on the bathroom floor. We moved the heavy stuff out of the father area Qian, in the North West and so on. We cleared the weed from the fountain outside the main door. Chi comes down from the mountain on the wind (feng) where it is held by the water (shui); most feng shui procedures involve water. We inhaled dead air and exhaled living. I did some mumbo-jumbo. She reminisced. He had been a difficult man and the more difficult he became the more she had protected him.

Then I sat in his favourite chair and just *felt*. To say he was still there is to overnarrow the metaphors but I was able to describe a man I'd never met and mannerisms I'd never seen. Like the building, he tended to twist around. This may sound particularly weird but buildings are like their inhabitants.

We talked about his failures and his successes, his self-righteousness and his wrongheadedness. She cried. Then she bought me lunch – a Greek place in Swiss Cottage – and as all her money was tied up in the apartment, I settled for lunch as my payment.

Then last week, some months later, her cheque appeared. The flat had sold some while ago but completion had been held up.

A nice surprise just before Christmas; that'll help towards the PSP*!

SIR JASPER AND OTHER GEMS

One bright sharp morning just before Christmas I surveyed Moira's house. There was an icy glare on the surface of the road. It was a day to move in a measured way. The Chinese calendar showed *Establish* –a good time for fresh starts.

Moira wanted to be free of her ex-husband, she told me.

I suggested the first step might be to stop sleeping with him.

Moira was herself a healer, using various forms of light work as well as massage. Generally when a healer is busy you can assume they are making a positive difference. Her practice was booked solid. Although they are picking up other people's stale energies all the time the best of such healers bounce with appetite for life. Which was not great news, all things considered, for her ex-husband.

The story was that he would turn up for a few days at a time and

---

* Play Station Portable for those without children.

whatever she did, they would end up entangled. Now she wanted to move on, she told me. She was interested in a relationship that had a shelf life. Which made the ex surplus to requirements.

She was an attractive woman in her late 50s who could have passed for 40. It is tempting to think of the ex as bewitched as Merlin by the evil Nimue but he, I figured, had the power of choice also. Nonetheless on balance the scales seemed loaded.

The feng shui told the same story. The house was full of shields and discs, yang metal symbols that in Chinese terms mean "mature man". These had been there since before he left. Simply putting them on ebay would have changed her life. And as a clincher, on the wall opposite her bed was a big metal wind chime. Wind chimes are also metal energy; the bigger and heavier the more so. In other words, the moment she woke, her eyes would light on a symbol of yang metal that virtually amounted to a portrait of the ex. This was not playing the game.

Of course these conflicting signals were unconscious – whatever that means. I don't make much distinction between conscious and unconscious decisions. For me consciousness is just what you happen to be attending to. What she was attending to was being free of him; what she was failing to attend to was the extent to which she was keeping him hooked. To her credit she laughed when I pointed all this out to her but I know the laugh of the redhanded when I hear it.

So we moved things around, altering the décor to bring water to bear on the metal, symbolically draining it to reduce the ex's presence. We talked at length about relationships. There remained in the way she spoke a shred of a belief that she had nothing to do with her ex-husband's persistence. *Moi?*

"You are talking to *me*," I reminded her as I sometimes do.

She coloured and I told her of a teacher I studied with briefly in the 80s whose *model* taught that women start and finish relationships. All relationships. There's something in that idea, I suggested. Broadly women are fantastically smart about what attracts men and most men are fantastically dim about what attracts women. Women learn early how to make an idea look as if it came from their man. Few men ever catch on.

But while one partner continues to manipulate the other, mutual respect must remain slight and true intimacy impossible. Furthermore if women are in charge of relationships then men are just helpless turkeys. This, ladies, is not the whole story. Nonetheless she could see it was a fair cop.

As it happened the guru behind this was shot by an ex-lover; he had clearly overlooked the great flaw in his theory: that men need to take the hint.

Next I activated for her a charm to attract the perfect partner. It's a tricky one. The Chinese symbols are ambiguous and you have to get the yin and yang right. The charm involves identifying the Chinese cyclical character that represents Moira's Mr Right. This character which has an elemental value, is gleaned from her ba zi or personal feng shui based on her moment of birth. The element corresponds with a colour. For the charm, we place this colour at a specific location in the house. As I say, the formula is ambiguous and you have to place symbols of the right polarity. Polarity means yin or yang, i.e male or female. Subtle and subdued colour is yin, yang is more bold and bright. This being about life partners, you can imagine polarity could be an issue. So we have to get it exactly right.

I explained to her as we set it up, that the first time I employed this procedure was for my friend Gitte in Bristol and I warned Moira that she would need to feed back to me what went on in her life from now on so that I could be sure I'd got it right.

"How will you know?" she asked.

"You'll start to meet guys that interest you."

"And if it isn't?"

"You'll receive money you weren't expecting and unwanted attention from women."

She took a deep breath. We placed some crystals to help her focus. Crystals are not a classical Chinese cure but the fact is they work. Tourmaline is the classic anti woo-woo™ crystal, moldavite supports creative magic and clear quartz, the vanilla of crystals, does what it is told.

Next I gave her a procedure to do at the heart of the house – the tai chi. We found this by carefully measuring the widest width and the longest length. Where the lines join is the heart. Sometimes the heart of a house is outside. An L-shape may do this. If the heart is outside, the house can be heartless. Such houses are very tricky. Moira's was not like this. It's very unlikely that a healer's would be.

I prescribed Moira an exercise in innocence; unilaterally disarming herself of feminine wiles in return for a spotless man. Being 99% innocent is dangerous but 100% is the safest state there is. If we will trust enough to be without defences we will attract people who do not want to harm us. This principle may be the single most powerful aspect in the creation of intimacy in relationship.

She sat at the tai chi with her knees crossed.

"Breathe," I suggested. "A nice deep one. Now imagine (the ex) about a yard in front of you. And just let him be there. Feel what you feel. Breathe again. Now bring him closer. Breathe."

She was facing North East – the direction of devotional work, gan the Mountain, contemplation, withdrawal, prayer.

"Now closer. Breathe."

Tears appeared in her eyes.

"Tears are bullet points," I said. "Your body gets it before you do."

More tears. My youngest son Joey once when asked what I do, said "Daddy makes ladies cry." Tears mean movement.

"Now let him go."

More breathing, more tears.

"Now bring in your ideal partner."

Repeat nightly between one and three am.

The central job of the feng shui master is to maintain *balance*. One measure of this is that the Chinese elements are represented in the correct proportions and are in their correct locations. Each of the elements – wood, fire, earth, metal and water – has a distinct individual nature and a whole body of symbolic meanings. A mother for instance is earth and a father yang metal. For a father also read mature man. The father "belongs" in the North West of the house and the mother in the South West. For healthy relationships both need attention. This is balance. Now we did a little work on the South West. Placing her private telephone there was part of it and also as she worked from home, we ensured her business phone was elsewhere.

I made to leave. It had been a long morning and I was feng shui'd out. Moira however had one last question:

"What happened to your friend in Bristol?"

"She got a huge refund of interest from her bank and her best friend came out."

MIDWINTER – THE END AND THE BEGINNING
A NOTE ABOUT CALENDARS

Most cultures with turning seasons mark the Winter Solstice. This is first of all practical. Before central heating and road-gritters there was only so much you could do while the snow was falling. Squirrels and bears had the right idea: pig out then sleep till spring. With the addition of reruns of old sitcoms, this doesn't sound unlike a traditional Western Christmas.

As you can see at the top of page 19, now it is dung gee, Midwinter – the shortest day and the longest night. The chi which has been winding down since midsummer is exhausted and then instantly regenerated. Of course life, energy, matter, chi, whichever model you want to work, can never be exhausted but here it plumbs its deepest trough. Growth comes to a halt.

The Chinese think in terms of process rather than end. So although dung gee is the moment of total yin where everything is dark, that moment is also the beginning of yang. The light is rekindled and gains power until it peaks at ha gee, the Summer Solstice in June.

For millennia, the Chinese have used the cyclical characters that appear in the date at the exact moment the year changes (like those at the top of page 19) in order to divine what the following year may be like. Again this is practical. If we can tell whether the spring will be wet or dry we can plant seeds accordingly. Derek Walters, who knows more about this than any other European, emphasises that the first almanacs were above all to coordinate dates so that buyers and sellers of goods would be in the same place at the same time. No good bringing my surplus chickens on Thursday according to my almanac if you're not there till Friday with your superfluous grain. As long ago as 4,000 BCE the Chinese were building houses with front doors on the ideal feng shui axis just off due south which happens also to be the warmest place in the days following the Winter Solstice. These are the practical conclusions of a practical people. We can accordingly be quite certain that feng shui survived because it worked. That is to say it made life more comfortable.

Midwinter is also the feast of Yule and in medieval England the twelve days of Yuletide were the period of *misrule*. At this time society was turned upside down and a serf became Lord of the Manor while the Lord himself ate at a lower table. In theory he suffered all the accompanying indignities but my guess is that these indignities were kept either to a minimum or administered anonymously as a feudal lord is likely to be nothing if not

a. capable of bearing a grudge and

b. possessed of a long memory.

This practice has its roots in the Roman mid-winter festival of Saturnalia but the interesting question is why such an upheaval should take place at this time. And it seems to be to do with the perennial attempt to square the lunar and solar calendars. The period of misrule is essentially the discrepancy between the two, thrown away as if it were not real. The pivot of this enterprise is the question of when we decide to start the year.

The earth revolves around the Sun once every 365¼ days. The moon revolves around the earth once every approximately 29 days. 29 is tantalisingly close to one twelfth of 365. In fact 30 *is* one twelfth of 360. If we could *force* the year to take 360 days and insist the moon slow down slightly we would have twelve lunar months in one solar year. And wouldn't that be tidy? Feng Shui with its interaction of horoscopes and orientations is among other things, an attempt to squeeze time and space into a single system. It is a fact that Chinese astronomers attempted for some centuries to work with a circle of 365 degrees precisely because of this; it would be so handy if the eternal cycle of the year and its physical representation were of identical proportions. It was only Jesuit scholars who by predicting eclipses more reliably, talked the Chinese out of it.

And this is no time to be smug, because our 60-minute hours and 60-second minutes are clearly also remnants of failed attempts at the same objective. In the West we developed an unwieldy system of leap years and uneven months which is hardly more elegant. The Chinese Hsia Calendar employs the *metonic* cycle which demands four extra months every nineteen years. The Hebrew calendar is similar.

So pulling all this together, it is perverse both that the Western calendar starts halfway through the midwinter celebration of chaos and that the Chinese appear to place New Year a month or so later in early February. I say *appear* because this is not actually the whole story.

The point of this digression is that the Chinese approach to the calendar emphasises repeating cycles. This emphasis has been blurred by Western systems. The procedures of feng shui follow from the attempt to connect the cycles of time and space. When we say water, we also mean the most yin, formless, dark uncontainable thing there is. On the clock this is midnight, on the calendar dung gee.

Once we accept this idea of parallel cycles we can say things about people's future by examining their houses. And, more to the point, change it.

Change the house, you change the person.

COMPASS MENTIS: BOOKS

I am often asked to recommend feng shui books, a hard task because there is so little that is both accurate and readable. If it's in English it's probably oversimplified. If it's in Chinese you probably can't read it. If it's authentic and it works it may not have been written down.

For the purpose of getting a fix on what the feng shui master is up to, I'd recommend Philip Pullman's *His Dark Materials*.

Lyra, Pullman's heroine, employs an *alethiometer* to divine what is happening. This instrument, like my luopan (Chinese compass) features a series of concentric rings covered in symbols. The trick, Lyra explains, is knowing which symbol means what and when. Yes it's written for kids and yes it's fiction. But then a lot of the feng shui material on the market is both of those things also.

When my luopan tells me a house backs on to say muw the Rabbit, in the East, I have to figure out whether that means the issue is movement, eyesight, the Eldest Son, one of a thousand alternative levels of meaning or some combination. By the end of a survey generally this will be clear and I can advise accordingly.

Pullman talks also of "dust" ebbing slowly out of our universe into a parallel one, taking all life with it.

At the physical level, "dust" is a good word for the chi (often translated "energy") that I work with. One reason that a feng shui master is concerned with front doors is that it is through the entrance that our own personal "dust" enters and leaves. By dust I mean nail cuttings, dead skin, hair and so on. It follows that these spores make the entrance truly ours and put our signature on the home.

Pullman ties Lyra's divination in with the I Ching (more properly Yi Jing) or *Book of Changes* which is indeed an integral aspect of feng shui.

I use the Book of Changes in a similar way to Lyra.

The orientation of a house corresponds precisely to a changing line of a Hexagram from the Yi. Each Hexagram contains advice. The changing line fine-tunes that advice. So by consulting the relative Hexagram of the Yi, I can get an instant assessment of the nature of a house. Number 39 (Jian, Difficulty) is indicative as is Number 12 (Pi Hindrance). I can work with either of these but when a door or house is at an angle that corresponds to Number 4 (Meng Youthful Folly) I generally take it as a sharp hint not to look for shortcuts and get back to the harder work of calculation.

Pullman's trilogy is about the ages-old separation between organised religion and spiritual practice. He is clearly angry with the self-righteousness and violence that have attached to religion down the centuries. The books' climax is a sort of shoot-out with God.

As far as books that teach authentic feng shui are concerned:

Derek Walters' *Feng Shui Handbook* is out of print but as with all of his work you can absolutely trust the information and it has been ruthlessly plundered by other writers, including this one. The books you get at the motorway stop which claim you can *Teach Yourself Feng Shui in Twenty Minutes* – in fact before you resume your journey – have usually borrowed extensively from DW, often without either credit or discretion. At least I paid him for a year's tuition.

Kwok Man Ho has written several volumes, many of which masquerade as potboilers, but if you just open them you will find he goes as far towards authentic usable material as he can. The pocket books produced by Dorling Kindersley are a really good example of this.

I can't overlook **Lillian Too's** books which of course are in their way wonderful. What worries me about them is that they support her crusade to empower everyone to do their own feng shui. I believe this to be misguided and the number of her readers I have bailed out who have found themselves halfway through a procedure unable to tell whether a Southern *location* or *orientation* was meant would surprise you. I think she may have unleashed a dragon that was best left in its basket.

For the advanced student **Stephen Skinner's** *Flying Star Feng Shui* is comprehensive, and well-researched though some aspects of it arouse controversy among professionals. **Gill Hale's** *Feng Shui Encyclopedia* is a clear and careful introduction. Finally **Joey Yap's** *Mastery Academy* books and DVDs are always reliable, clear and authentic.

There are other worthy volumes and I apologise to the authors of those I have overlooked. I have included nothing about clutter clearing or sacred space because the nature of such practices is instinctive and does not reduce well to the page.

Recommending books about ba zis, (personal feng shui or if you must, Chinese Horoscopes) is easier because despite the huge number of silly ones, there are even fewer worth serious attention.

Raymond Lo's *Pillars of Destiny* books are fascinating and *Discover Your Destiny* by his disciple **Hee Yin Fan** is essential.

Raymond, who is a genius, may be the best-known feng shui man in Hong Kong and produces his own yearly almanac, a few copies of which make it to Western shores each year. Do seek it out.

Derek Walters' *Complete Guide to Chinese Astrology* has if possible been even more plundered than his feng shui volume, making him the unwitting and unfeted founder of a whole industry. Every year dozens of new volumes based on a half-baked speed-read of his painstakingly comprehensive study subtract from the sum total of human knowedge: *Feng Shui Astrology for Dockers, Improve your TenPin Bowling with Feng Shui, Management Secrets of the Metal Rabbit* and so on.

Perhaps only **Jean-Michel Huon de Kermadec's** *The Way to Chinese Astrology* and **Man Ho Kwok's** *Authentic Chinese Astrology* deserve to be mentioned in the same breath although again **Joey Yap**'s *Master Academy* Ba Zi series is invaluable.

THE COLOUR OF MONEY

Catriona has asked me again about the application of feng shui to business cards and headed notepaper. There have been huge positive differences in her personal life since I surveyed but money is proving less forthcoming. On the other hand she needs to be clear as to whether she wants to make money for its own sake or to prove to her competitors that she is the better man.

Her home faces east, uphill into a T-junction and the work I have done to keep out this rushing chi makes it hard to access the chi she needs to run her business from the second floor. You can feel the pressure of car after car pointing its nose at her front door. On some level at least those who live at T-junctions live in fear of a bonnet in their front room. From the east comes fresh bustling energy but from the T-junction in this direction comes sha or sat – the poison chi that is traditionally associated with disorder and breakages. In short a T-junction is bad news.

Taking pride of place in her living room is a picture of her late father. He is in military dress and looks as if he will tolerate no slacking. Her ba zi has a distinctive pattern that suggests a strong attachment to her father but that's hardly unusual. And in what many people – none of them feng shui masters – would call the relationship area, is the toilet.

As I said, mixed motives. Her social life is booming but what she wants to be is a wheeler-dealer. Which is not to say she should not or can not. She is certainly smart enough but as long as she is proving a point to Daddy, progress will be, like her front door, uphill. This makes her attached to the fine detail of feng shui.

So for yours and her benefit, here's how to apply feng shui to business cards.

First of all the dimensions are important. 6½ inches is auspicious, as is 2.125 inches. These dimensions are hard to incorporate in a business card although I have seen feng shui masters employ ingenious folds for the purpose. More subtle adaptations of the principles of the lo ban ruler will not lend themselves to explanation here. You might however, consider a card of orthodox size and shape with a border 2.125 inches square. Secondly and if the effort of insisting on weird measurements is threatening to sour your relationship with the printer, just get the colours right.

You know that in the Cycle of Production (**see page 12 above**), wood supports fire which supports earth which supports metal which supports water which in turn supports wood and so on. Respect this in your design. To say this another way, green supports red which supports brown which supports white which supports blue which supports green. This, you will recall, is elemental theory.

Now you need to know what colour money is for you.

"How would I know that?" Catriona asks and it is a fair query. We are on the phone but I can see her father's face and his braided epaulettes.

Put simply, your ba zi will reveal it. I will explain how ba zi's work later in this diary. Meanwhile I can tell you that for me personally, because of my ba zi, fire is money. Generally fire is about curiosity, brightness and the intellect and most would say money is generally represented by metal. But derived from my ba zi, my money is fire.

Metaphor watchers will see some sense in this. Curiosity is the source of my livelihood, if you like. So to represent money I use red. Everyone is different.

So to personalise this, you need your ba zi drawn up although you can adopt the underlying principles right away.

Last time I was there, I spotted an alleyway a hundred or so yards outside Catriona's window. There was a bike parked in the alley, next to a dustbin. Some might simply have seen a bike and a bin. Some might have seen movement blocked by things that needed discarding. Someone else might have seen movement coming from the West. I suggested she tell me what it was *she* saw in the alleyway.

"Why?" she asked, which was depressing.

I think "why?" may be the most useless question in the world and I rarely answer it beyond handpicked company. All answers give you is more questions. What I'm interested in is positive life change. That generally does not emerge from the question "why?"

I explained to her the process of divination, of how we can read anything there is in the physical universe to tell us what is going on in it: the weather, random noise, tea leaves, half-heard conversations, mistakes. Even a newspaper may tell us something about what is happening in the world. She took it on trust but was not satisfied.

I asked her to let me know from time to time what was happening in the alleyway. This was not for her to marvel at my woo-woo™ gifts but to recognize her own. When we examine a metaphor we get less, not more information. Some people will queue round the block to have their power taken away and then fight like hell when you try to give it back.

To resume: the Chinese word for the relationship between the individual and money is choi. This choi is the same choi as in the New Year blessing gung hei fat choi. What may be a bit arresting is that in the unreconstructed format that is the Confucian family, choi also means *wife*. The implication is that a woman is a chattel. Not so enlightened. But when we consider the traditional attitudes of men to women, it makes sense outside the Chinese context. Men tend to use words like "pull" and "score" in relation to women. The Noughties New Wave Post-modern Ironic Ladette may be different but broadly women don't. I have toyed with translating choi as *booty* to connect up these ideas. But suit yourself.

The image of Catriona's dad, as surely as if it were in the *pensieve,* tells her femininity is weakness which is a pity for such a strong woman. She moved from the Middle East with nothing to her name when her country was overrun, set up a new life and established herself in business. She is astute and resourceful. Nobody's victim. She is also beautiful. But she is not a bloke. Thank the Lord.

Your logo or headed notepaper wants generally to feature the colours of your choi. But don't forget that it has to be supported by the background colour (i.e the card or paper) it is on. So, on white paper (a metal colour) I use blue or black (so the metal supports the water) for the main message as well as a splash of green (wood supported by water) and my name in red.

If my publisher has been paying attention, the principle should be all over this book.

Now those whose plan is to use feng shui simply for acquisition and who haven't invested in a ba zi may have noticed that the house colours of HSBC (originally the Hong Kong & Shanghai Banking Corporation) are red and white. As are those of the Bank of China. This represents the general significance of white (i.e metal) as money and red as its conqueror, fire.

Catriona is a whiz with ideas like these.

FORGET IT, JAKE, THIS IS CHINATOWN

And if you think this is fanciful, go along to the London city office of the Bank of China. You may have heard that in Hong Kong and Taiwan, big buildings are sited and built along feng shui principles. Which is true. You may have heard of faux cannons aimed at competitors like some frozen battlefield and of perfectly placed open space and water features. And you may have thought that this only happens in the mystic East. Not so.

On the fascia of the Bank of China, about a hundred yards east of the Bank of England and across the road, just above eye level there are six plaster circles. Both six and the circle represent Yang metal. Money. Go and see for yourself.

But why red (fire) and white (metal)? Interestingly, fire does not support metal but *clashes* with it. This is a more sophisticated idea. These wily Chinese institutions have deliberately *clashed* metal with fire. Why?

Because the choi relationship is a clash. How do I know that fire is money for me? Because the personal element of my ba zi is water which *clashes* with fire. Fire is therefore choi. What did you expect of something that both represents money and a very uh…. traditional man-woman relationship. Endless harmony? I don't think so.

The possession of money like the possession of a woman is in the traditional Chinese view, an aggressive land-grabbing sort of act.

Catriona is not so great with these ideas

Don't blame me, I say; I just work with this stuff.

A WORD ABOUT PREDICTION: WHAT IS ON THE CARDS

The basic unit of Chinese metaphysics is chi. This word is often translated *energy*. The Chinese express the character of a place or moment in terms of its chi. Every moment, every place and indeed every thing has an individual chi signature. On one level feng shui is simply an attempt to bring time and space into a single system. The symbol muw, yin wood, referred to as the Rabbit, represents the East as well as spring and the early morning. It is easy to see that these characteristics suit the Rabbit. And easy to see what the East, where the sun rises, has in common with the early morning and the first buds of the year.

Similarly the Rat that represents the month of December, stands also for the chi of damp, midnight and the North. The Chinese, like ourselves, see the Rat as a secretive creature of the dark. The Rat of this particular month, December 2004 is bing tze, the Fire Rat, sometimes known as the "Rat in the field". Although tze, the Rat, is of the water element, the stem bing brings yang fire to the party. Such a pairing – like the earth Rabbit or the metal Dog – consists of *stem* (bing) and *branch* or animal (tze) and is called a *pillar*.

Interestingly the character tze (or tzu – the Chinese don't have much respect for vowels) is one of the most frequently used in Chinese writing and stands also among other things for "baby" "prince" and "wise man". The tze in Kung Fu Tze (Confucius) Lao Tze and Sun Tze (author of the *Art of War)* are this character. There is a Chinese proverb that runs: "Tze, tze; ren, ren" which means something like "If the Prince behaves like a Prince, the common people will behave like the common people."

Not only are years given animal names but so are months, days, hours and even minutes. So as well as a Rat year every twelve years, there is a Rat month every twelve months (ie once a year) and a Rat day every twelfth day. Finally there is a Rat hour every twenty four hours (not every twelve because the Chinese think in double hours of 120 minutes.)

So how do we predict?

It follows from the above that any date can be written as a series of pillars: one each for the hour, day, month and year. The characters at the top of page 19 are the pillars for the moment of least light at the Winter Solstice 2004. This is the moment one year (2004) dies and the next (2005) is born, which many consider to characterise the whole of the following year. Another school of thought works from the corresponding moment at what is more commonly called the Chinese New Year in early February. We need not concern ourselves at least for now with such disputes but it is instructive to take on board that even feng shui masters disagree among themselves. What is also instructive is that a ba zi or personal feng shui is constructed from a birth date in the same way. Ba zi means "eight pictures" and the eight characters that make up the four pillars are those eight pictures.

As soon as we write Chinese characters we enter the world of metaphor. The language is constructed entirely differently from our own. The characters are pictures often made up of a series of component images that together make up an idea. They are not words in the Western sense, more like superannuated cave paintings. And each of the symbolic characters in the pillar carries as well as meaning, an elemental value.

A POULTRY THING

So the *pillar* with the word "wood" at the top and "Rooster" at the bottom is the pillar for the year – as opposed to the month, day or hour it starts. This year as you know by now, is a wood Rooster. The Rooster is essentially metal. Even if we know nothing about Chinese metaphysics, wood and metal sounds like a robust combination. And indeed it is. What we can draw from that is that the Rooster of the year 2005 is a very conflicted fowl.

The wood Rooster is sometimes called the Singing Cock. Roosters are renowned for their ability to warn of danger by crowing. It was a cock that warned Rome of the attack of the Etruscans and also that reminded St Peter of his failure to keep faith.

So, as we have discussed elsewhere, this is a dangerous year;

metal will be in conflict with wood. Warnings will be issued and swords will be drawn.

What else do we know?

The year pillar is commonly reckoned to apply to the whole year but especially the first quarter up to the Spring Equinox in March. Now the month pillar – the next one along moving right to left – applies to the second quarter as well as to December. This is our fire Rat.

The Rat in the Field may have derived its name from its habit of only being out in the open at high summer but the combination of fire and water is as volatile as metal and wood although somewhat different in nature. A way to expose this is to look at the Hexagram in the *Book of Changes* that relates to this pillar. There are 60 pillars and 64 Hexagrams so they share around nicely.

The Hexagram is Number 27 which is Mountain over Thunder, that is Yi#, which means "Nourishment" or "Jaws". It is often thought of as denoting *chewing things over*. It can refer either to the nourishment that goes into the mouth or the value of the words that come out of it. No surprise then that this is the year of making poverty history, of treating sub-Saharan Africa as if it mattered by ensuring sufficient food and medication. And notice that the influence of the Hexagram is in the second quarter of the year when we can expect a lot of talk* and perhaps even some action in aid of this.

Enough of this for now.

---

* This may seem tidy in the light of G8 and Live8 but these went out as part of my package of predictions in December 2004.

\# Not to be confused with *yi* meaning "changes". The characters are quite distinct.

2.
SOLAR FORTNIGHT BEGINNING:
SATURDAY 5 JANUARY 2005 13.52
Siu Hohn *Slight Cold*
Month: ding chou **the Fire Ox**

Hour	Day	Month	Year
metal	earth	fire	wood
xin	ji	ding	yi
wei	chou	chou	yuw
sheep	ox	ox	rooster

I Fought Velour and Velour Won

This is the stolen time between Christmas and New Year when no one knows what day it is. For some schools of feng shui, including the one I trained in, the New Year has started. For others, it doesn't come till February. I tend to keep a weather eye on this time of year, not rigidly defining it either way. The ancient Celts used to say that at Halloween the veil between the worlds of the living and the dead is at its thinnest. This time of year has a slippery dreamlike quality.

I receive a phone call from Chris.

A professional actress, I had surveyed her home two years ago, just days after she had moved in. Her voice is the seductive honey-brown of a specialist in speech work. Her house backs onto the North West with a little jutting-out piece to the West. West (yin metal) being the home of the youngest daughter is about parties and fun as well as the voice while the North West is about experience, respect and authority, so this is a pretty good configuration both for her and for her nineteen-year old daughter, Poppy. The yang metal of the North West also represents Qian, the Father and by extension the mature male. So although she was partner-free her relationship prospects had every reason to be looking up.

I had suggested to her a number of measures to support this benign metal chi and warned her against either *clashing* it with fire or *draining* it with water. Either would tend to get in her way.

Poppy had lived with her mother all her life. Just the two of them. She was beautiful, talented and worldly with a nice loud sense of humour. When I surveyed she had a boyfriend about whom she was apparently serious and her modelling career was on the up.

The back of the house called, I told Chris, for white and metallic colours. These colours represent metal and therefore support the qualities associated with it: fun, parties, voice work, money. Conversely blue would reduce its strength or *drain* it because blue represents water which is what metal turns to in the *cycle of production*. Put simply, metal is largely useless in its molten state so symbolically, to weaken metal, you introduce water. By the same token, fire would melt the metal and make it liquid even more rapidly: an absolute no-no, implying goodbye both to partners and work opportunities.

So: no fire at the back, no red, no bright light, no cactus, nothing pointy or sparky.

Poppy and Chris, I noticed, sparked a great deal, sudden sharp disagreements out of all proportion to the issue they were at odds over: who had the door keys or whether there were any teabags. In feng shui we might call this the meeting of two por kwans or "two sevens clashing." A por kwan is a catty type of energy. When my luopan spots two together I keep my eyes open for trouble. To alleviate this I placed miniatures of a classic earth shape: goy moon., which is like a rounded parallelogram and acts as a peacemaker. It is this sort of clash – the "two sevens clash" by the way, that lent Joe Strummer's band its name.

Speaking to Poppy, Chris would refer herself in the third person. "Mummy wants you to stay in and look after the cats...Mummy will be back later." All a little claustrophobic.

I had tried to talk her out of putting Poppy in the middle room which was a poor room for anybody to stay in long.

"Can't you do anything about it?" she asked mellifluously as if only a fraud would answer no.

"Better not to have to try."

Nonetheless she insisted on installing Poppy in this room full of morbid earth energy. It was too warm, there was not enough light, to enter it was to feel sleepy. A barred window looked out onto an open drain and a door that had been blocked in. Blocking a door is rarely a good idea. When a house has stood for decades with the energy entering and leaving along a single path, changing has repercussions. And the repercussions were in Poppy's room. As if that weren't enough, the xuan kong – current chi numbers or *Flying Stars* – showed **5:2** which means sickness.

Earth energy is by nature slow and hard to move. At its extreme it coincides with sickness, especially digestive and gynaecological. Generally it makes for lack of drive. Some might find this sleepiness comforting but it is at odds with focused activity. The owner of this room would, as I had told Chris, tend to gain weight and lose purpose,

"So what colours do I need to paint it?"

"If you made it pure white with blue accents you might have a chance of neutralising it."

As these words left my mouth I knew I should not be saying them. I was being pulled over a precipice. And that's no excuse really.

"What about cream?"

Cream is not white. It is not even a metal colour like white. It is an earth colour. It embodies probably more than any other shade the sleepy womblike quality I was at pains to mitigate.

"White."

She showed me a page of paint colours.

"That is white," I said emphatically, pointing at white.

"But I like this biscuit colour," she said huskily, don't you, Pop?"

"Whatever," said Poppy, seated on the bed lazily flicking through Vogue.

The next time I visited Chris she had hung a red curtain the full width of the back wall. The vast heavy curtain was at the North West where the life-giving metal was. Red is of course fire. It was velvet, a thick burgundy red; very beautiful but totally wrong. It was *melting* the metal. While she was asking me what else I could do to the house to make her dreams come true I tried to explain that the curtain had added to the problem. But she could not or would not see the connection. What she saw was a feng shui man who had failed her. She was not entirely wrong either.

Poppy was not well. Opportunities were not rampant in either of their lives.

Weakened metal: less fun, less money, no man, unhappy young daughter

"It's not *very* red, is it? I mean burgundy is almost purple."

I told her once more to take the curtain down. However you look at the causality, the curtain was a statement. She attempted to bribe me with a nice glass of claret.

"Not while I'm working," I said, feeling like PC 49.

Then we discussed Poppy. Her career had stalled and she had been inexplicably and constantly ill. She was putting on weight, spending much of her time in the warmth of her bedroom which was now a lustrous dairy cream colour.

The room was unbalanced in a clammy sickly sort of way. I could feel it and so clearly could Poppy. The solution was still to paint it white. This would introduce metal which as it resides within the earth is said to deplete earth by *giving birth* to it.

"But cream is so close to white," Chris said in her delicious voice.

"Close, yes."

"Could I use magnolia?" she breathed. She was drinking the claret herself anyway.

"Not really."

"Does it make that much difference?"

There are a hundred ways to answer this but her daughter's sickness was the most eloquent.

"Oh go on," she said breathily. "Couldn't I make it peach?"

Metal would relieve this, earth would exacerbate it. Peach was worse again.

To cut a long story short, her daughter could continue to expect stuckness and ill health in a cream room and relief in a white one. You don't have to agree any more than she did but it's a pity to pay me a fortune for the advice and then take no notice.

And take down the damn curtain!

Now as the New Year beckoned, she was ringing me to ask what else I could do. What *else*? The answer was to take the advice I had given her in the first place; make the spare room hers. Put Poppy in her room. Make what was Poppy's room the guest room, paint it pure white and don't ever let anybody stay there long.

She was not enthusiastic. She liked it as it was.

My basic model is choice. Everything in our universe is what we have chosen whether we take responsibility for it or not. We can have things any way we want them. This is not always easy to accept and of course I don't insist you do. England football managers have been sacked for less. But some cases are more clear than others.

Bringing up a daughter on your own in the inner city is no cake walk. One way to describe the energy of the house was "mumsy." Who could blame Chris for wanting company?

It is not uncommon for a client to try and persuade me out of what the chi is. And it is true that there are often two or more solutions. But if the chi shows a particular elemental combination, it doesn't matter how charming, seductive, forceful or persuasive the client is, it doesn't change. I have learned the hard way not to give way on such issues.

"What about lavender?" she crooned down the phone. It still gives me goosebumps.

THE NEW YEAR

Now the working year is underway. The Christmas hibernation is over. I survey early in the morning most days at this time of year. I like to catch the sunrise.

I used to hate getting up. That was when I still had a secret identity as an insurance broker. For more than 20 years I led a double life as pioneer in the world of woo-woo™ and purveyor of pensions. Twenty two years which was about seventeen too long. I had mouths to feed. When I finally sold my business after doing a deal with God (which I may elaborate on another day) I had enough to keep us for a little over two years. It was a little over three before I was making enough to keep us; me, my wife Sheila, twin daughters Jess & Hen, my son Joey and occasionally one or more of my other three grown sons from my first brood. I have known it be 21 December and not have any money for presents. One year I was Santa in a department store which is a good story too.

These days I often rise cheerfully at 4.30am because I love what I do.

Sheila isn't so good at mornings but then she doesn't fall asleep in front of the TV as often as I do. I usually look in on the kids before I go. Jessie has made the decision to drop out of the second part of her A-levels and be a fulltime actress. She is very beautiful and very talented but nobody is so talented that this is not a huge risk. She doesn't get up too early when she's not working but all her attention is focused on that big break. She makes calls, she goes to *meetings*, she tones up at the gym, avoids nourishing food. Many would say show business is a lottery but they don't know her as I do. Nor do they have the advantage of having drafted her ba zi.

"Goodbye star twin," I say and kiss her.

She shares a room with Hen who is equally talented but carrying on with her studies. Her immediate aim is three A grades at A Level.

"Goodbye boff twin," I say.

Joey is an unruly ball of potential. He has starred in two films but neither has seen the light of day. He is 10 years old and he doesn't really care. He loves Yugi-oh, his computer and reading.

His favourites are Garth Nix, Eoin Colfer and of course JK Rowling but the open PG Wodehouse on his bedside table is a healthy sign of broader reading. My father who died in 2002 loved Wodehouse. Joe is tall for his age.

"Bye, Shorty," I say.

I make sure my luo pan is in my shoulder bag, my iPod in my jacket and my moldavite in my jeans pocket. Moldavite is a *tektite* –a glassy fragment of a meteor that landed by the Moldau River around 15 million years ago. Moldavite is often prescribed for *centring*. I find that it supports me to get in touch with houses and people rapidly. There are times in a survey when I suddenly know a whole lot for no good reason. I am not very interested in ascribing cause but the moldavite may have something to do with that.

Today I'm placing a water feature for Singha who works in the Social Services in East London. Her office is drenched in stress even at 8am in the morning. If you walk into the waiting area during the day when it is full you could, if you are sensitive to these things be poleaxed. So much misery, so much desperation. Singha advises on what to do in cases of chronic debt; a lot of her work is in the even more miserable environment of a civil court.

That's what I call working for a living.

She insists she can get away with a small water feature by her desk in the open plan office. That sounds a little daring. On one occasion she interpreted my instructions over literally and ended up sandwiched between neighbours who were unhappy with the dramatic and not entirely appropriate changes she had made to her suburban garden. On the other hand it was then that her whole life turned around. I make clear that she can use a mirror in her office instead of water as long as her placement is exactly correct. I use an extension of a formula I have been using for several years. There are two compass directions that get rapid results in such cases. I have recently discovered a way to make it work even faster.

The principle is that certain points on the compass are what are called *low* guas – that is all other things considered, good locations for water and others are high, that is good locations for weight and bulk.

As well as the *low* gua that houses the water and the high one where I place something heavy, I am now putting something in a third position called an *active* gua which knits the other two together. There are numerological formulae for working this out but I have two or three pre-prepared for most situations.

Marking the locations takes moments. I am charging her at my hourly rate for this and I still owe her forty minutes but I can't stand to be here any longer. I am skilled at separating "my" feelings from those that belong to other people and places and I could make a permanent difference here but it would be several days' work and I have no brief to do it.

"Do you want to buy me cup of tea, then?" I suggest.

Her voice often has sadness in it; her husband is not well and she worries about him at home without her. But that tone, I sometimes remind her, is predictive rather than explanatory.

"Okay," she says, brightening.

We talk about the similarity between the ambient feelings in her office and her home and I ask her:

"Is this a coincidence?"

"I suppose not."

She is a brave woman with considerable spiritual awareness.

"We could not feel other people's feelings if they were not to some extent ours," I add.

"I understand that."

"But what happens is that when we feel something, we instantly start making up reasons for it. A feeling arrives. We explain it. We relate it to ourselves. Rapidly we have a story. We have culprits. We have explanation. Human beings very often prefer to be miserable for reasons they can explain to being happy for no reason at all."

"I know that," she says. "What do I do about it?"

"I'm going to give you two pieces of homework," I say. "One: when you are at work and someone brings you the worst story you've heard all year, notice the feelings that accompany it. Notice that you didn't feel them before. Notice that your tendency is to think of Rajul back at home and link the feelings with that idea. Take a deep breath and deliberately feel the distress, then in that moment. Notice how this lightens the load of the people you are dealing with. Notice how it makes you better able to help them. Notice that choosing to feel this stuff makes it less not more painful."

"Okay. And the Second piece of homework?" She pronounces the last word with just a shade of irony.

"On your way home…Do you travel in by car or tube or what?"

"Car."

"Pity. Public transport is better. Anyway, on the way home remember each of the most stressful moments of the day. And relive them. Feel the feelings. Breathe deeply into them. Keep breathing deeply – don't hyperventilate, I want you home safely – until the distress has faded. Then relive the next one."

"That's it?"

"Pretty much. All distress is an attachment to a reality other than what is real. In other words while we're trying not to feel what we are feeling we can't get on with our lives. The Tao is flowing one way and our preferences another."

I pointed racily at the Tao with my left hand and her preferences with my right – like an air stewardess giving out the safety procedure.

"Just get up to date and move on. If you do that at least three times every day on your way home, you might even arrive optimistic."

She closed her eyes and breathed deeply. Really this stuff is that simple. Then she opened them again.

"That's wonderful."

"All in a day's work, ma'am."

"More tea? Breakfast?"

"My work here is done," I said, like Christopher Reeve restoring a bus to the horizontal. I had a committee meeting next. Now that might be *hard* going.

COMPASS POINTS

The points of the compass both inside and outside the house are named for the Trigrams of the *Book of Changes*. Qian (pronounced che-an) who is the Father, occupies the North West inside the house and the South outside. So something happening at the South outside the house may involve the Father but inside it is generally the North West that is to do with him.

Qian's Trigram looks like this:　━━━━━━
　　　　　　　　　　　　　　　　　　━━━━━━
　　　　　　　　　　　　　　　　　　━━━━━━

three unbroken or yang lines. Pure yang, pure male as you'd perhaps expect of the symbol of authority and discipline. Qian stands for the literal father of the house as well as older and mature men generally. Being able to identify which is significant is one of the skills of the job.

These two arrangements of the Trigrams are called the *Early* and *Later Heaven* arrangements. The Early Heaven refers to a time before history, before complication, before life itself. The Later Heaven arrangement describes the chaos of the inhabited universe. This is one of the reasons that masters routinely remind us that most feng shui takes place out of doors. It is where the real power is; the power of mountains and rivers and seas and ultimately the power of early heaven. If we restrict ourselves to indoor feng shui, unless the exterior is very favourable we run the risk of simply moving tents in a sandstorm.

Historically feng shui masters traced the source of chi to the Kun Lun or Himalaya mountains. These vast heights are to the North West of China and both the great rivers of China, the Yangtze and the Yellow River flow South East from there. In this sense chi almost becomes equivalent to gravity or the scientific notion of potential energy, power deriving from sheer altitude.

It is an axiom of xuan kong – a method used to calculate temporary energies – that if the house has the North West missing there is little to be done with it. It is missing its backbone without which it can have no solidity.

Back in suburbia, the thing to take on is that an odd feature refers on some level to the member of the family who belongs at that point of the compass. So when we notice an eye-catching detail at the North West, we are to remember that this may represent either the Father in the Later Heaven Arrangement or the Youngest Son in the Early Heaven. Logically a chunk missing from a house has implications inside and out.

These ideas reflect the defined roles of the Confucian family. The Eldest Son for instance owed filial piety both to his mother and father but was strictly second-in-command until he inherited responsibility for the whole family from his father. It is reasonable to compare him to Thunder whose power grows constantly until it strikes. Thunder for the Chinese was a sudden force which would shake everything and everybody up – sometimes for the better, sometimes not but always drastically.

Daughters for their part were expected to marry in strict pecking order and the prognosis for the eldest daughter who could expect to marry an heir was far superior to that of subsequent daughters who might never rise above concubine status.

Hexagram 54 of the *Book of Changes* gui mei, *Marrying Maiden,* describes the cataclysmic outcome of a younger daughter getting above herself and marrying before the eldest. A great deal of the tension in Chinese society throughout history is to do with the conflict between the social organisation of Confucian ideas and the potential anarchy of the Tao. Some would say this remains true and that it is not the ideas of Marx but those of Confucius that have kept Chinese society alternating between slavish obeisance and mass murder for much of its history.

As in the case of both wife and money being choi (or booty) however much we may disapprove of its unreconstructed nature, this cultural luggage is the warp and weft of feng shui.

Early Heaven Arrangement	Later Heaven Arrangement

East:

li *Fire* 2nd Daughter   zhen *Thunder* 1st Son

South East:

Dui *Lake* 3rd Daughter   Xun *Wind* 1st Daughter

South:

Qian *Heaven* Father   li *Fire* 2nd Daughter

South West:

Xun *Wind* 1st Daughter   kun *Earth* Mother

West:

Kan *Abyss* 2nd Son   dui *Lake* 3rd Daughter

North West:

gan *Mountain* 3rd Son   Qian *Heaven* Father

North:

kun *Earth* Mother   Kan *Abyss* 2nd Son

North East:

Zhen *Thunder* 1st Son

gan *Mountain* 3rd Son

North East:

Zhen *Thunder* 1st Son

gan *Mountain* 3rd Son

3.
SOLAR FORTNIGHT BEGINNING:
THURSDAY 20 JANUARY 2005 07.09
Dai Hohn *Great Cold*
Month: ding chou **the Fire Ox**

Hour	Day	Month	Year
earth	wood	fire	wood
wu	jia	ding	yi
chen	chen	chou	yuw
dragon	dragon	ox	rooster

The Fire Ox

The Ox is yin earth which suggests stubborness and also fertility. The yin earth is the soil that gives life to vegetation where yang earth is solid, hard, dry and unyielding. Yang fire although it supports yin earth, will tend to dry it out. At the moment it is too cold for much plant growth to be visible but under the frost things are happening and a yin fire stem although it is more taper than blowtorch, can only help this process. An early thaw is augured.

The Ox is stubborn and home-loving.

Feng Shui tip: no hot-tubbing before March.

Cold, Cold, Cold

As I write, my eldest son Jaime is in Krakow. The city is knee deep in snow and also knee deep in luminaries there for the celebration – if that is the right word – of Holocaust Remembrance Day at nearby Auschwitz. It is ten below. I don't think I had experienced cold until I had stood out in the open during a Polish winter, at the mercy of the lashing wind that appeared to have travelled across five thousand miles of ice with the express purpose of finding the gap between my collar and my face. Beautiful though Krakow is, I am happy to be here in England complaining about temperatures significantly above zero than there braving the trans-Siberian gale. There it is an act of courage even to be outside.

That much must be acknowledged of the representatives of the great powers standing on a windswept podium at Birkenau – otherwise known as Auschwitz II – making plausible noises about the end of genocide without any obvious awareness that genocide follows the idea that people are different because they believe or behave differently. That misunderstanding remains as common as it ever was: in Darfur, in Kosovo, in Bradford and in New Orleans. And the idea of imposing democracy in the Middle East is surely no different. Religion has no monopoly on fundamentalism.

I have surveyed Auschwitz II. The feng shui is very distinctive. A number of things stand out. One is that there is no back wall to measure as a reference point. Such walls as there are are irregular, defying a fixed orientation. Jaime tells me the bricks were laid by Russian prisoners of war who were shot afterwards. No wonder they betray a shaky hand.

The dust that flies into already wet eyes is a suspect grey colour as is the soil around the gas chambers. Bodies burned and melted with lime have become one with the topsoil.

Another thing is that as you walk up the path familiar from photos, away from the *selection* area towards the ovens, there is a pocket of chi that is pure relief. If you are sensitive to these things you can simply breathe it in like air that accompanies sunshine after a storm. Jaime has explained that the trees here hid the bunkers. The condemned may have been deceived into believing for a moment that they had survived. For an instant they thought they had got away with it and the feeling is still here. These would be mostly women and children too small to be *selected* for work. I see the mothers comforting their children with sensible words and it breaks my heart.

Jaime has told me that one etymological analysis of the Polish *Oswiecim* renders it "the place that will become holy." The name dates from the 13th century. The xuan kong Flying Stars which measure temporary energies, show that the chi in the 1940s was quite different from today. Then it was full of wood/metal clashes. As water drains metal and fire clashes it, so metal itself clashes wood like an axe clashes a log. If we take wood as bone and metal as instruments of violence we have probably made this as graphic as it needs to be.

The Fei sin or Flying Stars calculations show how the chi varies from Fate Period to Fate Period. Fate periods last approximately twenty years. The current Fate started either in 1996 or 2004 and lasts until 2016 or 2024 depending on which school you subscribe to. In 2005, there is for once no arm-wrestling going on between feng shui masters over the issue.

The chi is expressed in pairs of numbers like the **5:2** that Chris and Poppy are confronted with. Today the Flying Star numbers at Auschwitz imply a spiritual purpose; the yin fire of the restless dead seeks worthwhile expression. If there is point to this monument and to this ceremony that is surely it. That might make a little sense of the six million deaths.

One more thing: Oswiecim/Auschwitz lies on flat land between two sluggish deltas; malarial in summer and hellishly cold in winter. There is a diagram in the *Water Dragon Classic,* a Tang dynasty document dating from the Middle Ages, and an ur-text of feng shui scholarship, that defines this as the least auspicious of chi patterns. That of course makes little difference today in the Polish cold where the unspeakable compound of ash and topsoil still forces itself under the eyelids.

The first time Jaime took me round Auschwitz – I've been three times but frankly once is too often – we stopped at the threshold of one of the blocks. Indescribable nastiness had happened here among the dark corners and subterranean pockets. There were still the dwarf walls where prisoners had been crammed into space they could neither stand nor sit in. Or were these Soviet reconstructions for propaganda purposes? The cruel ingenuity of man may be bottomless.

I felt such grief that I thought I would sob and took a deep breath to let it through. Nothing came. I have never otherwise felt such a thing. I can confirm that the birds do sing at Auschwitz, maybe there is a new generation of them that don't care for history, but this feeling of stopped grief was unique to me.

"It's despair," Jaime had said. "People die when they give up. When there is just no point in feeling any more."

By email I remind my son that his expensive education is only on loan. It's all very well having a series of degrees that make him more informed on the subject of the Holocaust than all but a handful of people. The point is to leave the world better than we found it. He went to Poland because he fell in love with a Pole, travelled there in pursuit of her and fell in love with Poland. He speaks Polish so fluently Poles don't believe he is British. Both of these affairs may be approaching their close.

I have a conversation with my 17-year old daughter Jessie who is on the edge of becoming a film star. She is still smarting from a disappointment, a major role that slipped through her fingers at the last moment. Her screen mother was recast and she no longer looked right. These things happen but for her it is like a bereavement. Nonetheless her ba zi (personal feng shui) is clear; the breakthrough is imminent. I remind her. Sometimes the truth is the truth simply because I say it is.

"And then you have to make a positive difference. No point being rich and famous otherwise. What the world needs is people with clout who care."

"I know Daddy. I love you."

I receive a return email from Jaime that says much the same thing.

It's damn cold, he adds. Britain never feels right with him so far away.

Fire and Ice

Back home the goldfish in the pond have woken up. They stirred early in January as the first full month of the solar year began. There's no fooling them. Most of us need almanacs and stuff but they just know. At the same time several of the prayer plants in the greenhouse have died because they were just that tad too wet when the temperature dipped. This is the time of dai hohn, *Great Cold.* If it's going to freeze, it'll be now.

In December my working day is seriously shortened. I have to start at 7am and end around 3pm as I can't do yang feng shui (for the living) after dark. The woo-woo™ stuff intervenes. But in January there is enough light to begin to stretch the day. And the quality of the light is so different, so fresh and so crisp. But when the sun does go down it is still pretty dim.

Mind, Body, Chequebook, Coincidence

Jessie has landed a TV part which will put a spring in her step for a while. The reason Hen didn't follow this path is that she could not stand the rejection. Luvvies receive a critical press but when you see your own kids putting everything they can into auditioning and then having to bounce back time after time when they don't get the part, you can't help but feel for them. We have agreed that Jessie has to find some Casting Directors who will help her jump the queue.Thanks to the cunning of her mother who is of course also her agent, she has found a couple now. Hence the TV job.

And lest you think "Easy for her, her Mum's an agent," let me tell you her mother has been an agent only since the day the two of them decided the 9-year-old Jessie was going to be a star. Before that Sheila was a social worker which perhaps qualified her for her next position as Mother de facto to the evergrowing number of children our house is overrun with. When you have six children, they just keep on coming.

These are the extraordinary women I live with.

I pay constant attention to the South and South East of the house with Jessie's career in mind. Feng shui for fame is pretty straightforward. Her ba zi shows success quite clearly. It's meaningful stuff that is more demanding. Such as Jaime splitting from his Polish wife and returning to Blighty. His ba zi predicted this happening around this time. Not that that helps him much. We talk on the phone; I actually go over there to be with him when he has to face a magistrate and his ex as the divorce is finalised. She looks guilty but there is no blame in this. I am for a moment tempted to hug and reassure her as well as him. This is not the moment. I doubt that I will see her again.

His is an unbalanced follow-the-fire form (for the feng shui anoraks out there) and this period of his life looks full of daughters. The character for this, otherwise called zeun kun or the enigmatic *Hurting Officer* can also mean he has serious work to do.

Of course nothing is inevitable and communication can solve anything. Love, as the Beatles insisted, *is* all you need. But sometimes we just can't do it, can we? The second-hand wrench of our children's heartbreak is a trying experience. I am before all other roles, a Daddy.

Henni now knows more about Elizabeth I than frankly is healthy and Joey is filming when he is not playing Yugi-oh. The rules of Yugi-oh are lengthy and complex. I have accused him of making them up.

I meet up with Ilse at the Mind Body Spirit Exhibition. Someone once called it the *Mind Body Chequebook* and it seems more like that every year. I play with finding the sweetest chi which in line with cyclical theory, moves all the time. And I find just such a spot, framed in light where the sun washes in through the high windows. It feels wonderful, a blissful lightness around the solar plexus. I can see the dust on the sunbeams.

There is almost no feng shui at the exhibition and I am not attracted by the electro-healing tongs or the regiments of reiki masters.

Ilse practises feng shui. Her practice has little in common with what I do. She is a smart, kind woman whose heart is open and she has a natural ability to sense chi but the entirety of her training consisted of a month in North Dakota with a Native American woman. It sounds wonderful: open spaces and making friends. We compare notes. She smudges, she anoints. She chants in dark corners. She locates the spirits of dwellings. No master would ever describe it as feng shui, but what she is doing clearly works. She tells me of her part in a friend's emergence from long periods of unhappiness into the light. It's a long way from compass measurement.

Although it can be complex and intellectually demanding, all Feng Shui is an attempt to second guess the Tao. Which of course is impossible. Oh, except when it isn't. This is as true of what Ilse does as of what I do.

Over several thousand years, a succession of Chinese geniuses have tabulated what appears to happen in certain circumstances and may therefore be predicted to happen again. From the earliest divination using the backs of turtles by way of the *Book of the Green Satchel* and the Flying Star innovations of Shen and Tan in the 1930s, what has been put together is a system.

And systems don't work. There are exceptions to all of them: Marxism, Behaviourism, gravity, physics. There is no method, no model within which there are no exceptions. So there are no rules. There is nothing that will change our lives other than ourselves. Although that is often not what it looks like.

My careful measurement, location and alignment, my years of study and my careful observance of rules some hundreds, some thousands of years old may coincide with a person's choice to heal, move, change. Just as Ilse's methods may.

"Disappointing, really."

She nods. She has a naivete about her that is extraordinary for a woman in her 50s. And if that word "naivete" sounds like a judgement, it isn't. I see it as a treasure.

I am facing posters that warn of "What the Doctors don't tell you" and "The Vaccine Conspiracy." I haven't got much patience with this; just as God is as likely to turn up in church as anywhere else, so there is no reason a doctor should not be a healer.

No model is anything other than a choice and these warnings are not advice so much as gossip.

Ilse used a big chunk of her considerable inheritance to fund a charity in Bristol relieving damaged kids. We talk about the old days in Bristol when we were all bothering people on behalf of the Exegesis seminar. Alive painful times.

She has driven from Bristol in her 2CV.

I explain to her how the cycle of years works. This has not been part of her training. A month is not a long time. We can expect the Rooster Year of 2005, I tell her, to be like 1945, which being the year of the Atom bomb is not that great a prognosis.

Her practice involves lot of *feeling*. The feng shui masters I have studied with would write this off as vague and meaningless. They would need luo pans and calculations. They are not in that respect much different from scientists. Show me the measurements, the consistent conditions, they all say.

What Ilse does may not be classical feng shui. What she gives is herself. She is a sweet, exquisitely sensitive woman who radiates kindness. She even pays for the coffee.

The huge hall is full of sunlight. The chi sweet spot has moved on.

If all feng shui consists of is giving love, why learn the authentic Chinese stuff?

My friend Kasan is driving the taxi that takes me home from the station:

"Why do you arrange people's houses when they can do it for themselves? I know this. I have meditated."

Kasan is an enlightened man, a Kurd, who has two beautiful acclimatised daughters and a successful business, having started from nothing when he left Turkey. His cars have been taking Jessie to and from Elstree.

"Kasan," I say, "In order to use any model we must embrace paradox. Whether we practise crystal therapy, rune reading or feng shui we have to treat with respect what we know, while remembering we know nothing."

And by the way I was telling you that back when you were getting excited about Sai Baba producing Rolexes out of people's spleens.

To do feng shui properly I have to both treat it just as a model and as if it were absolutely real. Who am I to say Ilse can or can't contact the Tao?

What is important, it seems to me, is that we make a difference for the better. I don't distinguish between feng shui, reflexology, aromatherapy, counselling and orthodox medicine. We seem to have been sent to this vale of tears, this rebel planet, to leave it happier behind us. This is my choice. I have been presented with this information. I choose to respect it. We all give love; this is my way.

When I get home, Henni is sweating over Tudor foreign policy and Jessie is just back from the gym. They have booked to visit Rome at Easter. Jessie hopes she can find a snow globe of the Pope to sit next to the White House Henni got in the States. Joe has done another voiceover, this one for the televising of a Grand Prix. These things earn him extraordinary sums for a few hours work. Henni also brought back from Washington DC, a George W. Bush talking doll. This seems an open goal for irony but no, the mannikin makes grave statesmanlike pronouncements, like Sam the Bald Eagle out of the Muppets. Sheila is charming a local authority into permitting one of her young clients to work somewhere glamorous during term time.

A few weeks later Ilse asks me to look at the charity's office building in Bristol. They are dangerously short of money. I measure the sitting position (back bricks), lap yum, pulses, direct mountain and so on. But I choose to report on the relative Hexagram from the Yi Jing. I want to give her a simple piece of information she can work with.

I tune in. The building is at odds with itself

It appears to feel bad about the money it is collecting. It is not providing as much value as it ought. This may be a question of overheads, inefficiency or distribution. But the building feels shifty.

I feed this back to Ilse. I suggest she raises it at Trustee level. Although her funds are the foundation of this foundation, it is an aspect of charity law that she cannot both work in and manage the charity. The Trustees have to be in charge.

To her credit she does. They spend a day talking the idea through. At the end of that week they receive over £100,000 from the Lottery fund. Someone had to work hard and smart to get this done but the timing is interesting.

I receive an appreciative email from her followed by another that informs me that the Trustees have ruled it a coincidence.

A Word about the Tao

It is little known and often denied by Chinese thinkers that Feng Shui is derived from the Tao.

The best known sourcebook of the Tao is the Tao Te Ching, the *Book of the Way and Virtue*. It dates from the 6th century BC and is attributed to Lao Tze. Typically even his name melts away into metaphor; it means something like "Old Chap". This volume of thoughts and insights reads like a book of poetry, skirting around the Tao, its poetry clarifying or obscuring depending on your point of view. If you believe that the world is made up of simple things that can and ought to be defined and stick to their definition, you will find it frustrating indeed. Little that is literal can be made of a prescription like:

> *The flow of the Tao is everywhere.*
> *It gives birth to all things but creates none.*
> *Its work is ceaseless but it looks for no reward,*
> **Tao te Ching**

Lao Tze was roughly contemporary with Confucius. Both lived during the Axial Age when a long-lived and well-travelled person might in addition to both of them have met the Gautama Buddha as well as Zarathustra and Aristotle. It is an astonishing fact that the ideas associated with each of these were developed inside three generations.

In China the era from then until 221BCE is called the Warring States Period. This is because the Zhou Dynasty which had been ruling an abbreviated form of modern China for over 500 years was losing control and China was breaking up into kingdoms. As the newer kingdoms and some of the older ones were unstable, turf war was rife. Chivalry, a given in warfare until then, flew out of the window. Appropriately the pragmatic military precepts of Sun Tze's *Art of War* date from this time.

Sun Tze is clearly drawing on the Book of Changes, (I Ching or more correctly Yi Jing) as is Confucius. The Yi originated within the distinctive culture of the Zhou. Its Trigrams (three-line figures) and the Hexagrams (six-line figures) they make up are the starting point for Confucius' *Analects,* the books of discussion for which he is known. Essentially these discussions are commentary upon the Yi. Much of Sun Tze's book is a discussion of Hexagram 7 – *The Army* – which deals with the appropriate uses of force.

The origins of the Yi Jing are at least 2,000 years older. Its yin and yang (broken and unbroken) lines were originally classifications of the cracks made in turtle shells when Zhou dynasty diviner-priests ceremonially baked them. Generally the turtle was withdrawn of course (and probably eaten) but nonetheless the practice was so widespread that at least one species of river turtle was made extinct. From the cracks, divination was drawn. Lao Tze's teachings come from this primal strain of Chinese thought. And like it, like the Tao, they are wild and without coherence. They are not making points. They are simply describing life as it is without the desire to make sense of it. Unlike Confucius they are not house-trained.

So it is no trick connecting Sun Tze, Confucius and the Yi. Generally Chinese culture, simplified by at least three reigns when books of record that did not conform to the way history ought to have been were burned, makes just that connection. But in doing so it has tended to leave the Tao on the fringes. Taoism – as much a theoretical nonsense as any other organised worship – has persisted as a fringe activity but the mainstream of Chinese thought is and has always been Confucian.

'Why would this happen?

Well, Confucius' work had a purpose which was social cohesion. Laudably he believed that an ordered and peaceful society was the highest goal. Accordingly his interpretation of the Yi Jing puts emphasis on filial piety, patriotism and duty.

The Yi however cannot be relied upon to do this unless it is viewed in a certain ordered, civilised light. And the Tao does not respect such notions. In other words the Yi interpreted neutrally reads like the Tao and is clearly drawn from ideas they have in common. For instance:

All arrive. The divination: good fortune.
Hexagram 19 ⌊in*: To Approach*, Line One
Yi Jing

Like much of the Yi this line is far too imprecise to offer life-lessons without slanted interpretation. It is if you like, too weird to be advice as we know it. Recent archaeological research backs up the idea that Confucianism was born of and draws on the Tao. As does a verse like:

The spokes of the wheel cooperate,
But it is not until the hub moves that the wagon does.
Tao te Ching

Here are ideas consistent with feng shui. They illustrate that feng shui and the Yi grow from a common root.

There is of course another aspect of feng shui that draws on two thousand years or so of records. These show what has happened previously under similar circumstances and allow us to predict that it will happen again. This in Western thought is called the *deductive* method. There is however a more fundamental aspect to feng shui and to Yi interpretation which leads to a different outcome every time.

This is the Tao. Which can not be predicted – except when it can.

So the Tao runs like the words in a stick of rock through Chinese thought but remains essentially unrecognised. Here in the West, unconstrained for the most part by the need to think along authorised lines, we can view feng shui for what it is: an attempt to second guess the Tao which of course is not possible but it's a brave try.

At university studying philosophy in the 1970s, I learned something (which you may find less surprising than my tutors did). What I learned was this: the entire long process of the development of human thought has come up with only two logical systems. If you like, there are only two ways of learning things. They are called the *inductive* and the *deductive*.

The inductive is expressed in logical tautologies:

Cars have wheels,
This is a car.
Therefore it has wheels.

This form is called a tautology because it only tells us what we knew already.

The other logical form works from the premise that what has happened before will happen again:

Because the sun rose this morning, it will rise tomorrow.

The weakness of this structure is that there is no certainty in it. It is probable to a very high degree that the sun will rise tomorrow but given any combination of comets, sunspots, aliens, Republicans and cosmic cataclysm it is clearly not certain.

This is the sum total of logical systems available to human beings. Upon these two pillars have been constructed astro-physics, political theory, architecture and medicine. There is no area of human thought that does not owe them.

And yet they can only tell us either what we know already or what is probable. They cannot tell us anything that is both new and certain. There is no logical tool that allows us to learn anything both new and certain. And yet we do.

This is the Tao.

Water, water everywhere

Helen asks me to visit a Victorian mill in Sussex; right next to a reservoir. The house belongs to Simon. The two of them have had an on-off relationship for close to a decade. Helen finds the place intimidating. She doesn't like to stay long so she maintains her own flat in Islington but Simon prefers it here. He is fond of darkness. There are Kenneth Anger and Aleister Crowley books on the shelves.

And there less than 100 yards away, at a level perhaps 10 feet higher than their living room is a reservoir. Millions of gallons of water; *I'd* have been nervous. But also he is

a scary guy in the way that only an English public schoolboy can be. Placing symbols opposite the water might wake him up but it might just turn him vicious.

These are both talented people. He is a sometime film maker. We discuss whether I am interesting enough to be a subject.

I place traditional Chinese jiu shapes in the South to tighten his grip on the slippery ladder of success. In a large basement under the house are stored the effects of his recently deceased parents. Here, 20 feet below the water table, you can feel the unreleased upset.

Public school is the traditional way English middle class parents ensure their children grow up as repressed as themselves. Wellington was right that the Battle of Waterloo was won on the playing fields of Eton. Only such an environment could generate the aloofness required to conquer the world. I speak as a public schoolboy, by the way, who knows the territory and I don't judge Simon any more than I judge myself. We all have baggage.

Gently I work with him. His upset at the loss of the parents he never really knew is trying to express itself. What he needs is a good cry, bless him. I gently nudge him towards it, he comes close but the waters won't break. The moment is left hanging.

I recommend loud music in the cellar followed by ruthless clearing: ebay and a skip.

Helen is an alternative healer, currently temping in the City. On the face of it she wants to get serious with Simon and he is resisting. But the physical universe does not lie: she lives 60 miles away from him just as surely as he lives 60 miles from her. If he is resisting, so is she.

She gets Simon to call me. The deal had been the one house. He wants two plus a discount. Reluctantly I agree. Clearly Helen has discovered his uses.

There is paradox involved in using any model: feng shui, acupuncture, reiki, psychoanalysis. All can make a difference but generally not without a choice on the part of the subject, I tell them. I suggest alterations to the chi of Helen's house to make it more open to a committed relationship. Simon wants me to explain this paradox. How can his intention have anything to do with it? Surely the system works or it doesn't?

But explanation gives metaphor less meaning, not more, and this sort of question is more likely to stem from a desire to stay separate than a desire to understand. I don't want to make this highly intelligent man feel stupid especially when he is witnessed by a woman who takes some dark satisfaction in his incomprehension.

I give them as much as I think they can handle and leave vaguely dissatisfied.

I recall when I had first received national publicity and I was in Sainsbury's. An old client from my days as an insurance broker spotted me.

"How's the zen mastery?" he asked me – as if I had ever made such a claim.

"Banana," I answered.

4.
SOLAR FORTNIGHT BEGINNING:
FRIDAY 4 FEBRUARY 2005 01.34

Lap Chun *Spring Begins*

Month: wu yin the Earth Tiger

Hour	Day	Month	Year
metal	earth	earth	wood
yi	ji	wu	yi
hai	wei	yin	yuw
pig	**sheep**	**tiger**	**rooster**

The New..ish Year

The Spring Festival that is lap chun or li chow, is on 4 February this year. Most people think of this as the Chinese New Year although as we have discussed, some have other ideas. Historically celebrations used to last fifteen days, spanning the whole of the solar fortnight or *breath* also called li chow (*Beginning of Spring*) but these days a less bourgeois three is normal. In modern China holidays, like lunch, are definitely for wimps.

Now if the courses of the sun and moon were tidier, li chow would also be the first new moon of spring. Sometimes it is and more frequently it isn't. This year it isn't. The new moon actually falls within the New Year on 9 February, which is generally considered dubious. The other way round is better.

Predictably, the Americans are rattling sabres in Iran's direction as the preening wooden Rooster gets underway. The spring chicken in the form of Condoleeza Rice may yet (as predicted) do significant good on her travels.

As Bernal Diaz said of his time with Cortez: "We came to serve God and grow rich". Nice work if you can get it.

The Spring Tiger...er...springs

This is the month of the Tiger. Although on the compass it is one of the North Eastern *Mountains* of late Winter, the Tiger belongs to the wood element of spring. Wood is growth, new stuff, freshness, early mornings and so on. Spring is in the air. This is an earth Tiger so probably more set in his ways than your average big cat. Those born in 1938 may confirm this and in 1998 we experienced a whole year of earth Tiger. Tigers are energetic and wear their hearts on their sleeve. Not perhaps the safest combination of qualities. There may be impetuosity to contain this month.

The term *Tiger* is also used to describe symbolically the yin side of a house which is to the right as you look out the front, making it (symbolically) West. On the left is the Dragon, at the back the Tortoise and in front the Bird. The Bird (symbolically) marks the South, the Tortoise the North, and the Dragon the East. When a house actually faces North this can be very confusing because for these purposes the four animals stay put whatever the orientation. On the other hand it is very straightforward if a house actually faces South.

It is such contortions that drive people to use feng shui manuals as fire lighters.

As the Tiger side is yin, this is the side to pretty up with flowers. The Dragon side calls for big green leaves and tree trunks. I won't dwell on the symbolism of this. When the yin side is neglected, which together with the orientation tends to pinpoint a member of the family, I look for trouble among the womenfolk. And conversely if the Dragon is unkempt. A house at the end of a long street will tend to be more fortunate for one gender than the other dependent on which side is inhabited and which side open space.

On one survey I did for TV's *Housebusters*, a house on Winchmore Hill in North London, the Tiger side was solid and the Dragon interfered with. There was an odd room on the Dragon side that went nowhere and an independent entrance. This led me to conclude rightly without entering the house or meeting the people, that the husband was hardly ever there.

Dreams Coming True: Cucumber Sandwiches

Zoe emailed me from Scotland this week. She is approaching 40 – young from where I'm sitting but I know the panic – and single. Ready to settle down and fed up with the raw material offered to date.

I located a water feature spot for her last August. She finally placed it in February and almost right away she met a man who passed the rigorous initial assessment. She is now on date three. As I was discussing with some very likeable ladies on a residential fitness* weekend last week, date three means business. One and it's anybody's guess. Two and they're considering it, three and you're probably away, we concluded.

Not by the way, I hastily emphasise, that I think that women are victims in this. It's just that generally they're more ready than men to see the joke.

I'll report as Zoe reports to me but clearly we have moved the energies along there.

---

*Them, not me.

However one thing she said pressed my caution button: that she was becoming *obsessed* with keeping the water feature going. Remember she's in Scotland where cold is a way of life and an outdoor water feature can easily freeze up. I know houses in Scotland where an *indoor* water feature can freeze up.

This obsession is worth looking at.

Another word for it might be "superstition". When people talk of "superstition" they often are not very clear what they mean. One feng shui authority sees reliance on symbolic figures as superstitious unless they resemble particular vegetables in which case they are, he says, definitely not superstitious. Go figure.

The Chinese Government uses the word to define pretty much anything inexplicable as well as a number of explicable things that they can't forbid any other way.

But superstition begins at home. It is a mental state. I think it is something like the inability to tell the difference between what we can and cannot control. There is little in this strange imaginary universe that we *can* control actually. Particle physics tells us that everything consists of molecules bouncing around. These molecules change nature and leap from place to place. Given sufficient time the molecules in your garden wall will turn into a cucumber sandwich. We cannot control such things.

What we can do is tell the truth about what is so and about the changes we want. This is the Tao. We can choose.

And Zoe has chosen. Her choice includes the water feature and it works to respect that as the medium she has chosen. But if she has chosen to move on, obsession is a distraction. It is not respect and it may even take her eye off the ball. Tricky stuff, having your dreams come true. Especially when it's still chilly and the Tiger is abroad

As Maggie Smith said in *Gosford Park*, obviously referring to this time of year: "Difficult colour, green."

World of Woo-Woo™

Daisy had been plagued by mysterious wet patches in her house. One, in the front room by the TV, was nowhere near a pipe or even a window. She has no pool, no pets, so there was not an obvious linear explanation. There is a ruined Cistercian Abbey nearby. Many of their wells still function so it is possible there is subterranean water but that doesn't explain a flood on the first floor!

At one edge of this fairly large house was an incongruous extension, built by the previous occupants only yards from the neighbour, unnecessarily close. Building it had been making some sort of point. It was an aggressive feature, a pointed finger frozen in brick. The North East where it was, is traditionally the *Ghost Gate*. If there is going to be woo-woo™ stuff, generally it will be here. There were also xuan kong 5s here which indicate spooky stuff in the ba chop or ba zhai calculation.

Inside the extension, which was a utility room with even its own two doors impeding each other, there was some sort of residual energy. If we deal with such things as metaphors and try not to pin them down too much as ghosts or malevolence or whatever, we do not reduce the means by which we can deal with them. The classical cures for this sort of stuff involve reds and noise. It's all very adversarial. I'm not interested in that. I don't want to do violence to anyone whether they are substantial or insubstantial.

This particular energy appeared to be female and short on humour. I could feel the corners of my mouth being drawn down.

And the accent I heard had flat Northern 'a's in it

"The people here before you, were they from up North?"

"Yes, they were," said Daisy. I took a deep breath to get further in touch.

"It's a sulk."

Sulks are not unusual in people or in stuck energies and I don't mean to imply they're regional either. We're all either in bliss or sulking, pretty much all the time but some more than others. When we stop sulking we disappear in a puff of smoke, I think.

"Still alive?"

"I expect so; they weren't that old."

She confirmed there had been friction between her predecessors and the neighbours.

I placed a t'ang lung shape in the utility room and gave her some crystals and some mumbo-jumbo to do and asked her to call me in a month. I left realizing that if we had insisted on a haunting we might have had nothing to work with at all or we might have been talking in hushed voices around the "ghost" of someone still living.

As I drove away I realized that I had described both Daisy and her husband, born in 1961, as "Rabbits". You are of course Oxen, Daisy, although as I am at pains to point out, the Year animal is only an aspect of the ba zi which describes the moment of our birth.

I make mistakes but this is a very basic one. It's meaningful when I am particularly stupid.

Lillian Too's World of Feng Shui

Feng shui is big business in Singapore and Malaysia. Stars like Lillian Too and Joey Yap fill huge halls with their seminars and workshops. Interestingly I attended a (very modest) workshop with

Lillian Too in London in the mid-90s. She was, in my judgement, a sweet, gracious and wise woman.

These days she publishes a magazine, *Feng Shui World* which I love. It's loud, colourful and brash and full both of offers for glitzy knick-knacks and useful advice. In tandem her daughter Jennifer runs a huge retail franchising operation called World of Feng Shui.

Reading the magazine this month I gained new insight into why feng shui should be so commercial in South East Asia and so low key in the UK.

There was an article on Martha Stewart who if truth were told, is probably a personal friend of Ms Too. US entrepreneur, Mrs Stewart, you may recall, was jailed briefly for financial misbehaviour. Now she is out and back with her own TV show and her lifestyle magazine is up and running again.

The article traces Martha's fortunes in relation to her personal feng shui, her ba zi (or *paht chee*). It shows how her incarceration reflects her elemental balance. The ba zi shows she was always going to be in trouble at this point in her career. The clash between her "self" character and her "fate pillars" illustrates this.

But there is no suggestion in the article that her disgrace had anything to do with her behaviour. It, in point of fact, asserts that she was not jailed for insider trading which is what most of us – including me – understood but for lying to the investigators.

I guess these self-made billionaires must stick together.

On the other hand there is something rather crucial missing here. I think it is an awareness of paradox. We do not need to choose between believing in Martha's accountability and her ba zi. Both can be true. The paradox is that the accuracy of her ba zi does not make her either a victim of fate or innocent of the charges. She, like the rest of us, remains responsible for her actions.

Paradox can be difficult because it involves holding two apparently contradictory ideas at once but it is a short route to wisdom. Paradox challenges the mind. How can we have free will as well as an innate character? Similarly, it seems to me, we enjoy choice as well as a heritage of DNA, accountability as well as destiny. If we forget we are the ones choosing, we become robots at the mercy of fate. Conversely if we forget we are part of the Tao we can easily hallucinate that we have a control over the universe that is just not available to human beings. Even self-made billionaires.

The article appears to imply that if you get your feng shui right you can get away with anything. Not only do I not believe that, I don't want to believe it. We can do remarkable things with no linear explanation but we remain responsible. At the heart of miracles, of magic, of truly practical feng shui is the humility of this knowledge. To miss one or the other is to not be balanced. This I think, may be the Tao.

And the magazine, as I said, is wonderful. I heartily recommend it. But let's stay aware that we are responsible.

Crystal Clear

Today is the New Moon. I don't have to rely on feeling this in my bones because I have a smart Moon Chart on my wall.

The New Moon is one of the times to charge crystals. The beginning of the waxing phase is a very constructive moment which you can lock into the cells of the crystal much as you fire shape into a clay pot. Except that you can do it over and over.

The full moon which heralds the *waning* phase can be useful for getting rid of things. Most of my feng shui however is about transforming, which is generally positive, so I employ the New Moon more.

Wash the crystals first in spring water, adding rock or sea salt for the rougher stones like rose quartz or amethyst. This helps get the *stuff* out of them especially if they've been working hard on your behalf. Don't put salt on the polished ones.

Some stones may have especially tricky *stuff* left in them from quarrying. Not all crystal mines in places such as Colombia are run by enlightened employers.

Leave the crystals outside in the moonlight. If the New Moon is so perverse as to manifest in daytime, leave them out for 24 hours before and after.

Then programme them: literally telling them what you want from them. Children may enjoy talking out loud to crystals – I often suggest malachite for growing boys and haematite for girls. These are specialist crystals but any crystal will do what it is told to the best of its ability. Simply carrying it around and touching it when an appropriate thought strikes you will make a difference.

Crystals live in the North East or the South West or at the tai chi, the heart of the house. These are the earth areas. Sometimes there are jobs for them elsewhere and certain houses have too much earth in the tai chi already but if your crystals are taking time out, these are the default locations to store them.

You can find the tai chi by measuring the widest width of the house and the longest length and noting where the lines cross. As long as your house is not oriented North-East – South West, literally grounding this spot with as big a rose quartz as you can run to is sound. Same cleansing and charging rules apply.

Swan Vesta

This week we placed Vesta the Goddess of Spring in my clients Paul and Donna's garden. The house had a very specific area missing in the SouthWest. When a house diverges from a regular rectangular shape it is always ominous and the gap here represented hard work for a Mother. There had been "tax" windows on the first floor overlooking the area, blocked as if the house did not want to look out in this direction. Paul and Donna had opened the windows up soon after moving in.

These windows had been blocked in towards the end of the 18th century to escape the proto-poll tax that was to compensate George III for the loss of the United States. It was assessed on the basis of the number of windows in a dwelling so predictably many were closed up. It's amazing how many still are. I see them every day above street level on Godalming High Street. While they remain blocked they trap a certain type of chi and obviously limit the light. Unblocking them can send a bit of a thrill through a house after two hundred years.

What the house didn't want to see perhaps was a blocked spring a couple of hundred yards to the SouthWest which was its principle receptacle of chi. Chi comes down from the mountain, carried by the wind (feng) and is held by the water (shui). This spring is at the foot of the *direct mountain* which is the local source of chi. Once open it will just *spray* benevolence. This costly job however will have to wait.

Paul has in the course of his ruthless climb up the ladder of success, a habit of jetting off for weeks at a time. I am used to receiving on consecutive days, his calls from places as far apart as Cannes, St Petersburg and Moscow. There are worse ways to earn a living but his travels leave Donna with the job of two parents. They live out in the wilds and though it is comfortable, it is lonely. And the house reflected this.

I had asked them to find an assertive female figure of approximate lifesize to fill this gap. It was important that she be powerful but not provocative. They chose a classical statue, one of a set of four representing the Seasons: demi-Goddesses, if you like, properly addressed as Vesta or Hestia.

As we wheeled her into place the chi instantly felt different. Actually it was Dean the handyman who did the wheeling, dug her in and made her safe for the children and placed the *Judges' Bench* at the other side of the house as well as completing with expert good humour a dozen other jobs I could not have begun.

Dean is an uncomplicated man, an old-style loyal retainer. When we talked about the phases of the moon and certain positions working for some sorts of activity and not for others, he was with me all the way.

When we sat down to lunch – cold fish and a wonderful salad – something had snapped into place.

It was a different house.

5.
SOLAR FORTNIGHT BEGINNING:
FRIDAY 18 FEBRUARY 2005 21.28

Yu Soi Rain Water

Month: wu yín **the Earth Tiger**

Hour	Day	Month	Year
water	water	earth	wood
gui	gui	wu	yi
hai	yuw	yin	yuw
pig	**rooster**	**tiger**	**rooster**

Ruling the Roost

I'm writing this listening to the Cars' album *Heartbeat City*. Recently I've been writing while listening to Keane whose blend of naivete and pure emotion brings tears to my eyes. But The Cars' *Drive* seems the right soundtrack in this year of ending hunger. Astonishingly a whole generation has grown up that doesn't associate this song with the Eritrean infant struggling to stand in the Michael Buerk documentary that inspired Live Aid. How did that change while my attention was elsewhere? It's as if all that effort and caring never happened and Bob Geldof had stayed with the Boomtown Rats.

It's not so of course. Africans are still starving but we no longer think of it as inevitable. It is not the way of the world but a function of the unfair distribution of wealth. The obscenity of a child dying every three seconds for mere want of sugar water is an option not a law. Having realized this, change must happen. We now know better. We can choose differently. Context is all. Just as way before his time, John Lennon knew that he could stay in bed for peace and (although I'm not recommending it for a variety of reasons) you could perfectly well eat Big Macs to end hunger once you have directed your intention. I'm a vegetarian by the way.

So this is the second chi, *breath,* or solar fortnight, of the month of the earth Tiger in the year of the wood Rooster. The opening day is a water Rooster too which is about as supportive as a day as this devious bird could hope for. Water supports wood you will remember. In a tricky year, this is not great.

So expect fresh liberties in the name of Liberty. Just as the Observer defined moral values as "unprovoked attacks on vulnerable minorities" so we might define Liberty as the restrictions the rich put on the poor. In Taoism everything is its opposite.

People have said to me several times this month words to the effect "I'm a Rooster, this is my year." Actually no, Roosters don't get on with each other. Go look in a chicken coop. If you are a Rooster, ally with a Dragon in 2005. Wearing a Dragon symbol is a way to do this especially if – God Bless You – you're also wearing a "Make Poverty History" wristband. Why? Because the wristband is white and therefore yin metal like the year. This incidentally is the finest of fine-tuning and depends substantially on intention. Or find a Dragon.

So in this precarious year, a month of conflict. Powerful idealism is active in the world but the odds are against it for now. The big openings won't come much before May.

Q: How many feng shui men does it take to change a light bulb?
A: If only it were that simple.
But hunger *is* over.

I used to be a Chinese Philospher but I'm alright Tao

I've been doing a series of ba zi *for Healing* sessions with Ken and Sue. A series consists of a ba zi – that's personal feng shui if you like – plus five one-hour sessions. These can be life-changing. The ba zi tells me what their parents were like: Sue's were disciplinarian in an almost random way, Ken's strangely absent – it turns out he was adopted. The pain is there in the Chinese characters. Our parents provide the template for our own relationships, so this is important stuff to see from this angle.

The ba zis also tell me how well they hang onto money (okay) and each other (exceptionally well)

Ken's a computer whiz. He's the sort of guy you ring when your computer will not do what it is told. If like me you instruct yours to search for the words "ba zi" and then an hour later it's still doing it on an entirely different document – maybe a letter to the local authority – you will appreciate his value.

To prove the Universe – God, Spirit, What-have-you – has a sense of humour, he got a plague of gremlins on his own computer this week.

It was Sunday evening. Sue rang and passed Ken over to me. His voice was coming from somewhere high in his head which is a sure sign of distress but even if it wasn't I could feel his upset deep in my chest. As if someone were standing on my ribs.

The Universe did not want you on your computer, I suggested. To his huge credit he ran with this idea. He had felt useless because the one thing that made him worthwhile was closed to him. Very painful. Taking him back to pain he had suppressed as a little boy, I suggested and he took my word for it. This can save a lot of time.

The Tao, I went on, is a system except when it isn't. You can't argue with it. Except when you can. My basic rule is that I go with the flow unless I have a better idea. You can't actually *control* anything. Generally the best you can do is get in touch with what you have chosen – however little you might like to own up to it – and work from there.

He was bemused but played along.

If we are to have any mastery over our lives, I said, we have to roll with the Tao, that is choose and accept what is so. The physical universe cannot tell a lie. Things are the way they are. And getting that we *have* chosen, we can start to get in touch with what we might choose next.

I told him the story of the American tourist lost in the West Country. Coming to the dead end of a narrow lane, he spots a local digging beet in a field.

"Say, pal," he calls, "How do I get to Bristol?"

"Well," says the native, "Oi wouldn't start from 'ere."

Ken's a very easy going guy and we were discussing a very painful parting. I heard a grown man at the other end of a phone but I saw in my mind a little boy coping the best he could with hurt he couldn't begin to understand; just crying till there was no more crying in him. There was something so *disoriented* about this cheerful man.

Sue and Ken's house is on the outside of a curve which implies not holding onto things. At the rear of their property the rhododendrons keep dying – as if they will *not* form a boundary. They will *not* hold onto the chi. There is even a swimming pool in the neighbour's garden behind the rhododendrons. And this is to the North West which because it represents solidity and the Father, is the very worst place for it. If the North West is missing, the cures we can place are seriously limited. Wet is nearly as bad.

Ken and Sue want a baby. This is what they want to hold onto. They have been through an awful lot: adopting and then returning an impossibly damaged child and then presenting themselves again to the adoption authorities for scrutiny. Meanwhile they pursue surrogacy as well as radical fertility treatments.

I have put a series of adjustments in place and now all we can do is wait and respond.

In his bright affable way Ken promised to *feel* this week. It even may be that simple. Simple (not easy); and calling for considerable courage.

Wishing on a Star

The *Imperial Heaven Stars* model is a system for aligning a house when we build from scratch. Some feng shui masters would say that is actually all you can do: find a location with perfect feng shui and then build so that the doors are correct. Alteration is always a compromise, they would say.

You need to find the *direct* mountain – that is the nearest major elevation – which will be the source of chi. This can be a hill nearby or a tall range in the distance. Then you need to find the water which will hold the chi. This will tend to be in the opposite direction of the mountain and echo its shape. Rolling hills give onto a winding river, mountains onto a torrent. They *will* be there.

Feng shui means literally *wind and water*. The wind carries the chi down from the mountain and the water holds it. Water is more a barrier than a source of chi; it ensures the chi doesn't float off. Since one of the implications of feng (i.e wind) is the *four* winds and by extension the four cardinal points of the compass, Western feng shui variations ignore orientation at some loss.

Many masters advise that if the doors of an existing building are wrong, you simply move on. This is certainly what the Emperors did. The Ming (14th century) Prince Zhao who is buried at Longquan in Hubei Province found his own mausoleum site while out hunting some thirty years before his demise. He is said to have left his ring there to mark the spot and gone home to alert his feng shui man. The feng shui man found and returned the ring, telling the Prince that it had indeed marked the perfect spot. This may be a tribute either to Zhao's skill or to the adviser's diplomacy. When the time came, Zhao was buried with all six of his wives and concubines. As his feng shui man, I would have taken no risks and found an urgent survey to do in Lhasa. All parties to the location of the Emperor Qin Shu Huang Ti's tomb were buried with him.

For many of us, changing houses if the doors are wrong is no more practical than changing cars when the ashtrays are full. Which is where the Imperial Heaven Stars model can be helpful.

Each of the 24 *mountains*, that is the 24 divisions of the 8 compass points, is occupied by an Imperial Heaven Star for the year and also for the *Fate period*. These Stars are external (not indoor) influences which both limits and multiplies their significance. They don't relate directly to the indoors but they are much more powerful for being in the realm of Early Heaven.

The bad Imperial Stars are always bad but they are different types of bad dependent upon the year or fate period we are in. The current Fate Period (8) runs from 1996 to 2017 (or 2004 to 2024 depending on which master you listen to). Fortunately this puts 2005 in the 8 Fate whichever way we calculate.

Give me an open field, the feng shui master would say, because pretty much all houses are wrong but the Imperial Heaven Stars allow us to make the most of whatever location we find ourselves in. We can create openings where there ought to be doors and elevation where there ought to be walls and we can neutralize the areas where there ought to be neither.

The mountain in the South East called zhen the Dragon for instance, is at tin diu or *Celestial Hook* during the 8 fate. *Celestial Hook* calls for any tree or structure that is disproportionately tall to be lopped; there may otherwise be dangers from above. These are not limited to curlew guano, branches or squirrels; Celestial Hook relates to aerial disasters, plane crashes and so on.

At other times zhen may be at tin sat or *Celestial Curse*. The antidote for tin sat is very similar to tin diu – tin means Heaven – and the baleful consequences of neglect almost identical. When tin sat is at zhen (April) the consequences are liable to be to the very young.

In the South West at the kun mountain, is the Imperial Heaven Star Bou din or *Treasure*, whose injunction is "Never put water here," the consequence being loss.

Each of the Heaven stars has a character. Some are good for doors (Gam Siang – *Golden box*) and some are not. Some suit the front of a property, some the rear.

To cut a long story short: they identify when any given orientation will flourish if it is ever going to. So before you build, locate your direct mountain and your water, then or otherwise plot your orientation so that you have loon loou (the *Imperial Dragon's Platform)* rather than ba mou (Eight – opposing – Armies) at your front door.

To cut a long story even shorter, if you are selecting a house avoid one with doors at the wrong stars. Or better still, call me.

Sam Going South

Sam's house faces slightly West of South. When I arrived, the front window was blocked with plants. Had she been a librarian, blocking it might have made sense. But Sam is an actress. Closing out the brightness of the sun and by extension curiosity, experimentation and recognition was clearly not appropriate. This woman's life is in the limelight.

"I can't stand people looking," she said and as if to make her point, a neighbour ambled by, inches from the pane. I noted exactly what she had said. People say what they mean. Often this is more than they think they mean.

So: an actress who did not like people looking. There was more to it of course.

It is a platitude that a woman has a deep relationship with her father. This is in my experience, pretty much always true. Sam's died last year. He was a complex man and not entirely without fault and she has been in mourning ever since. Little had been happening in her career and she remained uncommitted to her longtime boyfriend. Takes two to tango of course.*

Right away we pulled the plants out of the window. This, in a relatively small flat, left several feet of emptiness. As Lao Tze says, "Solidity is an advantage but it is emptiness that makes a vessel useful," and it is my observation that people with an expectation of abundance like unfilled space. You can generally spot budding

---

* Chuck Spezzano often says: "It only takes one to tango but it has to be *you*." And of course he's right.

millionaires by the space they allow themselves to move within: lots of space equals loadsamoney. Feng shui after all is an attempt to fit time and space into a single system so space available equals time available and by extension all sorts of other resources.

Classically at the front of the property the chi is "assembled" into a "pearl" within what is known as the ming tang or *Bright Hall*. This is where the space should be. Additionally some height is called for at either side. An enclosed apartment, even on the ground floor, generally has that. We also want a secure "mountain" at the rear, that is a clear safe back boundary.

As the front was West of South, the rear was East of North. Close to that in the North West, representing the father, there was a garage still full of her Dad's stuff. Lack of partition made it unclear what part of the garden belonged to her and which to the neighbours, so we placed conifers to define the border and agreed to empty the garage. Painful stuff, letting go. I'm not a great fan of evergreens but they make for clear borders.

What fence there was at the rear was falling over.

"Replace it with something solid at least six feet, ideally eight feet high," I advised.

We did some work on the rooms inside of course. Her bedroom is going to be very interesting and I applied some abundance band aid to the office.

It will be great to see her out in the world again.

Friends, Romans, Contrary Men

Katherine sees Roman Legionaires in her daughter's bedroom. But only when she eats pistachio nuts. The village shows clear signs of Roman occupation including a name ending in *-chester* (a corruption of the Roman word for 'camp'.) And the ba chop or permanent external energies speak of ancient stuff lingering. The core of the problem is water in the South West. A tricky one.

Earlier this year I was in correspondence with a student of one of the world's most respected feng shui teachers. She took issue with my observation that external water in the South West often coincides with distressed women. Her point was that in the current 8 Fate the chi passes on the wind (feng) down the mountain in the North East to the South West beyond which the water (shui) will not let it wander. The water which may in practice be a road or even a mirror, acts as margin or border. In other words the South West is exactly where the water should be.

I can't argue with her logic or her erudition. But I am surveying people's homes most days of the week and what I wrote is based on sheer observation. Submerged village ponds, pools of goldfish, flooded troughs; I have seen all of these at the South West coinciding with terrible upset for the women of the house. But it does seem to conflict with classic authority.

The reason for the contradiction – in so far as there are 'reasons' – may well be that the Imperial Heaven Star tin koon, (or *Heaven Hook* which is bad news) is in the South West next to bou din (*Treasure Hall*) in the (current) 8 Fate. Bou Din is actually rather fortuitous; it implies abundance as the name Treasure Hall suggests, but the orthodox advice is never to put water there. The South West of course, relates to the mature woman and the middle sector (sometimes known as SW2) is actually called kun after the Mother whose element is earth. Some people – none of them feng shui masters – call this the Relationship area.

As a rule earth and water should be combined with care. Their combination can imply the earth being sieved or washed. And I have observed that this is the sort of experience that a woman with water placed here goes through.

Katherine, herself suffering from depression and with a schizophrenic mother and Alzheimer's struck mother-in-law, seems to illustrate the point. They have an aggressive porch jutting out to the South and a perfectly good front door that they do not use. These are the sort of additional details I have come to associate with upset.

"I just don't like it," Katherine says of the door.

The Imperial Heaven Stars is a classical model which a feng shui master may use to orient a house when starting from scratch. It indicates the best locations of doors, site and so on during particular Fate Periods. So a house that was perfectly located in the 7 Fate (which most consider ended in 2004), may be suddenly not so good from then on. To complicate the issue, masters disagree over exactly when Fates begin and end.

Actually this is not as capricious as it sounds because the "good" areas are always good and the bad always bad, they just take on different types of good and bad from time to time.

In the SouthWest of the garden is a water feature. Historically there had been a pond and the house remains barely above the water table. Ancient energies often linger at these spots. Knowing this, the Celts negotiatied with the Gods by dropping goodies for them into ponds. Underground water often announces itself by tipping the needle of my compass. A major factor is the health of the water. Stagnant or subterranean and therefore blocked, water is unhealthy pretty much wherever it is. If it is too close to the house it may swamp and water anywhere may be inappropriate for the orientation of a particular house. Katherine's doors are wrong for this water when I check them against the medieval formulae of Grandmaster Yang.

What may also have some bearing is that the xuan kong method that distributes the Hexagrams of the Yi around the house, places Hexagram 47 meaning *Distress,* at kun in this Fate also. Here there are three women in three separate types of distress.

Katherine has been fed up and Tony has tended to be on the wrong end of it. Don't construe me as saying this is nothing to do with him. We always have our own responsibility for the situations we find ourselves in. Even men. But it is his beloved mother who has just developed the early stages of Alzheimer's disease. I watched my own epileptic mother's marble count reduce to zero over thirty years, so I have some idea of the heartbreak.

Katherine told me that her childhood had been punctuated by her own mother's stays in mental institutions. Having many times as a small boy, stood over my mother's prone form while she returned to her body, I understood some of the strain of this on a child. Dostoevsky suggested epilepsy was something of a window to God. He hadn't, I guess, come across Alzheimer's or iatrogenic dementia.

SouthWest water, three distressed women. The plot thickens; I prescribed as I often do, for Katherine to sit in the tai chi and *feel.* This ancient Taoist process involves letting go of the narrative that we add to our feelings to justify them. If this makes no sense, I am happy to enter into personal correspondence. Medieval thinkers called it the *Via Negativa.*

For the house, I prescribed more prosaically, turfing over the water feature and removing a vast outdoor mirror. It may take more than this. We'll see. For the Romans in the bedroom I am prescribing a jiu shape called a t'ang lung. This is not a breathing disorder.

Until (and beyond) next time, as I tell Joey my ten-year old son and Guru, keep a smile on your face, a song in your heart and a spring in your onion.

6.
SOLAR FORTNIGHT BEGINNING:
SATURDAY 5 MARCH 2005 19.45

Ging Jit *Excited Insects*

Month: ji muw **the Earth Rabbit**

Hour	Day	Month	Year
water	**earth**	**earth**	**wood**
ren	wu	ji	yi
xu	zi	muw	yuw
dog	**rat**	**rabbit**	**rooster**

The Rabbit Month

The Rabbit is connected in folklore with the moon. Its nature is tender and easygoing and the Jade rabbit at least, is reckoned to live a thousand years. A red one is particularly auspicious. Albino rabbits used to be so unusual in China that a sighting was considered very significant.

The Rabbit rises early. So as well as signifying spring it represents early morning and the East where the sun rises. In divination terms, this year, the Rabbit being opposite the year animal the Rooster, sits in the *Place Curse*. This is unlikely to be a great month in terms of global politics for the vast majority of us. Last month the Tiger heralded more indefensible shenanigans in Asia, this month the Rabbit may also be diving for cover.

Rabbits are noted for their fertility of course, a yin earth one even more so. Incorporate this in your plans as you see fit.

Alex (1)

Alex rang me this week. She is young and beautiful and refuses to get the idea that she can choose any way of life and most particularly any partner she wants. I surveyed her home when she was still living with her little daughter's father. It was full of traps for a man. He fell into all of them of course: too much time building his business and on the golf course, unable to choose whether he wanted to be committed to one woman and the sensible life of a father.

I have personally repealed Sod's (or Murphy's) Law because it is no use to me or anyone else but sometimes I'm tempted.

He's very young too.

Ultimately they split.

They have done a wonderful job with Abbie, their daughter. Abbie knows everyone loves her and that her life is perfect and she has a smile that that would charge batteries.

Now Alex wants a compatibility analysis for her and another guy. The analysis says Alex and he will be very happy together if she will just choose him. Unfortunately she is not about to do that.

Startled Insects, Toe fat, other delicacies

Excited or *startled* insects, the first *breath* of March, is my favourite name for a solar fortnight. As it happens it was adopted by a musical collective in Bristol in the 80s who specialized in soundtrack work, huddled away in a basement in Redland. Some of their number went on to work with Portishead and the legendary Blue Aeroplanes.

Lots of bands have plundered Chinese metaphysics for names, the *Clash* being perhaps the most prominent.

The reference is to the Jamaican phrase: "two sevens clash," used often in reggae lyrics and meaning serious power struggle. In feng shui two sevens signifies just that. The yin metal 7 por kwan stands for niggles and cattiness. The pits is two of them together. If you find this configuration in a Flying Star calculation, stand well back. There are going to be sparks. There is of course a large Chinese community in Jamaica. Harry Chung and Leslie Kong, if I remember rightly, controlled two of the major studios.

Cliff Bennett (of *Got to Get You into My Life* fame) called his regrouped 70s band *Toe Fat*, which is the san sat star of true love. That is to say that if it appears in the right place in your ba zi you will be so irresistible as to be able to pick and choose. This is the *Peach Blossom* find-your-soulmate calculation that is so popular in the US right now. One new age teacher I worked with banned the description *soulmate* from his trainings because he got so fed up with trainees turning up to workshop after workshop with new ones.

Ex-Byrd Gene Clark's album *No Other,* regularly nominated as the greatest album ever recorded, draws heavily on the *Book of Changes* and features the idea of Clark and the world simultaneously being high, low and subject to change. Confucius thought it before of course and Lao Tze before him.

Syd Barrett also plunders the Yi on the first Pink Floyd album *Piper at the Gates of Dawn* where he talks of things happening in six stages and the seventh "bringing return." Syd on the other hand, a prodigious user of LSD who has been *hors de combat* since 1967, may not be the best example of how to achieve mastery in a world in which the only constant is change.

The image of a *Piper at the Gates of Dawn*, incidentally is from the *Wind in the Willows*. Were it not so unlikely I'd speculate that

Kenneth Graham shared preferences in leisure activity with Syd Barrett. "Parp parp," said Toad.

A Question of Emphasis

People often have the impression that feng shui is about wind chimes and wall coverings. And of course it includes these but generally décor is fine tuning. I have watched a feng shui master spend a whole afternoon surveying a smallish house and recommend nothing but a reangled door. Then he was pretty dismissive of the lady asking where to put her holy pictures and what colour the carpet should be.

The reangled door radically changed the chi flow of the place, this being one of the single most powerful things you can do.

On the other hand, once the feng shui of a place is balanced, a tiny change can be crucial. And some of the most powerful formulae depend on distinctions of less than one degree.

So I was interested to read this from Sophie whose bedroom, I told her, was sending mixed messages:

"Hi Richard, you asked me to let you know of any coincidences etc…

As a single girl in today's world, I, like many, have been using internet dating sites to meet people. Before Christmas I spotted this very nice-looking guy. A couple of weeks later I plucked up the courage to write to him. No reply. In January I wrote again and again no reply. On several occasions I looked at his profile and admired him from a distance...wishing he would reply.

You came round to my house and advised me to put blue in my bedroom. So I went off to John Lewis and purchased a duvet set...coincidentally called 'Blue'.

That was 2 weeks ago and this Saturday I sent the guy one last email...and that night we were exchanging some very funny emails. It got to the stage where he sent me his mobile number and I sent a text. You can imagine my shock when he sent one back saying "Why have I already got your number in my phone?"

It turns out that we were set up for a blind date by friends 2 years ago and I hadn't returned his call!

Anyway we are actually going out on a date next week so I'll keep you informed."

By the way, I relate this partly as an illustration of the fact that sometimes although feng shui can put the ball on the penalty spot it is you that has to kick it.

Water Works

I keep surveying houses with showers in the North West which drains the metal that lives there. This tends to coincide with an undermining of fathers, lungs, throats, chests, voice-work, authority, beginnings of projects, direction and much more.

I say "coincide" rather than "have an effect on" because I've pretty much given up on causality. So often a house tells you about a person's childhood years before they got there. So often sheer attention to an issue gets it moving. Sometimes chi moves before the feng shui man arrives. It seems to me that a decision to change our lives may manifest in a hundred ways including feng shui and pretty much in any order.

As an example, Sunitti's new ensuite was about as badly

placed as it could be, at the North West of a North-facing house. And this was a very distinctive North-facing house. There are three different North-facing configurations; in two of them, water would conveniently drain nasty energy – **5:2** sickness or **4:3** lack of focus. But hers wasn't one of these, it was the third: toe far, which as I explained above, speaks of true love. To have this in the father's position and to drain it with water is truly sabotage!

I found myself thinking:

"She's paying me to change her life. I doubt that she had demolishing thousands of pounds worth of bathroom in mind."

As it turned out, Sunitti had been the object of repeated childhood abuse and this was her way of letting me know. As I have said before, the great thing about feng shui is that it not only shows us what is wrong but allows us to help. Change the house, you change the person. Here the afflicted area was the North West and therefore the culprit, I suggested, was her father. Which was the case.

Sunitti was so angry: with her father for the abuse. With her mother for turning a blind eye. With the rest of her family and the world for not coming to her rescue. With her husband because he was handy. But mostly with her father who was now an infirm old man.

"You have every right to the anger" I told her and held her hand which almost throbbed with outrage.

So as well as a father she loathed she had a husband and two small boys that she loved. What her bathroom told me was that all mature males would suffer in this house. The anger would damage her guilty father but also the innocent.

As it happened, the husband was suffering. There was a growing distance between the two of them. He was withdrawn and resentful. He'd always wanted to write songs but never got the time. Neither of her boys was 100% either; one was asthmatic and the other suffering developmental problems.

"It's all or nothing," I said. "You get to let all men off the hook or none. The price of nailing your Dad is nailing your husband. And ultimately your sons."

She shuddered. She could see the simplicity of the choice but it was hard for her.

While we talked we placed moving water indoors where it would ease things and a Buddha at the opposite corner of the house to hold it. This is li xi pai, the finest of fine tunings. The principle derives from landscape feng shui, or kan yu, the most powerful style there is which requires actual physical mountains and actual flowing water. Get the right chi in and hold it. There aren't any mountains in Mitcham so we employed a small water feature, a resin Buddha and a great deal of goodwill.

Then we talked for some hours. Sometimes when we appear stuck with poor decisions, all we can do is ask for help. And then we choose.

She sobbed for some minutes. And as she cried, the anger that had brought on the tears turned to grief and finally to release. Her face which had been screwed up, uncrumpled. Lines fell from it.

With extraordinary grace she chose to drop her grievance with her father. And for the first time in several hours she smiled. The sun came out, we worked out a solution for the sabotaged bathroom and I reminded her that without it I would have known nothing of this.

The point is this: if you are among the thousands who have put a shower in the North West and you've read a bit of feng shui and you feel like beating yourself up, consider how it is the choice of everybody concerned, not just yours. We feel guilt because we want to blame and we'd be better off without either. And until some distance in the future who is to say what lesson is to be learned from a shower in the 'wrong' place? Feng Shui is about nothing if it is not about patience. Sometimes waiting for the right moment is all that is required.

Consider the Imperial Palace in Beijing. It is oriented North-South and solidly protected at the back. At the front there is wide open space for the chi to assemble. The Emperor sits immobile at the rear. He awaits the correct moment.

A little while later I received an email telling me her boys were healthier and – which was progress – she and her husband were arguing. The withdrawn don't argue.

So homicidal bathroom – good thing or bad thing?

The Chinese Statesman Zhou-en Lai, whose breadth of knowledge was a byword, is said to have been asked what he thought had been the long-term effects of the French Revolution and replied: "It's far too soon to tell."

I like that.

A Future in Furniture Removal

We visited our friend Agnes this weekend. Agnes is 83 and registered disabled. We look after her paperwork; making sure her bills are paid on time and so on. It can take some attention to ensure she gets the correct allowances and clear up the paper trail each time another charming young man switches her utility supplier. She can be cantankerous and she holds strong opinions.

"Are you still moving people's furniture?" she asks me and I have to admit I am.

Agnes' working life was "in service." One patrician employer coughed up a couple of grand at her retirement and another now back home in the US, buys her weekly groceries via the internet. But she has no family. We are the closest she's got.

I have done all sorts of subtle chi movement for her over the years and for a widow whose husband left her nothing – not even a pension – she is doing pretty well. A few years ago we obtained a four-figure refund from the local authority to compensate for their misinterpretation of her benefit entitlement. She may even have to spend some money soon.

I've never placed any blatant cures because she has never asked me to. It's not because she has "beliefs;" she has communion brought to her every Sunday which is a pretty good way of guaranteeing at least one regular visitor. And she has experimented with what she calls the "spiritless" church. But I'm like Angel in *Buffy*; you have to ask me in.

And perhaps she has not needed to. What she does have is a South-facing home with naturally supportive feng shui; that is height at the back and a luxuriant open ming tang or *bright hall* at the front. It is a living illustration of the value of good landscape. The chi arrives from a healthy direction, is *assembled* at the front and held at the back. This is the essence of good feng shui.

Getting there is a bit of a hike and she is gracious enough to recognize it. Sometimes when I return from taking a binliner to her wheely bin or watering a plant, and I leave my jacket over a chair, I find a tenner in the top pocket.

Although she has gained substantially from the benefits reform since 1997, she is by inclination a clothcap Tory and she can bang on a bit about her carers. Her house is spotless and she still does her own dusting. If it took me forty painful minutes to walk round my bungalow I'm not sure my mind would be free of blame.

In keeping with my specialist skills she often has me adjust her Royal Wedding plates or plump up cushions.

Agnes claims she talks to Jesus every day and I have no reason to doubt her.

"That furniture, they don't always move it where you tell them, do they?" she says.

No they don't.

The Hunger Site

Did you know that each time you log onto *thehungersite.com* (for free) a cup of food is passed onto those who need it?

7.
SOLAR FORTNIGHT BEGINNING:
SUNDAY 20 MARCH 2005 20.41
Chun Fun *Spring Equinox*
Month: ji muw **the Earth Rabbit**

Hour	Day	Month	Year
water	**water**	**earth**	**wood**
ren	gui	ji	yi
xu	muw	muw	yuw
dog	**rabbit**	**rabbit**	**rooster**

Spring Equinox, Banana Skins

So already the nights are shorter than the days. Since about the 9th it has smelt like spring. There's just a tinge of pollen in the air, a certain dampness and a suspicion of warmth. We ponder whether Easter will be warm enough to re-colonize the garden, to sit outside or even to go away. Someone once said that the great thing about living is Britain is that we have weather rather than climate.

However, the elements (**above**) are still pretty conflicted and the cheerlessly named *Place Curse* of Ging Jit is succeeded by the equally unprepossessing *Calamity Curse*. Jolly stuff. Derek Walters*, the Western World's authority on this stuff says that the *Calamity Curse* brings *misfortune through natural catastrophe such as fire and flood.*

Right now the chi is too yin. In fact the way things are now almost describes the difference between yin and *feminine*. The

*Chinese Astrology (Watkins Publishing) ISBN 1-84293-025-7

extreme of yin is dark and destructive. The *feminine* principle emerges from the darkness to allow creation.

This powerful female energy – possibly the most powerful there is – may bring major change for the better later in April. It is already peeping out; probably best exemplified by the McCartney sisters in Northern Ireland who have revealed to the world the punch line to the IRA joke.

When their brother was being brutally murdered in a Derry pub, every one of the 60 patrons interviewed was according to their testimony, in the toilet. But this does not bring him back to life or widen the dragnet. Who else kills Catholics for being pally with Protestants? The McCartney sisters want to know. Not al-Qaeda, the Mafia or muggers.

A banana skin dropped decades ago is finally stepped on and that particular justification for killing is over. Only women work like this. When will we ever learn?

Right Answers, Wrong Reasons

As I usually do, I drafted a sketchy ba zi (or personal feng shui) for my new client Lizzie, last week. I arrived at 7am, in time to catch the **Dragon** chi as I surveyed her flat and the Victorian building it was set in and tried to work out how far the grounds had stretched a century ago.

I like to work at that time of day. There is a sleeping-in-waking quality about it that bypasses logic. We are more likely at that time, I find, to see the truth without the hard work of reason. And the chi is so fresh you can taste it.

Having braved the cold, establishing *facing* and *sitting* directions, I joined Lizzie for a cup of tea and started to pull information from the ba zi. Artistic? Yes. Very distinctive relationship with father and therefore men. One difficult relationship. Close to daughters. Yes, yes, yes. A new *Big Fate* started in January at your 48th birthday, I said.

She looked blank. I would not have guessed but I had flattered her by six years. The ba zi was drawn up entirely wrong. And yet I knew so much about her.

Divination is always some combination of good drafting, respectful reading of the symbols and intuitive leaps. But this was dreadful drafting. And yet.

So I owe Lizzie an accurate ba zi when I see her again and whole new possibilities have opened as to what is going on.

Teletherapy

A friend has been distance healing some clients on my behalf this last few weeks. Everyone can do this of course but it takes courage and honesty and the assistance of another person who is powerful and benevolent makes all the difference.

In one case there was a lot of woo-woo* to deal with; more ghosts than you could shake a censer at; the other a stuckness that I judged was best handled this way.

The problem is that getting hung up on the woo-woo can be a powerful obstacle to responsibility. We may decide that a ghost or geopathic stress or cutting chi is actually the cause of all our problems. It is and it isn't of course. But if we are to gain command of our lives we have to take responsibility whatever the landscape

---

* woo-woo™ : the inexplicable, the unknown, ghosts, hauntings etc. This term has travelled but, trust me, it started here.

looks like. It's a paradox. Just the sort of trick the Tao would play: this causes that, except when it doesn't.

I remember when I was an Insurance Broker in the 1980s and I was sold my first computer. The salesman said: "You'd be amazed how many people think their lives will work once they've got a computer." It stopped me in my tracks. That was *exactly* what I thought.

Runestone Cowboy

A crystal-healing lady I spoke to recently insisted that her skill with crystals boiled down to "intention". There is of course, something in this. If everything is illusion anyway then the difference is what illusion we choose. On the other hand as I said to her, "If it's all intention you might as well work with runes or prunes as crystals." Yes it's another paradox. Do I have an answer? Well obviously not.

Exchange of chi

I met with an agency this week that specializes in representing psychics, mediums and so on. Their business is putting TV and magazines together with weirdos like myself. While I was there I did just a tad of feng shui for them. "An elastoplast," I said. "You'll have to pay me though."

I explained to them the law of *exchange of chi* which basically says that you must pay me something to save me from resentment and to save you from taking the work for granted which will reduce its value to you.

This rule does not apply just to feng shui. It's a sound principle whenever we contribute or receive a service. If our experience is that we have got away with something, we tend to be diminished. Similarly if we feel unrecognized we are likely to judge the culprit and file them away under the heading "Bad".

Grudges, grievances, even wars start this way and prevention is so much better than cure.

Things go bump in the night

Simon called me because he thought he and Saida had a poltergeist. They planned to move and wanted neither to leave the entity behind in their flat nor take it with them.

Young, beautiful and talented, Saida had been on the brink of an exciting career in film and TV when she had fallen ill. Now she is in hospital.

My tape-recorder wouldn't work in the flat. I changed the batteries. Still no. Woo-woo™!

I try to avoid tight definitions of such things; as we apply labels we reduce the ways we can deal with them. A "poltergeist" dictates exorcism and ghostbusting and if they fail what do you do? Not defining it at all allows us to do anything we want.

This place was opposite a church and on a North East/SouthWest axis. These are clues in classical feng shui: the "ghost gate" is in the North East and a Taoist principle holds that wherever the trouble is we should look in the opposite direction.

Saida's ba zi was very distinctive, speaking of tremendous trials. I spent an hour or so working through it with her. It was very hard work. This very beautiful woman's face was disfigured with hives. As her ba zi calls for fire, I prescribed sunshine but her attitude was more disfigured yet: she was stubbornly negative. And the closest she came to a smile was a kind of grimace. Pain, pain, pain.

There were difficult choices there, family patterns that were very persuasive. Our families may be dysfunctional but often they are all we know. I felt her pain in my shoulders and back, as if it were a weight.

It turned out her career had stalled after a major break. She had been filming a TV detective series which had called for her to be pushed up against a balcony. It had all got a bit realistic. Her assailant was a big man. She had felt so helpless, she told me. That helplessness mattered a lot to her.

There was a pocket of very sticky energy in the South West which the ba chop and flying star calculations bore out. This was where their bedroom was. They had argued fiercely here, they confirmed. The arguments, they agreed, did not represent their relationship. It felt to both of them like other people fighting.

We – Simon and I – stood and breathed it in. He unsurprisingly has a gift for this. It felt angry in a suppressed sort of way. Another way to say this is that at that point *I* felt angry in a suppressed sort of way. For which I had no immediate reason. We cannot feel things for which we have *no* reason but the telltale that we are feeling something outside ourselves is that we have no *immediate* reason. All emotional stuff actually is within our experience but the trick is to know when an emotion is if you like, not "justified." And the mind is so quick to make up reasons, we have to be alert. Suffice it to say there was upset there that made no sense if it was mine. And I – that is we – just felt it. Then I looked at the opposite end of the flat: the North East,

This was the place to apply the bandage, so to speak: the bathroom that was on top of a bit of the flat next door; an odd twisted configuration, a dead give away. The light bulb had gone so often he'd given up replacing it. And smells lingered. Not ideal for a toilet.

I did some traditional compass feng shui here, placing a jiu shape called a t'ang lung.

In the living room I found a portrait of Saida on her wedding day, breathtakingly gorgeous, a deep light in her eyes. Sometimes beauty just makes me *smile*.

I took her the picture.

"This is who you are," I said and put it in her hands. Next month I visit the new place which is the acid test.

Welcome to the Jungle

Music is generally reckoned to be of the metal element although some masters judge it to be water. So where the problem with your house or part of it is to do with excess earth and the solution may be metal or water, music is a perfectly acceptable expedient. Often when I find basements or spare rooms that have gone yin I recommend music because it's so simply done and so effective.

And for your information, all houses on a South West/North East axis have this **5:2** problem at their very heart during the current Fate period.

Oh and Tibetan bells and tasteful flutey noises are fine but Guns and Roses really wake things up.

The Hunger Site

I'm printing this again so you don't forget: as you click onto *thehungersite.com* (for free) a cup of food is passed onto those who need it.

As we experience the extraordinarily fortuitous karma of living in the peaceful plenty of the West it's doubly important, it seems to me, to do simple things like this.

Spring in Iraq may not be so picturesque.

8.
SOLAR FORTNIGHT BEGINNING:
TUESDAY 5 APRIL 2005 00.48

Ching ming *Clear and Bright*

Month: geng chen **the Metal Dragon**

Hour	Day	Month	Year
wood	earth	metal	wood
jia	ji	geng	yi
zi	wei	zhen	yuw
rat	sheep	dragon	rooster

The White Dragon

This month's dragon is metal, a White Dragon. The Dragon is the most powerful animal of the Calendar, presiding over the expansion and fertility of late Spring. The earth of the Dragon supports the metal. This is seen in the Draining Cycle (page 13) as giving birth to the metal and thus weakening the Dragon. Furthermore Dragons conceal hidden treasure. Within the Dragon *branch* we find reserves both of wood and water. The Dragon month is actually known as the *tomb of water* and it enjoys a privileged relationship with the Monkey and the Rat whereby all three become water when they meet.

So for instance as feng shui is an attempt to put time and space into a single system, a Rat person at a Monkey location in the Dragon month indicates water.

Clearly months don't happen simultaneously but a Dragon day in a Rat month in a Monkey year and a Rat day in a Dragon month in a Monkey year provide the same conditions. This will happen several times next year. Check whether it's raining.

A metal Dragon, although sometimes referred to as the *Angry Dragon* is an expressed Dragon. Dragon chi – at the end of spring – is creative and innovative. The calendar character zhen for the Dragon actually means *thunder*. Explosive force attends this Dragon. Expect sudden change which may not be comfortable.

For Confucius, dragons among men were self-reliant and appropriately detached but dragons are also said to embody meteoric rises in social status. On the other hand, be cautious if you are positioning a dragon for this purpose. Chinese Imperial Dragons have five toes. Restricted results may follow positioning less patrician varieties.

Another Spooky Coincidence

There was a big mirror on the hallway wall of Lucinda's house. It was one of the first things I noticed. Mirrors are powerful, I told her. Placed right they are incredibly creative, placed wrong they are trouble. Hers was wrong but just a yard away was one of the best locations for a door or water feature in this Fate period. So we moved it. This mirror is on the money now, I said.

Her boyfriend could do with a boost, she told me. So we moved an image of him in and a mirror out of the tai chi (dead centre) to make her priorities clear.

This week there was feedback:

*"...he (**boyfriend***) placed a £6 bet last Saturday and won £1100, a week after the mirror being moved but no luck this Sat. Coincidence?"*

These are small figures of course but in a pretty desirable ratio. And these are the same principles, measurements and placing that I apply to multinational businesses.

What were those odds? 183 to 1? I suggested she might be a little hard to please. To her credit, as it happens, she knows she is. There's no such thing as coincidence of course.

This property was also interesting because it was on the ding/gui "showbiz" orientation. Time and again houses on these orientations conceal closet celebrities. In this case the man of the house, otherwise an unassuming gym teacher, has recently featured, appropriately clad, on the Olympic bid posters. I won't tell you which to avoid him being mobbed. He's a very fit boy.

Alex (2)

Alex rang me. She is in love again. This one's got an ecological and ethical agenda. Alex, you will remember, is young and beautiful. What she wants is a soulmate. And of course, he'll be that if that's what it takes.

She asked me to draft his ba zi. He is passionate about conservation and ecological living. So must she be. Or else. The ba zi shows a man in thrall to his father, a man whose every decision is in reaction. His father is probably a successful businessman which is what if he were following the Tao rather than trying to prove points, he would be himself. As it is he is defined by *not* being a businessman. And it's no real help me telling Alex all this – though I have. The heart has its reasons. And the last thing she needs is *opinions*: not from ladies who would never stand for this nor from blokes who can see his point of view. She needs to quietly form her own conclusions. But I do hope she gets it this time.

Abbie's fine either way.

And it remains true; the Beatles were right. Love *is* all you need.

Clear, Bright, not so Bright

The solar fortnight Ching Ming, *Clear and Bright* brings in the Dragon month. The weather with any luck will correspond. In the greenhouse, my sunflowers have started to sprout but the tomatoes are still shy.

Ming meaning *bright* is the same term as that adopted by the Emperor Hongwu to describe the Ming or *Radiant* Dynasty he founded in 1368. The Ming ruled until 1644, a period roughly corresponding to the combined eras of Plantagenets, Tudors and Stuarts; quite a while. During this time the Forbidden City was built and the matching Taoist complex at Wudang Shan a couple of thousand miles to the West. These complexes express the practice of feng shui at its full flower.

Wudang Shan apparently has two peaks which are approached from different directions. The easier can be reached after twenty minutes brisk walk. The other is 5,000 steps which is about 40 times the spiral staircase at London's Queensway Tube Station (which carries a health warning).

At the simpler ascent, the Taoist temples and shrines with their granite and jade and their curved tiles were mostly demolished in the cultural revolution. Pretty much all that stand now, I am told, are frames and felled columns.

On the steeper approach most of the buildings are intact. Fervent anti-revisionary feeling obviously cools after two or three thousand steps. It is astonishing how much damage can be done so rapidly by hotheads with a little gelignite and a few sledgehammers and how long it takes to make it good again.

I have arranged to study in Wuhan in central China in October. It is a one-month study tour that goes way beyond the pale of Shanghai and Beijing, right into the heart of China. I will be studying feng shui with Chinese academics and the course includes a visit to Wudang Shan: the real China if there's any of it left.

Things *not* Going Bump in the Night

Simon and Saida's new house was very different. Now out of hospital, it was wonderful to see Saida with a smile on her face. She fair bounced out of the car into the house and started showing me where her shoes were to be housed before I had time even to get fully oriented. At least one room will need to be redesigned to accommodate them. She may even need an extension. Good on her. When you're sick of shoes, my daughters tell me, you're sick of life.

And the converted attic was a revelation. The ceiling was quite distinctive. In fact I had only seen one like it once before – in their previous house. Where the ceiling broke up into a series of prism shapes was exactly like where the worst energy had been in the last place. But this new room was well away from their bedroom and the main living areas. That time was behind them. I went in for a sniff and placed anti-spook stuff including tourmaline and the traditional reds and arranged for the windows to be opened, noise to be made and so on. The room is physical evidence of them moving on from a very nasty phase in their life. They can watch the threat melting away before their eyes.

Job well done.

The Five Skills Rodent

Some weeks ago I observed that Chinese metaphysics in general and the *Book of Changes* in particular has been regularly plundered for song titles and band names. (Does anyone remember *Marrying Maiden* by **It's a Beautiful Day**?) This month I came across a name just busting to be adopted: the *five skills rodent*.

Some background: once a month I trek to Neal's Yard for Yi Jing classes with Peter Firebrace. The Yi Jing is of course the *Classic of Change*. The orthodox pronunciation I Ching is apparently one of those linguistic booby traps the Chinese delight in as it actually denotes a volume of pornography. So remember to say Yi Jing or simply Yi – pronounced like the old English "ye".

Relatively few people are aware that the Yi is also at the heart of feng shui. Every location on the compass relates to a particular Hexagram. Indeed the smallest gradations on the perimeter relate to the changing lines of that Hexagram. This is very useful. If we change the line we get another Hexagram. If we don't like the Hexagram our door is on we can change it. So if a door is inconveniently placed, we can put a mirror at the location of the Hexagram that the changing line implies and in effect open the door there instead. This is one of the myriad connections between the Yi and feng shui.

Peter is concise, authoritative, sensitive and flexible. He also speaks and writes Chinese. The current course which is always stimulating and often demanding, emphasises the changing lines of the 64 Hexagrams.

Last month I learned that line 4 of Hexagram 35. Jìn, *To Advance,* which refers to the *five skills rodent,* is actually alluding to the talents of the flying squirrel. *Five Skills* sounds pretty nifty.

The Chinese themselves however are dismissive. They consider that although the squirrel can fly and climb it cannot travel *far enough*, it swims *but not across a stream*, burrows *but not sufficient to conceal itself* and runs but not so as "*to outrun a man.*"

There's no pleasing some people.

North West Water: Latest News

Leonie has a shower in the North-West where it is splashing away the metal. After working on this part of the house her son's chest (also metal) is responding and she has more energy. But she and her partner are arguing more. Are things getting better or worse?

Rebalancing the North West will tend to regenerate father figures. All father figures. And often a woman with a tricky North West has issues with her father. As she heals this area, she will heal the father of her children as well as her own. It's all or nothing. And attention to this will tend to bring up disputes that have been long-neglected. If they are aired – however robustly – in a spirit of seeking the truth, this is very healthy. When the issues recur, the technical term is *bickering* which is unlikely to heal anything.

Bright Lights, Big City

To illustrate this let me tell you about two separate surveys I performed for two little-known actresses, one in South West London; one in North East London. As far as I know they do not know each other.

Both are married to older better-known actors. Both houses face ding in the South which indicates a taste for the bright lights. Both houses had oddities at the North West including big shower-rooms and a single-storey extension. Both women had small children who took up time that might otherwise have been expended on their careers. In both cases the husband was less successful than he ought to have been; their careers had been stop-start, up-down things – like the North West of the house. You'd know their faces but probably not their names.*

One of these actresses rang me straight after a *Housebusters* TV programme in which I had been telling a couple I still have not met, things about their relationship they had not told each other. The gist of it was that unless they communicated to some purpose there was little hope for them. And it was clearly the truth.

The actress assured me her own relationship was wonderful: "We laugh all the time. That's not why I have rung you." At 9.05 when my programme had finished at 9.

You and I know this is girl talk for "I'm in trouble but don't go there," so I was forearmed.

What I had not expected was for the husband to watch me all the way round the house.

It may have been the mistake I made when looking at his ba zi:

I said "You're famous too." Which was a bullseye of course. "Which side of the cameras?" Which was *so* not.

I can't really operate under scrutiny and it is tough to coax upset out of a distressed woman in front of an audience. I am not suggesting that we ought to have been plotting against the husband. Just that she might have valued the opportunity to get her thoughts in order without being too careful how she expressed them. To cut to the Chase Manhattan, this was not my finest hour.

The house was full of envy; the idea that she had *his* kids at the

---

* Both have become more prominent since my survey.

cost of *her* career was an underlying theme. Now she was pregnant and there were things in her ba zi and the house that made me fear for the unborn child. I did some mumbo-jumbo for the baby which they will not even have noticed.

She rang me three months later to tell me she had given easy birth to another healthy boy.

Metaphysical Stuff

Let's go a bit further. Read on only if you have an appetite for the metaphysical.

In the beginning is the Tao. Then follows a series of yes/no decisions. Dark or light. Matter or spirit, this sort of stuff. Then follow, as the Chinese have it, *the 10,000 things*.

This is an account of the beginning of the universe or of a human life. Take your pick.

When we are born, the illusion we are presented with is a series of decisions as to what we will do with our lives. The first is broadly who to use as a model: Mummy or Daddy? The second is whether we will accept or reject that model.

So it's Mummy or Daddy then Yes or No.

Then follow our own *10,000 things*.

We tend to this binary illusion because it provides us with a road map. But at the price of consciousness. And there exists a further choice within it: our own path. Rough or smooth, this generally comes without a map and involves radical trust. Faith is often associated with it. Faith in what?

Purpose, Higher Mind, God, the Tao, what you will. No wonder most of us prefer a map.

Now as far as paths go "Yes, Daddy" is no different to "No,

Daddy." It's just generally more comfortable. It is simply a journey in the opposite direction along the same path. Coming back to earth, you might say "Yes, Daddy" suggests a trouble-free North West and "No, Daddy" suggests problems there.

I don't wish to imply that this process is limited to women; it's an equal opportunities illusion. One way to describe feng shui is that it is such illusions made solid: I write as someone who spent 14 years in a North West-facing house with a bathroom over the front door, by the way. Thought you'd like to know.

9.
SOLAR FORTNIGHT BEGINNING:
WEDNESDAY 20 APRIL 2005 08.00
Kuk Yu *Grain Rains*
Month: geng chen **the Metal Dragon**

Hour	Day	Month	Year
earth	**wood**	**metal**	**wood**
wu	jia	geng	yi
chen	xu	chen	yuw
dragon	**dog**	**dragon**	**rooster**

Though April showers may come your way

The rain that swells the grain falls traditionally in this, the second half of the Dragon month: in China this too is the time of April showers.

As Jeremy Paxman said tersely, when forced to include a weather forecast on BBC's *Newsnight*:

"The weather. Rain. It's April. What did you expect?"

We are now only two months short of ha gee, the Summer Solstice, when the chi peaks. As 2005's ruling animal the wood Rooster, sits in the West, this is the direction to respect. The year animal (or branch) otherwise known as the tai sui, should never be faced directly. This becomes more crucial as the chi rises. So if you are improving your home, avoid the West. If you must refurbish there, start elsewhere and work round to it.

This principle transposed applies to every year.

Joey has a part in a big TV sitcom. He plays a child with an IQ of 210 which he has found allows him some of the status with his peers he might command were that actually they case. Henni is labouring through the curmudgeonery of Philip Larkin and Jessie has filmed an anti-smoking ad. They are off to Italy any day. My daughter-in-law Tracey who lost a baby last year is pregnant again.

Da Vinci Code Cash In

When I first approached the late Victorian apartment block where Miriam lived, one of the first things I noticed was the date *AD 96* picked out proudly in the bricks at the front.

Masonic, I guessed. I often notice the touch of master masons on Victorian buildings: they are precise and square and the dimensions and proportions reliable. And the alignment is often marginally off the cardinal points. Miriam's was no exception: just missing East-West. In China due North-South was reserved for Emperors. I imagine these facts are connected.

I guessed the date was a reference to some obscure event in Templar history. The temple in Jerusalem was of course razed by Roman legionaries under Titus in AD 70. Masada, where the mystic Nazarites fled, was taken the same year. As it happened, AD 96 turned out to be the year the *Book of Revelation* was written. Curiouser and curiouser.

There were two main entrances, both low and dark, set up so as to pull the visitor into the basement. The numbering was eccentric and I suspected corridors I couldn't quite locate. Miriam's flat was on the first floor. The house as a whole was an irregular shape missing a chunk of the North East: the *ghost gate* of Chinese tradition. Since it was purpose built, I supposed this was deliberate. Such a building will tend to be spooky which is what the amateur satanist often seeks. As Miss Jean Brodie says: "For those who like this kind of thing this is what they like."

Miriam's flat was oriented exactly opposite to the building which made it a rebellious sort of place. She is an artist with a very individual vision, so this fitted. Half the flats were oriented this way, the other half oriented the same as the block. This I have found to be a hallmark of residences built as a community; presumably in this case a community of 19th century freemasons.

Freemasonry claims roots in Egypt and Mesopotamia. And if the principles of feng shui are universal they can not of course be uniquely Chinese. It is just that the Chinese have the best records. You will see signs of the same learning in the Valley of Kings and in pre-Celtic standing stones. The Great Pyramid of Cheops and its two companions clearly mimic the stars of Orion's Belt, a constellation depicted at the centre of my luopan or Chinese Compass. Many observers (notably Derek Walters) have noted that Stonehenge is aligned South-West/ North-East, along the line of the *ghost gate.*

Sitting in the North East of the building then, it was predictable that Miriam's flat would feel quite unsettled. As I said, this was probably intended.

"How do you sleep?" I asked her.

"On and off," she said. "It's not that I'm frightened. It's just a bit..... busy."

"Busy," I repeated.

"As if there is stuff going on."

Whether we buy into literal ghosts or not, doesn't matter. If she wasn't sleeping I needed to address what appeared to be keeping her awake. My usual crystal for this purpose is *tourmaline.* I placed this and a t'ang lung shape by her bed. Then I prescribed the traditional red curtains.

"Against the woo-woo."

"Woo-woo?"

"The inexplicable," I said, "You know: woooo-wooooo" and I made a woo-woo sound, intended to sound like the soundtrack just as things are getting scary in a low budget horror movie but possibly sounding more like Thomas the Tank Engine.

We discussed how she might approach being left with this energy night after night. We agreed that woo-woo™ stuff wants love and understanding just like you and me. Going into spooky spaces and shouting is just silly. Energy is energy. I don't tend to see this sort of stuff, I feel it. But I feel the feelings of living people too. Which is often more scary.

The difficult rooms were her study and bedroom. The energy was pedantic and rowdy. It was very male, arrogant, a bit like a rugby club bar but only threatening if you took it seriously. It was the sort of energy you might expect in a gentleman's club. Which is one way you might describe a Masonic assembly. And the Long Room at Lords for that matter. Girls know about this stuff

What she hadn't told me about was her own heartbreak.

As it happened Miriam had parted recently from a self-destructive spouse and was still grieving. She had presented him with a choice: Miriam or his lifestyle. Her choice too of course but these are hard truths.

"Anything can be healed with communication," I said and she nodded, "But sometimes we just don't seem to have the resources."

Tears were forming in her eyes. I remembered when I had thrown my own life into the air in the 1980s: leaving my first wife, my three boys, my house in the country and my German cars. I know this stuff too.

I suggested she find the place in her that still held on and just give it love. Within herself she could locate the rather daft male energy. Her ex and the stuff suppressing her bedroom were one and the same type of chi.

"Deep breaths," I said. I know this is a cliché but there is nothing that gets you through upset quicker than correct breathing. "Can you just love it? Give it love. Let it be alright with itself."

"I've been doing that long enough," she said.

"Just a little while more."

The poignance in the room was palpable. You could almost hear generations of bored middle-aged men livening up their lives with rituals. To what extent were Masonic meetings just about getting away from the wife and kids? Might her ex have shaped up if she had given him one more chance?

There were tears; mine too. The energy lifted. It was quieter in here now.

"That should do it," I said.

With her artist's eye, she had clear ideas about what to do with the rest of the flat. We negotiated over the colours she would use, which given her strong tastes was interesting. The *Flying Stars* which indicate the nature and location of temporary energies around the house had put the pernicious **5:2** in her kitchen and this made for fun. But that's another story.

As far as all the Masonic/Rosicrucian conspiracy stuff goes, I haven't read Dan Brown's blockbuster. I don't want to. I know this makes me a bit precious but I was grailed out by the mid 80s.

I have visited Rennes le Chateau. I have peered into the Abbe Sauniere's garden. On a rainy day it doesn't look that mysterious. I really have spent days in the Languedoc locating the crypt depicted in Poussin's *Et in Arcadia Ego*; I don't want to go into it all again.

The *Holy Blood and the Holy Grail* authors placed the crypt on the wrong side of the road, by the way.

I have tried my wife's patience photographing Masonic tombs in the Highlands. I have pondered endlessly the connections between Dark Age Visigoths and the Merovingian kings. I speculated that the Papal interdict of 1307 could have left an open window through which the Templars might have entered Scotland. At Rosslyn I saw the carving depicting an ear of maize a century and a half before Columbus. Not again, please.

So, even if *The Da Vinci Code* is a cynical, indisciplined exploitation of mysteries that on examination slip through the fingers, there is something there. But I'm not going after it.

I was asked once in the 1990s when English cricket would be be world-class again. "When women are allowed in the Long Room at Lords," I said.

This happened soon after and was followed by the Cricket Academy, central contracts and a new regime. We regained the Ashes from the Australians in 2005. I rest my case.

Men need women so badly: to question them when they appear most certain, to prick the bubble when they stand on dignity. I am unable to believe in any centuries-old conspiracy because I simply don't see human beings cooperating over such timescales. Be that as it may, I find it hard to take seriously any institution that excludes an entire gender whether it's the MCC, International Freemasonry or The London Sanctuary. It is simply not balanced.

Miriam emailed me later in the week. She had been sleeping soundly.

10.
SOLAR FORTNIGHT BEGINNING:
FRIDAY 5 MAY 2005 18.23
Lap ha *SummerBegins*
Month: xin si **the Metal Snake**

Hour	Day	Month	Year
metal	earth	metal	wood
xin	ji	xin	yi
yuw	chou	si	yuw
rooster	ox	snake	rooster

The Snake Sleeping in Winter

The Metal Snake, otherwise known as the *Snake Sleeping in Winter* is this month's animal and like every snake, is a magician. Some see the Snake as the Sorceror's apprentice because it resides next to the Dragon, the miracle-maker of the Chinese zodiac. Each of us is far too complex to be defined by our year, month or even our day of birth but a Snake-Dragon marriage is an interesting and auspicious one. Only the Snake will be prepared to consider that the Dragon's power may justify his arrogance.

The girls, both Dragons by the way, are back from Rome. Jessie has a fine new Pope snow globe and stories of all the medieval fountains they wished in before finding the genuine Trevi. She has just failed to get another big movie job. She asks me to look at her ba zi again for reassurance. There is no question that her star is ascending but the world's immediate future doesn't look so clever.

This snake that rules this month, also ruled over 2001.

The Snake has inborn metal so this fire/metal clash is less

drastic than it sounds. The danger is that the metal snake may be the stooge of the wood Rooster which of course is this year's animal. In relation to the calendar this means that the destructive shortsightedness of much of this year's politics – international, domestic and in your home – may be exacerbated rather than calmed as 2005 approaches its height.

My son Jaime who is a between-the-wars historian has a theory that much of the hideousness of the retreat from Stalingrad was attributable to the cold. Very cold people will do anything to get warm, he says. My neighbour Henry Metelman who was there and wrote of his experiences in *Through Hell for Hitler*, says something similar. I did not question Hitler until I was flat on my face in the ice at Stalingrad, he says.

Heat may do the same, I imagine. I fear for our troops in Iraq. Lord knows those kids should not be there.

Husband in Bike Shed Drama

Tina's husband was in the bike shed. Before you ask how you get a husband out of a bike shed you perhaps need to know how he got there.

Their house is an irregular shape effectively excluding the North West. And outside, separate from the house, was a chaotic shed full of bikes and bric-a-brac. The North Western sector is governed by Qian the Confucian father. By extension Qian represents older men, the male side of relationship, also authority. So anything that happens in this sector represents what is happening under these headings. I believe there are Western systems that call the North West *Helpful Friends,* which is not that different.

Classically however, Qian's element is metal and therefore if we want to build it up, we add metal or earth (as earth creates metal in the Productive Cycle, you'll recall). If we want to lessen its strength we add water which drains metal. We can introduce fire to attack but this is more drastic.

First of all the shed needed clearing up.

And indeed her husband has been having a hard time. Her children (his stepchildren) had not accepted him. There is a new baby in the home. Things are tense right now. His vote, as they say, has been cancelled.

We can restore the North West by ensuring plenty of metal on that edge of the house. This can be white or metallic decor, round things, discs, coins and so on. By restoring the North West, we get the father back on track. Music is also metal. So are bikes, by the way. Things to avoid here are too much water or fire which will attack the metal. Logically a North Western bathroom is tricky because it means that the Father's energy is constantly drained by water.

If this doesn't work we can consider something substantial made of metal in the tai chi or heart of the house. His Suzuki perhaps.

11.
SOLAR FORTNIGHT BEGINNING:
SATURDAY 21 MAY 2005 07.22

Siu Mu *Grain Filling*

Month: xín sí **the Metal Snake**

Hour	Day	Month	Year
metal	**wood**	**metal**	**wood**
geng	yi	xín	yute
chen	sí	sí	yuw
dragon	**snake**	**snake**	**rooster**

Siu Mun: *Grain Filling*

A typically poetic description of the time of year. My sunflowers are shooting up but they frankly need a bit more sun before they flower. The experiment with globe artichokes hangs in the balance.

The sun enters Gemini today. The Chinese solar fortnights illustrate the correspondence between the Chinese calendar and Western astrology. The Snake month sí lasts from 5 May to 5 June. At its midpoint today, the sun arrives in Gemini which itself finishes on 22 June, the midpoint of wu the Horse at the summer solstice. Which allows anyone interested who didn't know this, to map the Western Zodiac onto the Chinese animals. QED.

The Princess and the Pea

Frances Hodgson Burnett wrote that *every* girl is a princess. And if I were to forget I have teenage daughters to remind me.

I was in Paula's house doing a follow-up survey. There had been huge leaps in her social life since my first visit but relationship remained the big question. A successful career woman in her mid-30s, very attractive, certain to make a lot of money, she wanted Mr Right. Right Now!

All in a day's work.

I corrected a water-feature here, inched a Buddha across the floor there, moved her bed a couple of centimetres to pick up relationship energy. Placed a tiny hand mirror as a temporary solution to a glitch. Everything now in place.

As we sat down with a cup of tea to debrief, the doorbell rang. A bouquet of flowers from an admirer. Fantastic, I thought, hard to argue with that. She read the card: "It's that bloke from down the road. Wants a date." Then she frowned: "I always get attention from the ones I'm not interested in."

What do you do?!

Her house as it happens is not right for her long term. I can do all sorts of things to support her for the time being but I could do a lot more in a house that was configured right. So I gave her a checklist of how the right house would be configured (which can be done for anyone given their exact moment of birth).

Obligatory Spooky Stuff

Zelda's house had been built for a surgeon in the 1950s. Although he was long dead, he was still there. The estate had housed doctors from the nearby hospital. Many top doctors are freemasons and the orientation implied Master Masonry.

She had been told she might find a body under the extension! And try as she might she had not been able to sell the house – which was why I had been called in.

The energy I found there was not wicked. It was self-righteous in a very male way, reluctant to admit errors so as to learn from them. But it was not evil. We don't on the other hand, I remarked, generally want our surgeons learning by trial and error. He was still there it seemed, because he would not admit some sort of major blunder. I did not want to speculate as to what. Without admitting the blunder he could not move on. But neither could Zelda. Every prospective purchaser backed out for some reason.

Looking at her ba zi which I had drafted sketchily on the train up, I asked whether she had had an artistic brother or sister who had been famous and died young. Her sister, a painter well-known in her native Slovakia, had died in her 40s, she told me. Sometimes I am amazed at what you can divine with careful drafting but the sister was not the presence under the extension. This was more of a James Robertson Justice kind of thing.

Taking a deep breath, I suggested to *him* that everybody makes mistakes and that wisdom starts with the realization that we are ignorant. He was not keen on this idea nor its corollary that alive, dead or hanging on, it's the same principle.

So move on already.

Zelda very bravely agreed to simply feel the bodily sensations she associates with the "presence" in her house. This is often uncomfortable and demanding but led she tells me, to an openness that is very fresh to her. The house sold shortly after.

Virginia, Water

Virginia had benefitted from distance healing I arranged for her. It had cleared ancient stuff from her flat after we had made all sorts of changes leading, among other things, to regular sleep for the first time in years. At the heart of the process was a conversation in which she got that feng shui, visualization, reiki, Goddess workshops, what have you, were all just distractions if she did not make a choice to change her life. Receiving this information took a great deal of courage and humility.

So after a decade of time out, her life is moving. But she has got used to the distractions. She's a very talented woman who is terrified of pursuing her purpose, which is quite high-profile. So I was unsurprised that a series of dramas happened around her as the energy was freed, culminating in a ludicrous farce involving a car chase around North Wales and an ill-tempered gay couple slap-fighting in her mother's front room.

I explained these were distractions, ways of not moving forward. The path was now clear. She could fly. As the distractions arise – minor illnesses, car breaking down – she has to deal with them appropriately but see them for what they are.

This week she had an infection and asked for more distance healing. I told her not yet; no more feng shui, no more distance healing for the time being. Feel it all the way through. As we do this the distractions run out and we can move on.

The danger of any model, any method, is that we can get attached. Any model taken too literally leads to dependence. People will often queue round the block to be disempowered and run like hell when offered their own power back. Funny old game.

Now if she'd only stop moving the water feature I placed so carefully for her around the flat and leave the mirrored cupboard covered, I could rest easy.

Cycles of Change

Feng Shui concerns itself with cycles, both in time and space. The idea is that similar types of chi will coincide with similar types of event. So as a ding (South) facing home often houses those with a desire for celebrity and a missing piece of a house at the East implies trouble for the Eldest Son, so a fire Dragon year or a water Horse month have distinctive meaning. I have put out before the idea that we can expect years like 1941 and 2001 (metal **Snake**) to have something in common. And indeed they do.

In both years the US was drawn by an apparently unprovoked attack into involvement in a war it had turned its back on. There are many more similarities but this may be the most dramatic.

Years run in cycles of 60 starting with the wood Rat (1924, 1984) and ending with the water Pig (1923, 1983). So do months. And this year we have a run of months that reflect the chi of recent years. In other words March was an earth Rabbit like 1999, April a metal Dragon like 2000 and this month a metal Snake like 2001. We can expect "echoes" in the month of the related year. On some level it may be that we receive these echoes in order to learn something. Which might save some of us from learning so much the hard way.

One such echo was the buzzing last week of the White House by a private plane followed by exemplary preventative action from the US Air Force. It turned out to be a harmless disoriented aircraft. Some learning seems to have gone on there.

I have received quite a bit of response to this idea. So let's take it a bit further

Q: What links the years 61AD & 1381? Both xin yuw years – metal Roosters

A: The Peasants Revolt and the Budiccan Rebellion, arising from similar issues and taking place in much the same geographical area.

In each case the dispute was about inequitable taxation and was fired by the abuse of the womenfolk. You will recall that Boudicca was maddened when she and her daughters were raped but you may not know that the flashpoint of the Peasant's Revolt was tax gatherers putting their hands up women's skirts in search of undisclosed assets.

Most of both groups of rebels were from East Anglia. Boudicca sacked the City of London. (The evidence can still be seen in the layer of ash encountered whenever the foundations of a new building in a London EC postcode go deep enough.) Wat Tyler's followers ventured further West to besiege the palace of John of Gaunt (whom they held responsible for their grievances) in what is now The Savoy Hotel. Incensed by his absence and the fact that strawberry teas would not be served for another six centuries they confronted the boy-king Richard II at Blackheath.

1981 being exactly 600 years and therefore 10 cycles later, is also a metal Rooster and there are those inclined to shoe-horn in the Miners' Strike of 1984 as another case of this rebellious energy. These pundits account for the 3-year discrepancy by way of the *precession of the equinoxes;* a thought-provoking explanation that I will not tax your concentration with here.

History is peppered with these similarities. I can't pass on without mentioning Ian Wallace's proposal that Tottenham Hotspur Football Club always prospers when there is yin metal in the year pillar. 1961 and 1971 for instance. On this theory 2005/6 will bring their best showing in a generation.* Their emblem is a Rooster of course.

---

* Soccer-lovers may feel this sounds convenient but it was written

almost a year before Tottenham were deprived of their first place in European competition for 20-odd years by a lucky Arsenal win and a freak defeat of their own.

Ending Hunger

I received an email from Natalie Imbruglia this week. When I saw the sender's name I assumed that opening it would bring me a virus, a compromising photo or the usual help with my physique. But on behalf of **makepovertyhistory** she was inviting me to take various sorts of action. They are focussing on the G8 summit in the first week of July. I think however that action is much more urgent for reasons I will happily outline in one-to-one correspondence.

I haven't watched *Neighbours* since Kylie Mynogue left.

12.
SOLAR FORTNIGHT BEGINNING:
SUNDAY 5 JUNE 2005 22.45

Mong Chung *Grain in ear*

Month: ren wu **the Water Horse**

Hour	Day	Month	Year
fire	metal	water	wood
bing	geng	ren	yi
zi	shen	wu	yuw
rat	monkey	horse	rooster

Grain in ear and a word in yours – The Water Horse

The stem/branch combination or *pillar* (above) for this new month is ren wu, that is mixed water and fire chi. Internally conflicted, this *pillar* is called *Willow Tree*. Like the willow, it is more associated with flexibility than with robust, gregarious behaviour or strength.

This however is the peak of the year and the chi is at its strongest. If you are skilled you can really get things done this month. Conversely don't install feng shui remedies unless you know what you are doing. *Willow Tree* sounds promising for The Ashes but I have already committed myself on that.*

The shorthand *Willow Tree* is called a lap yum and it allows us to give a combination of elements a single name. This can be very useful. In drafting a ba zi or personal feng shui for instance, it can be important to identify the body element which is the lap yum of year and indicates tendencies to ill health and what to do about

---

*England to win.

them. Comparison of the personal lap yum with the lap yum of the sitting direction of a building (the back bricks at waist level) is also one of the simplest tests of whether a house supports its owner.

I used to be in an origami group but it folded

Feng shui gets an interesting press. Everybody knows that tai chi, chi gung, tae kwon do, even origami are lifetime studies but we are encouraged to believe that we can master feng shui in a weekend. This month only the imprudent will act on that belief. Above all do not start in the West or the East!

Northern Light

Lana is a painter. She is 30ish, wise, beautiful and very ill. Some months ago I surveyed her house and delivered several hours of analysis of her ba zi (personal feng shui based on the exact moment of birth). Her health and especially her attitude have improved significantly but not enough yet. I worry about her.

On one level feng shui is simply divination. Divination is the process whereby we inform ourselves of the whole universe or an aspect of it by studying what is close to us. Some do this with tarot cards or tea leaves. There is not much difference in diagnosing what is going on with someone, between "reading" tea leaves and houses. There was a woman on Living TV who "read" bottoms.

"Drop your trousers," she'd say, "And I'll tell you your life story."

No cheap jokes, please.

There is no reason she should not do this accurately. Whether we do it by close attention to birdsong or ink blobs or something else, all we are doing is informing ourselves of the universe we are in.

The great difference between buildings and tea leaves, tarot cards and indeed bottoms, is that you can rearrange a building and thereby change what is going on in the subject's life. Feng shui offers not only diagnosis but also remedy.

Authentic Chinese feng shui has developed over millennia a body of procedures and principles but this is at the heart. And I say this, having both studied with a Chinese Master and spent time on the appropriate Classics. The Forbidden City is based on the human form just as are the principles of good design developed by the Father of Architecture, the Roman Vitruvius. It is perfectly good feng shui to deduce things about the head from the roof of a house or about the mouth from the front door. Sometimes these derivations will stretch: a stuck front door is unlikely to speak of conviviality for instance. Sometimes it can be literal; I have heard a feng shui master accurately infer dandruff from blocked gutters.

When I am doing a ba zi or personal feng shui based on the moment of birth, I am used to incorporating everything that is going on at that moment. In Lana's case one of the characters refused to be drawn properly. I messed up the same one twice, hours apart and at different points in the drafting. Many Chinese have laughed at my clumsy calligraphy. For that matter only my children can read my handwriting consistently but the mis-shapen character in Lana's ba zi looked like a particular type of growth and indeed growths were the problem. The orthodox interpretations of the relationship between the hour of birth and the year were interesting but none a bull's eye like this.

The Chinese have developed feng shui into something very complex indeed over the millennia. But at the end of the day all they have done is work out more and more complex ways to second-guess the Tao. In other words, the Tao, the way of things, the flow, is going where it is going and 6,000 years of invention have not changed that. None of us has lasting control over it. The best we can hope for is to identify it and surrender. That way our will becomes the Tao and we cease the fruitless pursuit of having it the other way round.

I reminded Lana of this. Brought up a Confucian, it was not news to her. Born a Buddhist, the notion that all pain derives from attachment was no revelation either. As a particularly stubborn and feisty girl, she was attached to her own view of how the universe ought to be. This is by a margin the most popular attachment: the attachment to our view of how the world ought to be in the teeth of the facts. Or as Robert D'Aubigny used to say: an attachment to what is other than what is.

Lana's attachment was to a universe in which her neglectful but wealthy father got his come-uppance. In real life it never came. Instead her body mimicked the world she insisted on and punished the parts of her body that related to her father.

This way of thinking follows in several sound traditions and led, without any logical right to the information, to what was wrong with Lana. I'm just concerned that it should also heal her.

She showed me that the front of her house boasted perfect "northern light," the natural light that has illuminated European painting. From any other direction it is either too glaring or casts shadows that mislead. I now get another level of meaning from the title (*Northern Lights*) of the first volume of Philip Pullman's *His Dark Materials* trilogy. Silly old me; I thought he just meant the aurora borealis.

After a day and a half with Lana, I take refuge in the pie shop at

Selfridges. My second son Alex sells expensive suits nearby and I often meet him there. The adolescent grunting phase of his life lasted into his early 20's and he's not a man for small talk but these days he is outgoing and full of ideas. He is very good at what he does and drops the names of an enviable list of celebrities he has outfitted. What glamour! They come back to him because he has style but also because he takes such care.

We never stop worrying about our kids, do we? My father said the first 40 years were the hardest.

Once You've Got a Name, You've Got a Label

I have been working with young Donald for 15 weeks. I normally restrict a course of ba zi sessions to five because I don't want to create dependence. In the 80s and 90's I attended workshops with a number of world-class healer/guru/teachers/what-have-you, a decent proportion of whose audience appeared to come back again and again to retain rather than heal their stuff. Eventually it dawned on me that I might be among them.

Donald's family want him *defined*. And weak yang wood is not good enough. Weak yang wood speaks of wilfulness. And you will know by now that weak yang wood wants water or more wood to strengthen it. Water would be both talking and listening. He's a good listener but a dreadful talker. Wood could be movement, exercise, new ideas. He's keener on his Nintendo.

Is he manic-depressive, sociopathic, schizophrenic or what? The more I see of him, the less I know. He is not keen on risk taking but that doesn't mean he needs valium. He fears that if he gets too enthusiastic he will be disappointed but then so do I.

When he came to me he was spending most of his time in bed.

Now he plays computer games and he has signed on for Job Seeker's Allowance which means his mother is not totally responsible for his upkeep. And signing on was just the sort of death-by-paperwork that for him characterises adult life. Simple enough to you or me but for him it was the Matterhorn.

I suspect that his best chance is not to be diagnosed and put in a box but to keep talking. And I'm perfectly prepared to do that indefinitely for nothing.

People are often labelled so that we don't have to consider them as real people. It's tempting to agree that Donald is a paranoid schizophrenic like one brother or a dreamer like another. But the great thing about Chinese elemental theory is that to say a house or a person has too much metal or too little wood implies a solution. If you have too much of this we can drain it with a little of that.

Michael Breen once said to me that people are verbs not nouns. We cannot be defined in any final way. By the same token, helpful description is adverbial: it modifies the verb of behaviour rather than pinning down the noun of who we are. He *behaves* this way or that; not he *is* this or that. Once you've got a name you've got a label.

Myspiritradio

I've been burning the midnight oil writing feng shui items for *myspiritradio*, a new new-age digital download podcast web radio station thing. I put on Marvin Gaye's *What's Goin' On* and ramble. There are worse ways to feed your children.

The people involved are goodhearted, skilled and smart. The idea, a digital magazine covering subjects from crystals to the *Course in Miracles*, that is both up to the minute and incremental is ingenious and deserves support.

Interestingly I did a little feng shui for Suzanne who is behind *myspirit*: "You need an office at the front of this building: put a water feature here and a Buddha there." Now a month or so later, they have the new office. Stand between the Buddha and the water feature and you're pointing at it.

Alex III: Alex's Kitchen

Alex had two floods in her new house this month, both shortly after my survey.

The first was in the kitchen she was planning to make over. The water came up through the floorboards. The second flood was in the bathroom.

Her house faces wei the Sheep in the South West and backs onto chow, the Ox in the North East. This is among the most stubborn configurations. And the back door is about as malicious as I have seen.

She is such a bright curious woman and the kitchen is in the South which is the fire element representing enlightenment. Elementally and otherwise water puts out fire. So by implication these qualities are threatened.

The second flood was in the South East which represents the 1st Daughter. A flood in a yin wood area is like new grass swamped with rainwater. It exhausts something that is small but not necessarily weak simply because it's small like the fun and freedom of a young woman. Or Abbie's smile. It's too much. Exhaustion by duty sounds like the sort of message a thinly stretched (voluntarily) single mother might send herself. But 27 seems a bit early to shut down.

She has another man now. This one is not "on a path," she tells me. Soon will be.

If she were less young and beautiful, I tell her, it would be so much easier for her. The millionaire Oscar winner Halle Berry was quoted as saying that beauty gave her no advantage. Alex's conundrum is not quite like Ms Berry's.

It's this, I tell her: she wants a soulmate. And young men want a shag. Not that she's averse to sex but that for her it comes as part of a more meaningful package. And young men will get just as meaningful as they have to in pursuit of a shag.

Cycles of Change III: why England won't win the World Cup till 2026

1966 was a bing wu double yang fire year. Its closest equivalent to date has been the ren wu year of 2002 when you will recall, England were beaten in the last eight by the eventual winners. We will probably do well again in 2006 and again in 2014 but probably not in between.

England did of course win a minor sporting competition with a different-shaped ball at the end of 2003. Don't ask me.

13.
SOLAR FORTNIGHT BEGINNING:
TUESDAY 21 JUNE 2005 15.17

Ha gee *Summer Solstice*

Month: ren wu **the Water Horse**

Hour	Day	Month	Year
wood	fire	water	wood
yi	bing	ren	yi
wei	tze	wu	yuw
sheep	rat	horse	rooster

Ha Gee: *Summer Solstice*

The moon is full on the 22nd also, so in a sense we have full moon and full sun at the same time. This obviously does not happen every year. It is a particularly powerful time for processes that harness solar or lunar energy; that is everything from tides to the growth of the maize that forms your cornflakes.

Crystals can gain a particularly powerful charge at this time: left out for the six nights before the full moon they pick up the growing power of its waxing. This can be done any month but left out by day over the solstice, they also pick up the aggressively active chi of the sun at its height.

All in all this is a very powerful time for movement

Up the mountain, down the river, round the houses

Sue's house is on the outskirts of Edinburgh. She had been telling me how nervous Edinburghers(?) are about the huge numbers of visitors due next month for Live 8 and G8. A small price to pay, I would have thought, but then I'm not the one paying it.

For herself she had a simpler objective: finding Mr Right.

The night before this visit, my own mother had died in hospital in Bristol. Although she had been ill most of my life it was surprisingly sudden. I had been correct in expecting her to see out my father despite his robust good health (even after a bypass operation) and her fragility. Their relationship was nothing if not competitive.

One phone call and she was gone. There was little point trekking West to see her warm body. Those procedures I can perform for the dead work best immediately after death and just like my father who also died at midsummer, I had missed it. So keeping my appointment with Sue seemed the right thing to do.

There is just one experience going on at any time. This is the Tao. So my own grief was bound to be reflected in Sue. And the best way to use pain is to relieve it in others. I asked her whether someone close to her had recently lost a parent. They had, that week. Then I asked about her own mother. Had she been troubled? There was a glitch showing at 5 years old in her ba zi. She denied it but there was something in her eyes. She was not telling me the whole story.

Sue's house was unusual in that the front door was 90° to the facing direction. That is to say it was not at the front. Furthermore the configuration was what the Chinese call shang shan hsia shui, that is *up the mountain, down the river.* This is a specially demanding configuration usually coinciding with upset. As if this were not enough, the chi was collecting in a filthy etiolated stream at a very poor orientation from the house. Its flow awash with knotted contraceptives and chip wrappers, it was no good as a collector of chi. What it would collect would be sparse and nasty like the rivulet itself. It spoke of nastiness that was better shunned than disturbed. I would have to look elsewhere.

The day was by turns warm and wet; not wet enough to change that stream. It was never going to be that wet again. I thought of my mother shrivelled and cold in Bristol and breathed in deeply to feel the grief. Grief doesn't hurt; it's reasons for grief that hurt. This is what we resist.

The orthodox cure for shang shan hsia shui is water at the rear of a building and some sort of blockage at the front. This flies in the face of the teaching of the landscape school which is generally reckoned far more powerful and you have to square that with yourself first.

When you place water outside a house and nearby, according to Grandmaster Yang, the author of the *Book of the Green Satchel* from which all written feng shui theory derives, you affect the doors. What happens is that they are said to change *palaces*. This can transform a perfectly innocent front door in the palace named dai wong (*the Peak*) – which is pretty good – to mou kuk (*dirty linen*) which, implying scandal and hanky panky, is not so great. As it happened Sue had enjoyed her fair share of hanky panky and was currently nursing a heart broken by an adventure with a married man.

We agreed quite rapidly that her broken heart was shorthand for blame and that if she was to be happy, she would have to apply quality control.

"Live by the sword, die by the sword," I told her. She knew that already.

Then I calculated a position to place water. I was nervous about it not only because it was going to be by the back door which is much like putting a deep hole on your back doorstep but also because the eccentric front door and nasty stream made the bases of calculation uncertain. When I had made a decision as to what was there, I asked for help. I work on the premise that when I have done all I can in a good cause, I qualify for divine grace. And when I say "divine", so that we can avoid bloodletting, I mean God, Goddess, Spirit, Higher Mind or whatever force blows your hair back.

I did the calculation. It worked. If I placed water outside the back door, the doors remained safe and the house would energize.

Sue reported "a change of energy within the hour" and gentleman callers seemed to emerge rapidly from under flat stones.

I heard from her three more times that year: once when the pain of the five-year-old became too much for her and once when she found a decent, attractive, single, suitable bloke. They aren't a glut on the market apparently.

And one more time when she reported that a man had been murdered down among the french letters and styrofoam. She had against the odds remained undisturbed and unlike her neighbours, unthreatened.

Sometimes I think I might be making a difference.

On the way home I allowed myself the luxury of crying for my mother.

Whizz for Atoms

I took part in a radio discussion forum this week, featuring myself, Shila, a healer who has been working with Tsunami victims and an ex-GP, Dr Gummi who has some fascinating ideas about the science underpinning traditional practices. I managed to upset her in record time by suggesting that science had "got too big for its boots." We really needed a longer time slot in order for me to explain myself and give her a fair chance to batter me with her handbag.

My point was this: We want scientific explanations for things so that we can repeat them. Understanding how and why, for example, Pasteur's experiments worked, allows us to apply them elsewhere. That is a good idea.

On the other hand when science takes it upon itself to decry a procedure that works because it can't explain it, then it is ceasing to be useful.

I remember debating with a physicist whose view was that astrology was "unscientific." I countered that since the phases of the moon clearly coincided with the tides and women's menstrual cycle as well as the best time for sowing and harvesting as any experienced gardener will tell you, to *dismiss* it was unscientific. There are also hard statistics showing that certain types of human behaviour coincide with sunspot activity.

I don't actually believe in causality at all which makes me a bit of a wild card and is why I use words like "coincide" but I don't think that astrology needs science's permission at all. And astrologers mostly don't seek it.

But when scientists take it upon themselves to proscribe homoeopathy as some have recently, because they can't explain the underlying theory, it is actually dangerous. It is not so long ago that acupuncture, now proven under test conditions to work in the reduction of pain, was subject to the same attacks. Because no one knew *why*.

There are aspects of feng shui that might one day be explicable in a scientific sense and masters like Joey Yap call it a *science* because the precise procedures they perform are identical every time.

But frankly, I don't care.

Sometimes people would sooner be ill for explicable reasons than healthy for none.

Summer Magick

I have been installing some subtle feng shui procedures at home over the last month, following a traditional map of positions around the house. On this pattern some locations need to be low and busy, some high and quiet. Where low and busy is required I may put water or mirrors. If there is a door there, so much the better. For high and quiet, walls and trees are ideal but I may place Buddhas in an empty space that should be occupied.

This particular procedure has been focused around the South, which is about fame of course. Mine is a South-facing house. Not surprising then that not only are they suddenly without warning showing editions of *Housebusters* that I had forgotten about* but my whole family is on your screens as the "Sky family".

In Godalming nobody gets Channel 5, so I am in little danger of being mobbed on the strength of *Housebusters* but everybody sees the Sky ads! For my children who are all performers and my wife who is a theatrical agent and to blame for all this, the Sky ad is just another foothill in the ruthless assault on the mountain range of success. For me the sidelong glances are a tad embarrassing.

But an excellent reference for the effectiveness of feng shui.

For your own use: the fame bit of this procedure consists of

---

*This week I get to boss Janet Ellis about in her own house.

placing 9 things ideally red, ideally pointy, that are relevant to what you want to be famous for, in a South-facing window. The strongest fire chi of the year is right now, so get on with it!

When I was dabbling with feng shui theory in the 90s, trying to conclude what was folklore, what true feng shui and what nonsense, I used exactly this procedure. On a single night one of my sons was on University Challenge and both my daughters and my wife on the Esther Show. You might retort that this is hardly spooky when your daughters are aspiring actresses, your wife an agent and your son probably an attention-seeking smartarse like yourself. But if I tell you that I had that same day happened to be in Wakeling's the butchers in Godalming, when unknown to me ITN were interviewing Roger Wakeling about beef on the bone, so that if I had cared to move a yard to my right I would have been on News at Ten myself and add that I am a vegetarian, you might just shift your position a wincy.

Love All

Last week I was asked to provide a prediction for Wimbledon. Followers of my annual predictions may recall that I am already committed to England winning the Ashes – though I swear I have no money on it.

For this prediction I drew on the fact that the central "pillars#" of the birth chart for the year 2005 both correspond to 1934. There is a lot more to it but broadly these "pillars" cover the middle

---

A "pillar" is the elemental formula for a unit of time such as a day, an hour or a year. At the top of this document are the four "pillars" for the Summer Solstice.

quarters of the year from March to September. So the middle of the year will show "echoes" of 1934, which was, you may recall, the year of the "Bodyline" Series when the MCC had to change the laws of cricket to make them fair to Australians*.

Interestingly it was also the year that Fred Perry, the last Briton to win Wimbledon, recorded the first of his three consecutive championships.

So an upset and a British winner.

Not knowing anything about tennis, I was totally unaware of Andy Murray, incidentally kitted out with Fred Perry gear, until he had won twice. And then he lost – which implies an "echo" rather than a duplication of 1934. A smaller upset and some British wins but not a British winner.

Does this mean that England, having beaten the Australians twice now, have already peaked? Watch this space!

Ending Hunger

Although significant debt has been dropped, the conditions attached remain arduous and it won't do more than scrape the surface of the problem. We still need an absolute commitment at G8.

---

* As it turned out the correct year was not 1934 but 1933. Embarrassingly I realized this while talking on the phone to a ruthless hack from the *Guardian* Diary. But I was still *right*!

14.
SOLAR FORTNIGHT BEGINNING:
TUESDAY 7 JULY 2005 09.08

Siu Shu: *Slight Heat*

Month: gui wei **the Water Sheep**

Hour	Day	Month	Year
wood	**water**	**water**	**wood**
yi	ren	gui	yi
si	chen	wei	yuw
snake	**dragon**	**sheep**	**rooster**

Siu Shu: *Slight Heat,* **Exploding Sheep.**

Some chi changes are gradual, some sudden. From water Horse to water Sheep is on the face of it, not that drastic. The embers of the midsummer fire become the yin earth of the Sheep. What could be more peaceful? After all, July is the "silly season" when there is usually so little news that the papers have to make it up. To shed light on this unusually explosive change we need to know the nature of the *stems* that qualify each animal.

The *stem* is the upper character in each of the four *pillars* above. This Sheep month is water because of the yin water *stem* gui. Gui is volatile and has a unique relationship with wu, the yang earth stem; combined they make fire. And just as gui appears every 10 hours, every 10 days, every 10 months and indeed every 10 years, so does wu. Along with a whole month of gui we get a whole month of sudden fire combinations whenever wu appears. And the Sheep branch certainly did open explosively: as the chi was changing, bombs were going off in Central London.

I'm always banging on about the cycles of Chinese metaphysics so a reasonable question is: "Was an attack on London predictable?" And just as with the tsunami, I have to say yes, but I didn't see it. Here's how. Non-anoraks skip this page.

The *Imperial Heaven Star* ⌊in ᴳa which appears at the moment set out above, is to do with transport. Whether it presages good or not-so-good depends on the cyclical characters accompanying it. On the day in August 2001 when Concorde crashed, Lin Ga appeared with the Lunar Mansion* *Bird*. Indeed I remember noting that it did not look a good day to fly as I boarded my own rather slower plane at Luton. And on another occasion, Lin Ga coincided with the Madrid bombing. A friend of mine used exactly this raw information to predict transport-disaster-Spain in the right fortnight. On 7 July, however, Lin Ga coincided with the Lunar Mansion, the *Well*, whose significance is ambiguous. On the one hand it is generally fortunate; digging and building are encouraged, for instance. On the other it is about purging and moral uprightness which presumably represents the thinking of the sociopaths behind such brutality. Hard to call.

For myself, as I was saying to my 10-year old son last week while he successfully persuaded me to accompany him on the new rollercoaster at Legoland: "I find life quite frightening enough without deliberately inducing fear." Fortunately he is prepared to humour me.

The question is this: "When are we predicting and when are we creating?"

---

* There are 28 of these, of differing durations. See Derek Walters' *Chinese Astrology*.

Psychic Psephology

Some sort of answer to that question# came to me after surveying Hanne's house in South London a fortnight or so before the General Election, when I was sitting waiting for a tube back into Central London. It was a baking-hot day and a demanding call. She owned two houses; one she wanted to move into, one she wanted to sell. She had had difficulty selling. There had been one pretext after another and she was becoming impatient. On this particular day I had covered mirrors in the old house* and placed a big water feature in the back garden of the new one. We were both worn out by the time she dropped me at the station.

Sitting on the bench my mind focused on the election. I thought: what is ideal? What serves the world best? Not a Labour landslide. Their neurotic need to manage the news has pushed me over the edge into a cynicism about politicians that I had escaped all my life. In 1997 I really thought they were different. Silly me.

Not a hung parliament. That'll just mean election after election.

Not a Tory win. That Michael Howard! Hammer hath no horror like this.

Not a free-for-all for the small parties. Lord preserve us from the Independence Parties. Britain for the British! Don't these people know any history?

What I was looking for was balance.

So with these parameters I worked out what split of the votes would keep Labour in power with a reduced but workable majority.

Also raised by my accurate prediction of an Ashes win based on the wrong information. See p 156

* It sold a month later.

Then I divided the other votes.

The station is on the line between London Waterloo and Ashford in Kent. Every quarter of an hour or so the Eurostar train to Paris and Brussels rushed deafeningly through. Everything shook.

When I was clear exactly what result I wanted, I wrote it down.

Two weeks later after the poll, I happened upon the piece of paper. I had grouped the votes into Labour, Tory, Liberal and others. Each grouping was right within five votes.

Only a Prawn in their Salad

It is a creative act to see the G8 summit as positive if we want a lasting positive outcome. Aid doubled, trade restrictions lowered, commitment to distribution of basic health support is a 100% improvement. Not long ago the dogma was that it was all Africans' fault for having so many babies. The simple maths that infant mortality of say two in three means a mother must conceive three children to keep one was not understood until the mid-80s. This vicious circle may at last be broken. And if we have to deal yet again with Pink Floyd's internal politics, it's a price worth paying isn't it?

As Margaret Mead said: "Never doubt that a small group of committed thoughtful citizens can change the world. Indeed it is the only thing that ever has."

Trumpet Blowing Department

BTW: followers of my annual predictions will notice I predicted a "Live Aid II" in December.

Fighting a Corner

Soraya's house is on a corner at the end of a terrace. This usually means there will be winners and losers inside. At the North West, the realm of the Father, a high fence divides the garden. This is on the Dragon or yang side; suggesting a rift between yin and yang, male and female, mother and son, husband and wife.

Soraya is a smart, attractive woman. "Why is my teenage son underachieving at school?" she asked.

"How is his Dad getting on?" I replied.

"Hard to tell," she said.

"Frustrated?"

"Yes."

"Missing opportunities?"

That too.

"Do you argue with him a lot?"

She agreed they did and I rapidly reassured her that after decades of marriage, argument was probably a good sign. "But you've got to let him win sometimes," I said.

She looked at me coyly, with what some call a "busted smile."

"You win, your son loses. This man suffered the hail of blows it took to win your heart. Give him credit. That way, you make it worth your son's while to be like his father. Support one, you support both."

There were mirrors all over the Eastern wall. Too many. The East represents movement. I was reminded of another house which had been floor to ceiling with self-improvement books bought by the wife for the husband. The message she intended was "Life could be so much better" What he received was "You're no good." Here the mirrors were telling the menfolk: "Change because you're not alright." What sort of motivation is that?

We moved several mirrors.

Soraya's job as a casualty nurse was very demanding. Casualty nurses are a very special breed. They have to be strong, calm, decisive and compassionate. After a decade she was ready to move on. I told her I thought a new opportunity so challenging she might fear to pursue it was in the offing. She admitted that just such a job had been in that morning's post. She had not been planning to apply. I advised her to give it a go.

That she got the job was one thing she told me when she rang a few months later. That and that her son had risen from Dungeons and Dragons and was now stringing the odd sentence together. Even the old man was smiling every now and then.

All in a day's work.

15.
SOLAR FORTNIGHT BEGINNING:
TUESDAY 23 JULY 2005 02.21

Dai Shu: *Great Heat*

Month: gui wei **the Water Sheep**

Hour	Day	Month	Year
water	earth	water	wood
gui	wu	gui	yi
chou	shen	wei	yuw
ox	**monkey**	**sheep**	**rooster**

Dai Shu: *Great Heat*

After *Slight Heat,* we get – wait for it – *Great Heat,* though the actual process here on the ground appears to have been the other way round. The water-butt to watering-can to sunflower patrol has given way to Slugwatch. And no I don't squish or poison them – who knows what else slug pellets pollute? I put them gently over the fence into the long grass. All they can complain about there is an unvaried diet.

What else did you expect of a pacifist vegetarian? Napalm?

Children are God's Way of Keeping Us Anxious

Carol is of the American persuasion. She is an attractive, dignified woman; still frisky at 50. She and her son Dan are hiding out from her abusive ex-partner. She has been beaten up, poisoned, burned – you name it. If I had not heard it first hand I would have attributed the story to Stephen King.

One of the first things I did was to ensure that the entrances to her home were safe. There are ways of making a house hard to enter. And I have ensured that the back garden is prosperous.

She is a skilled nutritionist and to put the tin lid on it, the British powers-that-be have defined her mile-long US CV as irrelevant, rendering her unqualified to practise.

What all suddenly-single mothers have in common is money issues. The mutual dependence of the nuclear family pretty much ensures that.

Carol has chosen the house well; it has mou kuk, the *Guardian*, at its heart so it is watched over by a stable male presence without the need for an actual man. Nonetheless she feels safest in the back with the house between her and company.

She calls late at night. Dan is out joyriding again. What can you do? I have six children of my own. I know that not all grow at the same rate. Children are God's* way of keeping us anxious. And anxiety of course, is God's way of letting us know we are not alone. She is very not alone.

I tell her that as there is nothing linear to be done, her best bet is to admit defeat and ask for help. Divine grace is always available if we will ask for it. Sometimes I think there is a qualification procedure but even that can be waived in certain circumstances. We are never given tests we cannot pass.

Unsurprisingly I have been at home working on her feng shui all day. So she was on my mind already and we have an appointment the following day. I will be reviving her outdoor water feature (which is perfectly placed but stagnant) and installing other

---

* Tao, Higher Mind Spirit, Goddess, Primum Mobile; pay your money, take your pick.

protections.

When I arrive Dan is asleep upstairs. We get a chance to do some heavy-duty soul work.

Her ba zi shows that this woman has been in three abusive relationships. Is that correct? Yes. More than her fair share, I say. I ask her about the family she grew up with. Her mother would beat hell out of her as would her elder brother. By an inexorable route we start to unearth the decisions that have run her life and that we can – Tao willing – change.

Virginia: Take me home Country Roads.

Virginia calls me again. Sometimes she calls three or four times in a week. She won't use email.

Last month she had cosmetic surgery. It remains sixteen years since she risked appearing in public. I reassure her she looks a million dollars.

When I first surveyed her flat she wasn't sleeping. Her bedroom was a classic case of quietening a room down with earth. Then it was full of exotic glass pyramids and snaky murals. Now it is low, flat, sandy-coloured and quiet and she sleeps.

All this fussing is just delaying the day she must tread the boards again. As Legolas says in *The Return of the King*, unable to resist the obvious any longer: "Aha, a diversion."

She has every right to her fear but now is the time to come to life. Call your agent, tell him you're back, get on with it. Her flat is full of fresh energy, courtesy of an immaculately placed water feature. I suggest gently that there's not much point paying me hundreds of pounds and wasting the chi walking the dog.

"I know that really," she says.

"I know you do."

Generally feng shui will put the ball on the penalty spot but you may have to kick it.

Alex (IV): New Facing Direction

Alex has cut her arm badly. She was gardening at the front and the door threatened to slam with Abbie still inside and she reflexively reached to stop it, putting her hand through the glass. She has quite a cut; dozens of stitches have been needed.

The survey had revealed that her back door had a vicious streak. And it was positioned so that I could not move it by placing a virtual replacement elsewhere. Because every Hexagram of the Yi Jing belongs in a particular place on the compass, each door in effect sits *on* its own Hexagram. In fact more precisely, each door sits on a particular *changing line* of its own Hexagram. When a door is wrong which may mean, for instance, it does not readily cooperate with other entrances or that it faces something nasty outside, I try to change it.

This change is effected by changing the line to its opposite which gives us a different Hexagram. So if the door is at "Heaven over Thunder" in the East which looks like this:

and sits precisely at 39½°, the *changing line* is the bottom one. If we change this to its opposite we get:

```
━━━━━━━
━━━━━━━
━━━━━━━
━━  ━━
━━  ━━
━━  ━━
```

which is Hexagram 12 and belongs in the North West. So in theory I can place a mirror at around 312° in the North West and in effect 'move' the door. But I don't want to place water in the North West because that will make things even worse.

There are two further possibilities: the locations I get if I invert the Hexagram, either by standing it on its head or by swapping the top and bottom Trigrams (i.e the top and bottom three lines). Neither of these work either.

This is unusual but not *that* unusual (the same was true of Catriona's house) but it speaks of a very stubborn house. And as people are like their dogs so they are like their houses.The orientation **NE:SW** underlines this. In the current fate period there is a swathe of immoveable earth, cutting a diagonal along its length.

Stubborn houses, stubborn people.

There is no knight in shining armour to take her to A&E. I wish there was but I don't see one arriving for a while yet and this stubborn vicious house is not helping. She is taking time out, she tells me with an embarrassed smile.

Abbie's smile is not dimmed though.

Of Human Bondage

Olivia is a mother of two, born in West Africa. For a variety of reasons both her children were farmed out to family when small. She tortures herself that due to this they are not "bonded". You can bond any time you like, I suggest. Why not now?

Her house faces North over a fast roundabout which suggests dissipated energy as well as repetition. The sins of the fathers... that sort of thing. Her daughter's ba zi shows a capricious child. But one with huge potential.

She doesn't always tell me the truth, Olivia says. Olivia's ba zi suggests she may have been like that herself once. But you learned. So can she.

Here's an idea: make a deal. You will always trust her and she promises to always tell the truth. Think it through. It's a benign circle neither of you can get out of unbonded.

We revise the colours of her daughter's room: one scheme to compensate for what is there already, an option that costs almost nothing, another if Olivia feels able to start from scratch. I compensate for the new, immaculate but incorrect living room with crystals.

She can't stand to sit and watch TV with the kids. She has been withdrawing to her room. I point out to her that this is an opportunity to bond: a bit of quality time. Can't they compromise on what they watch? She bravely agrees to stay in the living room in the evenings. I notice the photographs of the kids at a theme park. She had actually worked it out before I arrived.

Harry Potter and the Critical Pontiff

So according to a statement from the Vatican, the Pope is against Harry Potter. Not much in His in-tray then. But what about the timing of these books hitting the market? Midsummer last time –

surely a consciously chosen release at the moment of maximum yang. And doesn't the way Harry Potter has stormed the world feel a little trancelike? I no more share the Pope's position on this than on the need for unprotected sex in the Third World but I am interested.

Guardian Diary

Stitched up by a cynical *Guardian* sub with a quota of words to meet. He christens me "Mystic Mug." Adam, my agent assures me that any publicity is good publicity. No one who is interested in feng shui reads the back pages of the *Guardian* on a Wednesday – if indeed anybody does – and I can now put "consulted by the *Guardian* Diary" on my resume. Thanks, Adam.

16.
SOLAR FORTNIGHT BEGINNING:
SATURDAY 7 AUGUST 2005 18.51

Lap Chow: *Autumn Begins*
Month: chia shen **the Wood Monkey**

Hour	Day	Month	Year
metal	water	wood	wood
xin	gui	chia	yi
yuw	hai	shen	yuw
rooster	pig	monkey	rooster

Lap Chow: *Autumn Begins,* **Monkey Business**

The beginning of Autumn, a depressing thought, also the start of the Monkey month. The Monkey is ingenious and full of tricks and he has a particular affinity with the Rooster of the year, both being metal in nature. Metal is competitive, it can be quite aggressive. The Rooster's yin metal at its worst is bitchy, what the Chinese call por kwan. At its best it is convivial and chatty. Vanity is the Rooster's downfall. The Monkey is a useful ally and a devious enemy. Too much cleverness is his problem.

These are the characters that rule August 2005.

As for the characters from which we might predict – the *Imperial Heaven Stars* – they are fun gok and bou din. The first is the *Queen's Holiday Mansion,* which is a nice thought for August but actually implies a window of girl power like the one earlier in the year which brought us Live 8 and the Make Poverty History campaign. Bou din is the *Hall of Jewels* – boundless wealth. Who for and how, I wonder?

As far as the things we want to be able to predict are concerned: the Monkey could easily be represented by a confused Imam and fun gok by burka power. I would not be surprised if someone with access to the version of the Koran with the word 'mercy'* included – probably a woman – made a powerful and unifying statement from within the Muslim community.

Ignore this please, *Guardian* Diary.

Celebrity Squares

It's a funny thing being a z-list celebrity.

Parking pre-survey outside Nick's home in Brighton I scrape the bumper of a rather smart 4x4 with my very scruffy Espace. It is 6.50am, I've been up since 5 again. Intuitive as hell but with the sort of co-ordination that makes me likely to turn my cassette over twice and lose half the consultation. Fortunately I'm the world's slowest driver.

I leave one of my leaflets under the wiper with a note. When the owner calls me, he addresses me as "Richard" and we talk as if he has known me all my life.

Then I am in London returning to Waterloo by bus, from a survey in North London. The bus terminates in Trafalgar Square because of a security alert at Aldwych. The woman in front of me remonstrates with the driver and does not understand his explanation. Her English is fractured. I remind her simply about the explosions last week. There could be more bombs any time, I explain. She nods resignedly, turns and looks at me:

---

* Let us not forget, by the way, how many Bibles seem to have been printed without the word "forgiveness".

"Hi know hugh. Hugh are de feng shee man."

This astonishes me; no one watches Channel 5 in Surrey. As a matter of fact, my mother-in-law disapproved of ITV on principle.

Rebel Rebel

I used to be terrified of celebrity, whether it was being on TV or having my books published.

I would imagine myself being lionised somewhere and a voice coming out of the crowd saying: "I knew you when you were an insurance broker/crap guitar player/tosser. You're a fraud!" Worse, I imagined a feng shui master telling me I knew nothing at the same time as a particularly bossy space-clearing lady letting me know that I was not spiritual enough. Don't you just hate it when that happens?

These days the vision bothers me less partly because of my son Thom and partly because of Adam Lieder.

I told Thom: "Being famous seems to involve dispute and I don't want to be fighting people."

We were sitting in a train. I was on my way to a survey. I think he was going into London for a casting. Thom is a musician but he'll do acting jobs if they pay enough. If he goes for a casting, he gets the job. His ba zi is a doozy.

As the railway line widened between Clapham Junction and Waterloo, he suggested: "Why don't you just choose to succeed *and* be agreed with?"

That is a very good idea.

Feng shui of course, divides broadly into two approaches: the strict mathematical Imperial feng shui that I trained in and the clutter-clear, sacred space school of thought that comes out of

Western New Age thinking. I also spent more than a decade exploring this. Each tends to think of the other as invalid and each is defined by what the other group thinks of them. Classical feng shui people working in the Chinese tradition tend to see space-clearers as vague and careless. They suspect that what the space clearers call intuition is just a reluctance to learn feng shui properly.

Space clearers often see compass style practice as heartless calculation by people who are not in touch with themselves.

These days I am of the opinion that it doesn't matter a damn but my worry used to be that one side would say I didn't know my ying tongs from my ping pongs and the other that I had no heart.

So now you know.

Just as I have sought out and learned from most of the major feng shui authorities, Howard Choy, Joey Yap, Raymond Lo, even Lillian Too, as well as a period of fulltime study with a Master, so I attended workshops or read books by New Age authorities from L Ron Hubbard to the Guru Maharaji. I completed the Exegesis instant enlightenment course – which may have been the most valuable experience of my life – as well as spending a year in the business community that grew from it. But that's another story.

I have concluded we can give love as well with a smudging stick as a luopan and indeed a thousand other ways.

These days I receive constant emails and calls from people telling me what is wrong with their houses and their lives and asking for help. Their house tell me about their lives and vice-versa. They have a toilet over the front door – Lillian Too makes a very big deal of that – or their stairs open directly out onto the street. Both main camps of feng shui have strong views on these. They have no back fence, they overlook a garbage dump. The house is axe-shaped, wedge-shaped, pear shaped.

What most people don't know is that Classical feng shui masters disagree among themselves as well. Some swear, for instance, by the power of mirrors to move energy, some insist mirrors do nothing. Some recommend a lot of symbols and knicknacks like foo dogs and wind chimes. Some say these are not feng shui. One thing feng shui masters are united in is the view that space-clearing is not feng shui.

I used to proudly believe that in a war between the schools of thought, I would be shot by both sides. I have since decided there is every chance I might belong to both. And frankly it doesn't much matter.

It was Adam Lieder who taught me that.

Adam was a pension client of mine back when that was what I did. Like many of my clients – but not all – he would come to me for love and understanding and the price was a little more money into his pension scheme. Eventually the tension between these two motives became too much. But for over 20 years it held. In many ways what I did then was not much different from what I do now but it *looked* a lot different.

Adam would come into my office in the city, roll a cigarette in liquorice paper, smoke it and talk. He could be quite pedantic. Like most opinionated men he was asking to be talked out of his opinions and I can always help with that. He wasn't that smart and on a level playing field I would not have sought him out as a friend. Also he was very frustrated: ambitious but not educated, skilled but not clubbable. His job was something I never understood in the back room of a stockbrokers. Arbitration? Aberration? Arbitrage?

His career was going nowhere and there was – on the face of it – little to be done.

His marriage was shaky and although he loved his young son he was always at loggerheads with his wife. Doubtless she has a story and as a client he was someone whose ego always needed building up, so I imagine he was not easy to live with. But to hear him tell it, she was a shrew. He never made enough money. He was never there when he should have been. He didn't pay attention. He was a disappointment. Once or twice she locked him out of the house.

He would present himself as being as calm as a ninja, but his pain was palpable. Somebody said that smoking is an outer sign of inner tension. Well so is breathing. But there was something about the way he leaned back in my client chair as lackadaisical as you like and chewed at that cigarette that gave away just how wound up he was.

If I had not in any case been able to feel it.

There was a deep agitated pain about him. A pain that wanted to keep moving every moment, that believed that a moment stationary would be unbearable. He knew only sleep and movement; there was no stillness about him. Even as he sat and smoked, his legs twitched or his fingers drummed.

I gave Adam what I could and usually sent him away with a smile on his face.

I saw him once a month or so for about six years. I knew all about him, his preferences, his football team (Spurs, by the way), how he liked his coffee (black, sugar). I was just his insurance broker but I may have known him better than anyone, including his wife. He had political views that didn't make much sense. I never disabused him. What's an opinion? He liked to dress a bit rakish:

pointed-toe shoes sometimes or a narrow tie. The office politics he talked about were predictable and tedious, his holidays routine.

You'd never have known it to look at him but this was a man on the edge. I did know. I saw the look in his eye, a mad flick that spoke of dreadful distress. I saw knuckles made white by the fist he formed as he talked. I felt that rollercoaster panic and I did with it what at that time, I knew how.

Towards the end of those six years, he left his first wife and son. He had met someone else. She was a listener. She cared. She understood. She gave him respect. They settled far enough from his first wife to start again but close enough that he saw his son. They married, he became the father of another child, a second son.

For a while he was less tense.

Meanwhile in March 1984 I threw my own life up in the air and left my wife, my three sons, my house in the country and my German cars and made a determined effort to wake up. I could no longer pretend to be ambitious. I handed my clients to my business partner whose agenda was more straightforward – he just wanted to make money – and left.

After a year at Programmes, the business community that grew out of Exegesis the instant-enlightenment seminar, I was ready to face the world again. That as I said, is another story.

So I returned to my office in Bristol. The job was the same but I was very different. I took up with my clients again. Although I was back in business my heart was in a very different place. Making plans, I looked for Adam's file, which was nowhere to be seen. I had to ask my business partner why.

During the year I took out, Adam had made some radical decisions.

It turned out the new wife wasn't such a great listener after all and early one morning Adam beat her to death with a hammer. And then his infant son. After that he threw himself under the upline at Barnhurst.

Compass style, intuitive, hands-on hands-off; what's it matter?

Lakshmi Part One:
A Simple Tale of the Dangers of a back-to-front West facing house in a Rooster Year

Lakshmi has deep spiritual gifts but she is desperate. So hugely in debt that it makes no difference if she spends more. And her husband is ill.

The house is the wrong way round; that is to say that the front should be the back and vice-versa. One powerful indication of this is when the back garden is lower than the front. Hers is drastically low.

To make it worse the house is East-West oriented. This year the tai sui (or year animal) is in the West. This is the orientation of the Rooster and it means the urgent changes I must make can not start at the East or West. This is even more true so close to the Summer Solstice. Catching this, I make major differences to the South East and North West before we part but I will leave a long list of changes for her to undertake.

Thank heavens, the chi is falling now Midsummer is past; these changes will not keep.

The heart of the problem is at the tai chi, the heart of the house. A house on an East-West axis has money built into it. It should be hard to be in financial trouble here but I've seen this wrong-way round thing before. Money out instead of in. So I perform procedures to turn it round.

Lakshmi herself remains anguished. Her first job is to stop beating herself up.

Why do we beat ourselves up? Because we cannot live with our choices. Why can we not live with our choices? Because we do not or will not believe them to be choices. Sometimes this is so hard.

"How could I have chosen such a series of disasters?" we ask ourselves. Lakshmi asks me several times. I set her the initial task of sitting at the tai chi and simply feeling. The important thing is to feel without attribution. That is: do not explain.

Mystical Stuff : Approaching God via the tai chi

Explanations generally lead to more questions. I sometimes think the question *why* is the most useless in the language. I don't really care *why*. I just want positive change.

At the tai chi where all the different pockets of chi intersect, there is no hiding place from feelings – no moving of furniture, no painting, no re-decoration. To feel openly is not pain. Pain is not in feeling; it is in not-feeling. The problem with anger is not being angry but trying not to be. The problem with anguish is being anguished about anguish. But we do feel the way we feel and we do have to start from where we are.

For reasons I am not egregious enough to second-guess, we appear to arrive on the planet with a series of lessons to learn; a curriculum if you will. These lessons come wrapped in feelings, many of which we don't like much. As we open to them we progress and they are less and less painful. If we really choose the feeling before us, above all things, however unattractive it looks, things move quickly and we are more awake, less pained and more in command of our lives. This, I think is the Tao.

Lakshmi needs to feel past the feelings she dreads. I assure her this will not hurt. It was Blaise Pascal who said that most of the world's problems are to do with people not being able to sit still. Some of us never take the few moments of stillness that would change our lives forever. Mystics call this the *via negativa*, or the *apophatic approach* to God.

It is the expressway to change. It consists of identifying what we consider important and seeing that it is simply a choice. Choices arrive in moments that appear to be separate from normal time. They hang there like a helicopter above the facts. The facts call for us to stumble through further facts. The moment allows us to fly over them to a point we will never reach by logic.

A Moment

Paul McKenna, the hypnotist, was on TV today. I don't know Paul but I used to know some of his collaborators. He is a very gifted man. Tonight he was talking to a group of the reluctant overweight. He had a large woman up on the podium with him. Her demon apparently was chocolate. He had her imagine he had covered the chocolate with slime and hair and all sorts of unmentionable stuff. Now she did not find it so attractive. After a short dialogue she was cured. Three months down the road, the programme showed she had lost several stone and only ate sparingly of health food.

Some see here smart NLP language patterns, the induction of trance state, attachment overbalanced with aversion.

I see a moment.

It is a moment of choice when all those desperate people see that their obesity is not an act of God or gravity. It has been chosen, mouthful by mouthful and can be un-chosen. In these moments an un-choice can be made.

Nothing is fixed or forced upon us. We can change ourselves, our feelings, our lives any time we want.

A ba zi will identify it in time and feng shui can locate such a moment.

We simply need to respect it.

This is the Tao.

17.
SOLAR FORTNIGHT BEGINNING:
THURSDAY 23 AUGUST 2005 09.17

Chu Shu: *Limit of Heat*

Month: chia shen **the Wood Monkey**

Hour	Day	Month	Year
earth	earth	wood	wood
ji	ji	chia	yi
si	muw	shen	yuw
snake	rabbit	monkey	rooster

Chu Shu: *Limit of Heat* **Not on my watch.**

Last fortnight there was a window of girl power (fun gok). This fortnight's *dial plate* character is *Heaven's Amulet* which may be characterised as *heavenly intervention*.

And appropriately Mrs Cindy Sheehan interrupted George W. Bush's holiday in Crawford, Texas. Mrs Sheehan, the mother of a soldier killed in Iraq, has vowed to stay on his doorstep until George W. answers her questions. Meanwhile the US anti-war faction has topped 50% for the first time with the homely soccer Mom as focus. When opposition to Vietnam topped 50% it never went down again.

Dubya has adopted the dictum "Not on my watch." I think this means that he will not allow a terrorist attack while he is President. But if there is one fact that will enter the history books it is that the first major attack by foreign terrorists on US soil happened on his watch. This reminds me that Tom Lehrer gave up satire after Henry Kissinger was awarded the Nobel Peace Prize. Bush has a mandate until 2008 but I doubt he will see out the Year of the Dog (2006) in power. There are forces of balance in the universe that even a sociopath as insulated as he is cannot escape. Check back with me in 2007.

Gategourmetgate, more fun gok

In the same fortnight, BA workers in Britain struck in sympathy with the preparers of inflight meals, mostly women from the Punjab who on average nett less than £12,000 a year. Although they work long antisocial shifts in conditions that are often stifling, they really want the work. It means their children get educated and they have some sort of future. Meanwhile, squeezed by Virgin and BA, Gate Gourmet aim to pay new contract workers even less.

This complaint has now been taken up by baggage handlers and check-in staff who themselves struck last year during BA's period of maximum vulnerability.

How did the women who juggle children and home-management with the thankless task of checking passengers onto crowded planes become involved? It seems that hard-pressed women doing their best in the face of insensitive management recognize others in the same boat. Ethnic, philosophical, cultural and linguistic differences are dwarfed by the commonality of women managing under difficult circumstances.

Is it only me or does this suggest a route towards peace? Watch for further fun gok.

A Dog's Life

Kate was a successful career woman who had recently parted with her husband. In her matter-fact Northern way she explained that he had just not been *responsible*. He was American. Their mutual misunderstanding was made worse by a common language.

"If he had sounded foreign I'd have known we didn't understand each other."

In his absence she lavished love on her terminally ill terrier. She had got him a pair of wheels to replace his useless back legs. We both had tears in our eyes as the little dog hauled himself around the house. What a soft pair of Jessies!

There was sat (poison chi) at xu in the North West. This means pretty much precisely "sick dog". Sometimes the Tao is very literal.

Kate's house was close to the Thames so it was, as riverside houses usually are, overwhelmed with chi from several directions. A river holds the chi, acting as a massive storehouse, but as the chi from each direction is of a different nature, a house may receive several contradictory types. This can be uncomfortable and confusing. The key is blocking off the water as opposed to installing it, which is more usual. Riverside and seaside communities are often predominantly "artistic." An explanation is that there is so much chi of such wildly different types that artistic expression is almost forced on them. For "artistic" we might read "bonkers."

The house was not tidy but it was full of stuff; some very expensive stuff: designer clothes, Habitat accessories, some in unopened boxes, and at 11am the rooms were still dark. I suggested she open some curtains. Windows too. The windows are the eyes of the house and the front door is the mouth. Opening them leads to movement. I know heartbreak when I see it.

Sandy: Shore

Adrian's wife had been having affairs for years. Everybody knew but him. Now he and his three children are setting up home with Sandra and her two. Brave people. His beautiful Jacobean house backs onto a disproportionately large swimming pool. At the North West. This can mean *man undermined.* Under no circumstances place a swimming pool at the North West.

Adrian's ba zi (personal feng shui) showed a character called mo yuk which is most simply rendered as *hanky panky.* So did Sandra's. I had a hunch I would find the same character on the house plan. So with half an eye on the Test Match and the Aussies – in fulfillment of prophecy – receiving a long overdue thrashing, I clarified this with some more than usually arcane calculations. I was right. Hard by the swimming pool.

So far so ingenious. Now to alter it.

If I shore it up, I shore him up. And Sandy too.

Spades, Hearts

Denise and Gordon put me up at a beautiful medieval pub deep in the Dorset countryside. Their office was relatively straightforward. A chunk of the very stylish 18$^{\text{th-}}$century building had been nicked by next door. The walls narrowed by feet towards the back. The missing Eastern chi was to do with younger men, thrust, ambition and so on. Denise and Gordon had thrust in spades but not their staff: there were no males and a shortage of ambition. I advised them to replace the missing East with plants, colours and so on.

Their home was another story; one of the toughest I've ever surveyed. They had not been there long so the energy was largely inherited. But equally if the lessons in the house were irrelevant they would not have been present. The house was arguing with itself. The previous incumbents must have been in serious distress.

The heart of the house was an unusual courtyard affair which is just about perfect feng shui but extensions to the house had shifted it. Twice. How would you or I find space for three hearts? What if ours kept moving?

And there were three separate sources of chi. For the lay reader this means the house had three alternate natures. Once I had identified them it became plainer sailing. I settled on just the one heart. This meant separating out a lovely little pond in the South West. Water located here is associated with unhappy women. We didn't want any of that! So I effectively placed it in the South East of a water garden now distinct from the rest of the property. Here it will produce healthy chi that Denise and Gordon can go there to enjoy.

Denise has three children about whom she worries constantly. As I have said before, children are God's way of keeping us anxious. The children – all grown – obligingly get into scrapes that she can sort out for them.

This brave smart and powerful woman has two cats. She never lets them out of the house.

When you email I ask her, always tell me about the cats.

Tai Sui Storm Warning

I have found this year's tai sui – the year animal – particularly fierce. The Rooster of 2005 faces West so once again, take care with alterations in these areas. If the West must be included, start somewhere else and work round. And sympathy to those with East-West houses where remedies are taking longer than usual. The worst will be over by the early October. If your house, car or door faces this way and you have had a tough time, just reassure yourself it's only once every twelve years!

18.
SOLAR FORTNIGHT BEGINNING:
WEDNESDAY 7 SEPTEMBER 2005 21.35

Bak low: *White Dew*

Month: yi yuw the Wood Rooster

Hour	Day	Month	Year
wood	wood	wood	wood
yi	chia	yi	yi
hai	wu	yuw	yuw
pig	horse	rooster	rooster

Happy Ever After

I'm often warned that a client – or more often their partner – is sceptical. Which I welcome. If what I'm saying won't bear honest scrutiny of what value can it be?

So I was particularly pleased this week to be asked by a very old and sceptical friend to do a compatibility exercise for him. Had he at last found the love of his life?

Establishing compatibility can be very fiddly. First you draw up two ba zi's: personal elements drawn from the exact moment of birth. These consist of what the Chinese call *stems* and *branches*. The date at the top of this page is expressed in *stems* and *branches*. As you can see, the *branches* are the Chinese animals. Each *stem* and *branch* is either yin or yang and belongs to an element.

Together stem and branch are called a *pillar*. Above are the four *pillars* of the late afternoon of 7 September 2005.

If you have read just a little about feng shui, the odds are you know the animal sign you were born under. Few however know their *stem*. Are you a water **Rabbit** or a wood one? Even fewer have any idea of the *stems* and *branches* of their month, day or hour of birth.

A master would tend to identify your central characteristics via your day *stem* which of course is quite individual, rather than the year animal.

Once the ba zi's were drawn up, several hours drafting, I could start to make some sense of them. It was pretty good news. All the three approaches I took said much the same thing. These two would get on. There was work for them to do but there was every chance of a long-term fulfilling relationship.

Feng shui is much like this. Whether you're looking at a house, a date, a person or a potential couple, whichever approach you take the same picture tends to emerge. A house with the South West missing for instance will tend to lack compassion. The ba zi's of the occupants will show a certain isolation. The mother may be absent for long periods. The road is likely to be a rapid one and so on.

These ba zi's said much the same thing whether I matched the pillars, the individual *stems* and *branches* or the relative Hexagrams of the Yi Jing. Bless.

Elephants and other animals

Last week someone asked me where to place elephant figures.

The NorthWest, the domain of Qian, the Father, is a candidate. An elephant on its side according to Master Peter Leung, helps a father to listen. Classically however, the elephant lives in the North East. Broadly this is the area for withdrawal, meditation and prayer. It belongs to the Trigram *Mountain*: *Stillness*. As this area belongs to gen the youngest son, paying it attention will tend to settle the minds of the younger males in the house. Keeping the area still will tend to reduce hyperactivity elsewhere.

The Chinese character siang stands both for elephant and wisdom – as reflected in the Western tradition that elephants never forget – and also divination. In Hindi of course the elephant figure is *Ganesh*, the favoured son. Hindu tradition incidentally, places Ganesh in the North West.

Now the year progresses into the month of yin metal: yuw the Rooster. Interestingly, for the Chinese, the Rooster is the beast that serenades our sleep rather than the one that wakes us. The Rabbit is the early riser. Legend has it that they swapped places at the request of the Buddha.

So it is that autumn arrives with the Rooster. The Rooster represents the nights drawing in, the lights going on and the windows closing. Now is the peak metal time of year. We can feel this in the changing of the light. Although it is hot, the sun is lower and the shadows longer.

The nature of metal is competitive. Positively this can signify excellence and increase: negatively disagreement. Yin metal can be argumentative, yang metal can be warlike. If I remind you that the monkey is metal too, you can see (above) that there is an awful lot of metal in today's date. Now is a time for patience. Misunderstanding is just too easy.

The *pillars* of this afternoon, as the chi changes, can be used to divine the month to come. We can expect a more-than-usual concentration of metal. To divine the events of September we can look at the way these characters interact. It is always the interaction of the elements that is meaningful.

This is the wood Rooster Month in the wood Rooster year. I've gone on and on about the wood Rooster – internally conflicted, uneasy, likely to explode into violence of all kinds including natural – but the point here is that the month now has the same nature as the year. It's like a summary. And its last few days will therefore imply what the last few months of the year promise. That is to say that this month typifies the year; so we have had, for instance, some of the worst violence in Iraq and a hurricane crisis in the American Deep South. With a son in Tennessee and an in-law in the RAF, by the way, these are not neutral issues to me.

19.
SOLAR FORTNIGHT BEGINNING:
FRIDAY 23 SEPTEMBER 2005 06.41

Chow Fun: *Autumn Equinox*

Month: yi yuw the Wood Rooster

Hour	Day	Month	Year
earth	metal	wood	wood
ji	geng	yi	yi
muw	xu	yuw	yuw
rabbit	dog	monkey	rooster

Chow Fun: *Autumn Equinox*

The wood Rooster month in the wood Rooster year: violent, unpredictable, time to keep your head down. Especially if you are in an East-West house, expect little forward movement before 8 October (12.59 GMT). Enough about the wood Rooster already!

Jake the Peg

This month I surveyed Jake's house. He is an adviser to government. Brought up by a single mother in a Northern two-up two down, Jake is an example of exactly what a man (or woman) can make of him (or her) self. We are as they say, all self-made men but only the successful ones admit it!

Brilliant, powerful, handsome, relatively wealthy, Jake has been living a life consistent with these qualities. And now he is beating himself up because he is 40 and has not found Ms Right. Yes, girls, he's single and lonely!

Jake does not know his hour of birth. So it is a challenge to predict his future from the ba zi. After talking him through it for a marathon four hours, I go home and study the chart some more. There are two possible hours of birth. One brings him the change he craves: stability, true love, peach sunsets, the other brings him more of the same. I choose him the better hour for a variety of reasons chief among them being his confessional to me. Can I really do that? I remember once asking a feng shui master whether we can change Heaven Luck – immutable fate – and he said "Of course, but we are not God."

But the place of prediction is a place of creation. In other words we get in line with the Tao – by whatever means – and we can choose. The Ashes, elections, what you will.

If we want to know what Providence has in mind for us, we can ask ourselves: what do I want? Not what do I need, what am I desperate for, what am I addicted to, what must I do to feel alright or to gain approval but what do I truly want? Often we make it so much more complicated but it's that simple.

This is the Tao.

Jake's bed on the first floor puts half of his body into an overhang on stilts on top of a porch. This is dreadful feng shui. His restlessness may be as much to do with sleeping over an abyss as remorse about his wild wild ways. I suggest he sleeps at the other end of the house while I set up some temporary cures.

For You the War is Over

Martha talks to her father often. That would be quite normal except that he died crash-landing a fighter-plane over East Anglia in 1942. Ironically he had survived the Battle of Britain when life-expectancy was measured in days. He never spoke about those times even to Martha's mother. And especially not to Martha who was two when he died. I know little about Western astrology except that I am a Virgo which apparently explains why I adjust other people's furniture and crave symmetry – but I believe that Western astrologers call this the *Saturn return*.

The Chinese simply work with 60-year cycles. What I have found is that many people born in the years 1939-45 are reliving those years. The chi of 1999-2005 is identical because it is exactly 60 years later. As most of the world was at war at that time, this can be very unpleasant. One lady whose father was a sniper was mugged several times between 1999 and 2003, including having a breeze block through her windscreen. And this was in West Surrey; hardly the inner city.

For Martha I implement some classical feng shui cures. There is a substantial water feature in the back garden whose positioning teeters on the incorrect. I redirect it. In the North West an archway leads out of the garden onto the street. There is no gate, just a gap and no path to the seldom used front door ten yards away. The North West of course is the area of the Father. Door closed, gate open, no path; the Father is here and yet not here. She is waiting for him. I suggest they restore both a winding path and the gate.

Then we talk awhile about her father to resolve the ill-health and uneasiness she has been feeling. And then *to* him. Wherever he is or was he wishes her only well. Her illnesses are simply a misunderstanding. As we start a radio turns itself on.

"That happens a lot," she says.

Compatible Houses, Compatible People, Compatible Dates

I generally include in a full report, personalized dates for major changes such as turning on a water feature or building a wall. This is based on consideration of a number of issues. One is simply whether it is an appropriate day according to the calendar for this type of activity. Do the *Mansions of the Moon* favour it? Then there is personalization.

For each of us there are rises and falls of usable chi. This relates to our kwa which is an abbreviated expression of our elemental make up. A building has a kwa too which can be compared to that of the owner to establish how compatible inhabitant is with building.

For instance Rosie's kwa is the same as that of the house she is renting – which she likes – while she refurbishes the one she owns and doesn't like so much. There's more to it but her kwa clashes with the one she owns. What's just as interesting is that her refurbishment, which was all planned before she found the rented house, is clearly an instinctive attempt to make the layout of her home like that of the rented one. Some of this is possible and some isn't. She has actually moved the back wall, which in feng shui terms is quite drastic. The house she is renting is a place of recuperation. In her newly redecorated home she will have work to do: on her relationship with her husband and father, on seeing that all three of them and the rest of the extended family achieve health wealth and wisdom.

Her father is a world-famous songwriter. So is her husband except for the world-famous bit. And her brother as well.

I place a band-aid water feature in her husband Nick's tiny home studio and a Buddha at the opposite edge of the compass. Collect the right chi and hold it. It's only a miniature but it should give him a rush at least. It's a hard row to hoe, living up to Daddy.

How has Nick been doing? Not so great. She tells me how much she *supports* him. I ask her whether she has considered she may be creating weakness in order to compensate for it. To her credit she is not outraged. The beds are set up so that their daughter sleeps on the same alignment as Rosie's desk while their son is aligned to Daddy. Daddy's team and Mummy's team. This appears to fit the facts. We make some changes. Some vast mirrors come down.

She picks things up very quickly and is amused by her own unconsciousness.

"How could I have missed that?"

There's no such thing as a mistake.

That's a lot of hard ideas all at once with no warning. She makes tea. We integrate the ideas and I get her to move her fridge.

Askin Martin

Martin's car business seems at first sight, very well placed. It sits high on the valley floor with water in front and hills on two sides. There are probably only two better sites in a valley several miles in extent. One of these is to the North where the hills are highest and the view longest and the other is to the South at the other extreme of the valley. And the factory straddles rather than dominates the valley. It is an odd orientation with hills to the West and water to the East. So Martin's showroom like his business and indeed his life is between two stools. Although by most standards he is doing well and he loves his business, he has an indistinct feeling he is going wrong somewhere.

We approach the site; his car winds down the valley. The view is bracing: dry stone walls and rolling hills. A few sheep, otherwise little company. He is keen that his warehouse should be at one with the environment. He likes the proximity of trees, river and wildlife.

He is very enthusiastic about his business which is American Cars and about Americana in general. He and his wife like to holiday in the States off the beaten track. He is one of the few English people I have met who loves the Appalachian Mountains from whence my once prospective daughter-in-law, the lovely Ms Prilla, hails.

The warehouse, he explains, was a pipe works. It closed following the Thatcher years. Half-a-dozen movies have been made about the anti-manufacturing dogma of those years so I won't dwell. But whatever view we take of the long term strategy, the short term outcome was misery. This, he tells me, indicating his vast echoing show room, pregnant with Lincolns, was a happy bustling factory. Here was assembly, here welding and so on.

Again the metaphors coincide. Better days have been seen here. Although cheery middle-aged men shuffle back and forth across the shop floor, I have yet to see a female employee. The gender imbalance nags at me.

His business fills a unique niche with brio but he is uneasy. Possible reasons include the recent deaths of his father and an old friend as well as his own 60th birthday. I remind him that I don't actually believe in causality at all.

The whole valley was devastated by flood in the 19th century, he tells me.

In Chinese terms, age 60 represents the completion of a full cycle. The Qianlong Emperor abdicated at this stage rather than upstage his late grandfather who had died at it. Interestingly the grandfather's reign roughly coincides with Louis XIV who enjoyed similar longevity and Qianlong with our own George III (1760-1820).

Time, some might say, for a fresh start. I tell Martin that I have also noticed that a number of clients in their early 60s have found themselves reliving to a greater or lesser degree, their earliest years. This seems to relate to the cycle of years which repeats every 60. Echoes.

One found herself talking with her father who had died in 1942 and another was mysteriously prone to assault during the years that coincided with her father's career as a sniper. Disinterest in causality is a plus when you reel off stuff like that.

Martin's father was a bandleader who enjoyed a privileged war. This does not write him off as the host of the uneasiness but it suggests that following his example might not be too traumatic. On the other hand some of the most apparently carefree fathers have fathered some of the most worried children. Read about Bing Crosby if you doubt this.

Martin has philanthropic ambitions and his crew are a happy bunch. One is delighted that I grasp quite quickly his contention that not voting is itself participation in democracy. But not a female face in view.

The factory site naturally faces South which is generally a pretty good idea. I notice however that of the six vast double doors, none of the south-facing ones are both open and unimpeded. The most obvious threshold is locked shut and two others are blocked with lorries. So the Southern aspect, which most would say was about publicity and promotion, is unexploited. There are some signs but they are a bit scruffy and varied. On the other hand he has chosen red and white for them which symbolizing as it does, fire melting metal, that is money being freed up, is very commercial.

Then he shows me the pond. It is quite deep; 20 feet or so and its surface is 10 higher than the factory floor. It is delimited on its West side by a levee. In other words to the East of the car warehouse is a flowing, babbling threat of flood. Martin's cars are all beneath the water table.

Now the East is generally considered to be about movement. So I have always tended to class cars as Eastern and to do with wood even though they are so clearly metal in a structural sense. In this case it doesn't matter. The metaphor is that movement threatens overwhelm or that a large body of water is swamping the metal. Either would account for a lack of dynamism.

I notice that to the West of the site there are cottages built on a ridge that is higher than the pond. They are post-flood but pre-pipe works. As a rule of thumb, older buildings that are still standing must enjoy good feng shui.

I notice also that the river that winds between the factory and the pond, that is West of the pond and East of the Lincolns goes under a bridge that itself leads to the ideal but closed doors. The bridge is not perfectly placed but it is in effect the jade belt that crosses the water in the approach to the ideal feng shui site. So again its use has changed but it's a pretty good feature. There is the potential, using a few tricks, for a near-perfect feng shui site. All we need is to build up the back a bit, deal with the water and respect the Imperial Heaven Stars. It may not be everyone's cup of tea but to me this is very exciting.

I have already been here four hours. I must find the tai chi – the heart of the building before I go.

I once received directly the information that the tai chi is 27" in diameter. I take this as an instruction to take great care locating it precisely. In this case, given the size and the division of the rooms, it is a demanding task. When I find it, it is predictably, blocked with great chunks of metal. I ask Martin as a priority to clear the area six feet around it. I can then be sure even if I am little out, that the heart has been cleared.

A blocked tai chi of course speaks of stuckness and holding onto the past. I suggest that employing some women would start to restore balance right away. There are, I sense, unspoken reasons why this may not be a popular move. I have a feeling of my advice bouncing off Martin, the human chi, the willingness to change does not seem to be there. Sometimes I can touch people deeply, easily. Sometimes I can't.

I tell Martin I will send him bullet points but that I will have to return to deal with the water and the Imperial Heaven Stars which demand a complex calculation and precision placing onsite. I congratulate him on the colour scheme of the signs and suggest he makes them consistent. I don't insist on more or that they are more prominent, which would be to cross the border into the world of the business consultant. His style appears to work and it is above all his business.

"They are the same colours as at least two of the major banks in China including HSBC which is currently among the world's most successful."

He smiles; good feng shui often calls for a sense of humour.

It is a long train journey back from Yorkshire and gremlins appear to have been at my iPod's shuffle feature. *Four* Abba songs in a row?

A further word about the Tao.

Feng shui has its roots in Taoism which comes, if you like, from the mystical wing of Chinese thought. As Quakers, say, are of Western Protestant thought and the Sufis of Islam.

The Tao is the flow of things, the process. It is everywhere and nowhere, baby. It always was and always is. The Tao that can be named is not the Tao. The Tao is both precise and vague.

For the Chinese there was before all things the Tao. Then came yin and yang. Then there was yin with yang. And yang with yin. And yang with yang and yin. And yin with yang and yang. And then *the ten thousand things*: that is the whole of creation.

Feng shui is the attempt by a series of Chinese geniuses to second guess the Tao. Which of course is impossible. You can no more see your own eyeball. Another way to say this is that it is an attempt to wrench time and space into a single system. So it can be used to predict and prescribe right time and right place.

And now we have reached the time of the Autumn Equinox, one of the turnings of the year. A new **Hexagram from** *The Book of Changes* rules over this time: Pi *Hindrance* or *Obstruction*. Not an easy **Hexagram:** we may be facing the most demanding part of the year but possibly the most rewarding also. This is the nature of change. This is the Tao. On the other hand there are still three months to go.

Feng Shul

I have been in Poland working on the Galicia Jewish Museum in Krakow, a radically different museum. It is situated in Kazimierz, the ancient Jewish part of Krakow, an area which has entertained many film crews over the years. This is where much of *Schindler's List* was filmed; the girl in the red coat came within yards.

It is not the ghetto which was a mile or so South across the Vistula, this is a historically wealthy area. Shown the map, any feng shui master would tell you this suburb nestling on the inside of a bend in the river is the very best place to trade. A tributary slightly to the north was covered over in the19th century which would have made this doubly true. Beyond it, the centre of Krakow has to reach across Kazimierz to the river for its chi.

This was an area of commerce, wealth and culture. It was noisy, crowded and full of life. Now it is very quiet. The Galicia Jewish museum is just yards outside the medieval boundary which is marked by a half-destroyed wall. It is a busy building full of young, keen staff but most of its visitors arrive in tourist coaches.

The purpose of the museum is to identify, celebrate and even recreate that lost culture. They hold concerts of *Klezmer* music. Hebrew lessons are taught here. The heart of the exhibition is the photographs of Chris Schwarz, the Director: he has captured lonely gravestones lost in woodland as well as the predictable sites of massacre but there are also striking images of restored synagogues. Despite everything it is an optimistic place.

When I was identifying the source of the chi, I was surprised to realize that it was not coming from the river. It was coming from beyond the boundary wall, from within the old quarter. My luo pan confirmed for me that the museum's source of energy is in the ancient suburb. All that lost life and culture is reaching out for revival. It will source its own future.

There were 40,000 Jews in Krakow in 1939. Now there are

perhaps a thousand. And wrestling with the burden of public works demanded by EU convergence, with inflation and high unemployment, Poland has seen better times. But I expect these things to change for the better as projects and jobs filter through from the West. This country has been buffeted between East and West for a thousand years. It is time it came into its own.

As you can see above it is the *wooden dog* month now, and the moment it started had an awful lot of 8s in it: 8.08 on the 8th of the month whose name means "eighth." It is from the elemental make up of this moment that we divine the meaning of the month.

8 signifies hospitality and meditation, as well as gen, the youngest son, known as **Mountain** whose location is in the North East. The current *Fate Period* which started in 1996 is an 8 *Fate*. During this *Fate* many Chinese employ 8 and 3 – in that order – as lucky numbers.

Do with that information what you will.

The *8 Fate* is the *Fate* of the North East, of the youngest son and by extension perhaps it is also the *Fate* of Rumsfeld's New Europe. It's about time.

20.
SOLAR FORTNIGHT BEGINNING:
FRIDAY 8 OCTOBER 2005 12.59

Hohn Low: *Cold Dew*

Month: bing xu **the Fire Dog**

Hour	Day	Month	Year
water	wood	fire	wood
ren	yi	bing	yi
wu	chou	xu	yuw
horse	ox	dog	rooster

Chow Fun: *Autumn Equinox*

Interrruption to Normal Service

This month I go to central China.

Between the years 1959 and 1961, Mao Zedong's attempt to impose a command economy upon Chinese food production led to around 30 million deaths. Throughout China people starved.

In 1960, the American sinologist Edgar Snow was allowed to wander pretty much freely on foot all over China. From Henan to Qinghai, peasants were eating leaves and sawdust but he saw none of this and wrote that he had searched diligently and could find no sign of a famine. China is a big place.

Today China is the fastest-growing economy in the world. The press releases indicate that hunger has been abolished and more and more people are achieving something close to what we would call comfort. I have for some time been keen to see the Chinese economic miracle first hand; what if anything, is being brushed under the carpet?

For most of October I will be studying at Wuhan Normal

University in Hubei Province. Assuming all the plugs and relays are available I will maintain the diary from there.

Divination of all kinds including feng shui has been frowned upon for 60 years. Which is why masters generally come from Hong Kong, Taiwan, Singapore or Malaysia. Alfred Huang, author of the *Complete I Ching,* * was imprisoned for 15 years. So I am fascinated to find out what practice has survived and learn what they know that we don't. Also we are due to climb Wudang Shan, the Taoist holy mountain, where centuries-old Taoist shrines still function.

More importantly my daughter Jessie has demanded that I find her a Mao Zedong snow globe to join the Pope and George Bush on the toilet windowsill.

I am a little daunted; Wuhan is not a tourist area. It is not Hong Kong or even Beijing. China has moved into line with Western ways of doing things extraordinarily rapidly in the last few years but I still hear rumours of communal cutlery and traditional methods of toilet paper disposal. My studies are government-approved presumably because the authorities see European money in it. But don't except anything radical in the next couple of entries.

On the way there I am to attend the *First International Conference on Scientific Feng Shui* in Hong Kong whose keynote speaker is Stephen Skinner.

I am afraid I remain sceptical that the authorities who brought us the massacre at Tiananmen Square (and still deny it) can truly be the authors of a bloodless revolution. But I want to believe; really I do.

---

* One of the two most useful translations I know: published by *Inner Traditions*, Vermont 1998.

Richard Ashworth
Feng Shui **Diaries**
Hohn Low: *Cold Dew*
Solar fortnight beginning:
Saturday 8 October 2005 12.59

Hour	Day	Month	Year
water	wood	fire	wood
yum	yute	bing	yute
ng	chow	sute	yuw
horse	ox	dog	rooster

"Solidity is an advantage but it is emptiness that makes a vessel useful."
Lao Tze. *Tao te Ching* **Chapter 11.**

8 October, Saturday
Malaria tablets taken: 6
Huazhong Normal University, Wuhan

As I arrive in Wuhan, the month chi changes from the *wood Rooster* yi yuw, to the *fire Dog* bing xu. Wuhan is an industrial city, not pretty, with a skyline that reminds me of the ex-Soviet bloc. Its population is eight million. There are 20-odd cities of this size in China and you've probably only heard of three or four. And not this one. As it is a port on the Yangstse which connects the urban East with the rural West of China it is a busy place but it is not on most tourist routes. Its major attraction for the culture seeker is the Yellow Crane Tower, a repro masterpiece of trompe-l'oeil architecture, about which Mao Zedong wrote a dreary poem.

From my room on the campus of Huangzhou Normal University, the view is miles of flat roofs of grey and faded pink. On the horizon are smart new highrises but this is very different from the neo-Manhattan of Hong Kong.

Something tells me this is not Kansas, Toto.

I am here for a month to study feng shui at the University. It is the first ever such course to be certificated by a Chinese university and I am more than curious to discover what they have to say. Although in 1927, Sun Yat Sen had feng shui men design one of the most sumptuous mausolea in Chinese history, divination of all sorts has been frowned upon since. The Taoist *I Ching* scholar Alfred Huang was released from a decade of imprisonment only quite recently.

This ambivalence, that the rulers exploit feng shui while denying it their subjects, runs like a seam through Chinese history. Qinshi Huang, the Emperor who first burned the books, spared divination material and his tomb, eternally guarded by the Terracotta Army, observes feng shui principles. Rumours persist also that Mao Zedong, although he proscribed popular use of the art, ran his life according to its precepts. He slept it is said, in a round bed that allowed him to orient to whatever was the best direction of the moment, personalized by his own feng shui advisers. As we are due to visit Mao's birthplace and hideaway, I am optimistic I will have a chance to examine some of the evidence. The story is that the feng shui is excellent but I have heard that it is the positioning of Mao's grandfather's burial place that is truly remarkable. It is reputed to be in a spot that is just about perfect in relation to the rules of all the major schools of feng shui. This raises many questions.

About this and China in general, I have no firm preconceptions. It is high time I visited the 'real' China whether I learn anything new or not. It seems to me that if the principles of feng shui are real, they must be universal. They are exemplified in long barrows and earthworks in Europe and in the terrain around Uluru in Australia as well as the Forbidden City. It is just that the Chinese, with their unbroken civilization, have been able to preserve the records. I want to conclude for myself exactly how old those records are.

And there have been a lot of – pardon me – Chinese whispers.

The popularity of feng shui has waxed and waned in Europe. I think this is because the principles were watered down for European consumption by the impatient, the naive or the unscrupulous. It seems straightforward that feng shui, like tai chi or chi gung, cannot be mastered without application and yet it is often presented as if an afternoon workshop is enough.

Equally Chinese Masters have presented the teachings as the monopoly of "lineages" when repeated accounts imply a respectable academic tradition. There is a body of information derived from the Classics that is accessible to anyone who can read the language. Joining what amounts to a cult and learning in hushed voices under dim lights is just one option. Many New Age Teachers, Gurus, Healers, what-have-you, choose this. And it always ends in tears. I know this first hand. I have done cult. Never again. But that is another story.

So I want to define that body of information and master whatever is new to me. I don't necessarily expect all of that on this trip.

Secondly I want to know where China is at in relation to its own heritage. In the late 60s the Cultural Revolution devastated much of what remained of Chinese art and architecture from the millennia either side of Christ's birth. Many died; estimates vary but thirty thousand is at the lower end of the scale. Compared to the tens of millions who died during the *Years of Hardship* 1959-61, this is chicken feed indeed. Actually I doubt even chickens got fed in those years. I suppose it is numbers that tell but there is something so outrageous about death by ideology that it seems to transcend the maths. Either statistic makes Mao a bona fide mass murderer in any case.

In the Cultural Revolution, whatever was not consistent with the reductionism of Maoist-Marxist-Leninism was smashed. Virtually overnight thousands of Buddhist and Taoist temples were demolished and artefacts trashed. At Wudang Shan, the Taoist refuge in the mountains, everything that could be reached on foot was laid waste. The perpetrators were mostly very young. The younger they were the more callous their behaviour appears to have been. Imagine at 14 or 15 the chance to rough up your teachers without retribution. Teachers, poets, intellectuals, hardly any were safe. The youth were rabble-roused and encouraged from the very top. Mao was up for retirement; the Cultural Revolution seems to have been his leaving present.

His thinking seemed to go like this:

Decadent Western culture is too attractive. We can't affect that. So we'll destroy our own. Like the jilted Sergeant Bilko in the Phil Silvers Show: "I'll go out and get drunk.....but I don't drink....I know; I'll over eat."

This is not unlike the contemporary face-off between Islam and the West. "Those who will not learn from history," as Santayana wrote, "...are doomed to repeat it." A recent poll in Egypt revealed the US as the country both that most people wanted to visit and that most people hated. Extremism happens just when and where the alternative becomes most attractive.

Perhaps I have got this wrong but I want to see for myself just how much or how little the Chinese value their own culture.

What I had been struck by already was the Party line on Chinese metaphysics. I had by chance spoken at length with a young Chinese postgraduate student working at Debenhams in Guildford. We discussed feng shui and the *Book of Changes*. He told me that such "superstition" had been outlawed because wicked men had used it to fleece the people. The same term surfaced at the Symposium in Hong Kong: the Chinese Government, the organizers made clear, would tolerate feng shui as long as it steered clear of "superstition." Whatever that means.

So there is much I want to know.

I am also keen to visit Wudang Shan, the Holy Mountain, for its own sake. Wudang is a haven of Taoist practice and the cradle of the *soft* forms of martial art. I have heard that Taoist monks at Wudang have despite it all, continued to divine using the Yi and that they draft ba zis. There are several conventions for drawing up a ba zi, my own being realatively unorthdox; I am interested in the styles the monks may use.

All of these objectives are subsidiary to my primary purpose which is to get an official Mao Zedong snow globe for Jessie to join the Pope and George Bush on the toilet windowsill, of course.

I leave my room and take a walk with a small group from our party to sample *dim sum* – filled dumplings – and noodles. There is Mario, Carla and Guido, from Italy, Irving who is Chinese-Australian and Wilhelm, a German. They are all architects.

The pavement is thick with people. So is the restaurant; young girls rushing back and forth with steaming trays. My Mandarin is very slight but the menu has subtitles. Even in a small fast food joint in suburban Wuhan, Central China, English is useful. On the other hand I am still only yards from the campus of a university with a pretty big Department of Cultural Exchange. This, I guess, also explains why our European-ness isn't that interesting yet.

The *dim sum* is excellent and the noodles pretty good. I wrestle with the chopsticks though. Noodles were not designed for consumption by chopstick. Although I have brought disposable Western cutlery, it seems a bit early to concede defeat. There is a respectable theory that a Roman legion made it to the East coast of China. I don't believe this. There is another that the Chinese invented noodles which entered Europe as pasta with Marco Polo. I believe this even less.

The dog month xu is unique. Although its nature is earth, its third week conceals a pocket of fire as if the summer will not admit when it is beaten. This pocket is often an explosive time. The three sharpest stock market drops of the 20th century happened around this hot spot. Here in Wuhan, it is unseasonably warm: 20-odd degrees Celsius.

The Italians are used to this of course. They appear to laugh about four times more than anybody else: Mario is charming and likeable, Carla effortlessly sexy and Guido whose English is less good has a dry sense of humour that doesn't always translate. Irving is the leader of the party. Mandarin appears to be his first language.

The previous evening in Hong Kong, Carla told me about the complications in her life.

Her husband is having an affair with his secretary. She is not sure how she feels about it; angry, relieved, guilty. All of the above.

The lights of Hong Kong Harbour twinkled as she told me her story . The skyscrapers are so different at night, lit like jadestones in a display case. This place should always be illuminated. Daylight does it no justice. The sea air wafted over the table where we sat and ate deep fried rose petals.

"Frita, tutta bona, anche una scapa," Carla said. "Anything tastes good fried, even a shoe."

A woman marries her father or she doesn't, I suggested, either choice being equally interesting. She has been, I could tell for reasons I cannot explain and don't question, run by a choice of this sort. And I was painfully right: her father died two years before. She believed she had let him down; because of this she believed she could not find him within herself anymore.

She told me about her childhood and her parents' complex relationship.

I held her hand.

"He is there. Wherever that is. And wherever that is, whoever he is, all he wants is your wellbeing."

And she cried.

My son Joey sometimes tells people that: "Daddy's job is making ladies cry." He is not far off: tears usually accompany healing but it's not a gender issue. Except that generally women are smart enough to cry instead of breaking things or punching each other.

Gently I pointed out some cyclical patterns. Chinese Metaphysics suggests that everything is binary; reality is composed of yeses and no's. First there is the Tao, then simultaneously yin and yang, the opposing principles that compose everything. Then there are simultaneously yang with yin, then yin with yang and then the

10,000 things. But we always retain choice. Always.

She could see that she had made a mistake, a mistake that could only make her unhappy. Not too late to change though. We always retain choice. Always.

"Your husband is a silly arse," I said, "But that's not much use to you. If you work from your choices, he's got nothing to do with it. On one level there's only you involved."

"Seely orse," she repeated back and laughed.

By then it was late.

We walk further from the campus. Wuhan was where the first shot was fired in the Revolution of 1911 that overthrew Pu Yi of the Manchu Dynasty, the *Last Emperor*. The Manchu of course preferred to call themselves by the more Chinese epithet *Qing*. Wuhan is also where Mao ordered the first road bridge across the Yangtse. Mussolini made the trains run on time; Mao got traffic across the Yangtse.

There is a lot of history here but you'd never know. Nothing has been preserved. Even the Yellow Crane Pavilion was rebuilt in 1985. Count has been lost of how often it has been destroyed. It still stands out from the skyline south of the river but knowing it is a reproduction makes it hideous.

In the shops and restaurants the staff are so young. You could be forgiven for concluding that China's workforce is mostly teenage girls. Where are the older people? And the businesses are drastically overstaffed. I enter a small record shop which I expect to employ two or three and there are six. They greet me effusively. This does not seem predatory or even particularly commercial; just a desire to grab with both hands whatever work might appear. The greeting is sweet and enthusiastic. I buy "Hell Freezes Over" by the

Eagles for 12 yuan which is about 1 Euro. There is no way royalties have been paid on this.

We are joined by Julian, an Australian Doctor of Geology, a likeable, earthy, outgoing man with a brilliant mind. He has travelled up from Hong Kong by train which costs a fraction of an airticket but takes confidence and fluent Mandarin. I observe that one of the four tones that make Chinese speech so demanding for the Westerner is like the so-called "Australian interrogative".

"You guys have a head start," I say.

He smiles and shares a story about teaching underprivileged Doctoral students in Sydney.

At the symposium I have just attended in Hong Kong, he gave a remarkable paper on earth energies. Some of his ancestors were cannibals from the Solomon Islands. "It is the ultimate way of settling a dispute," he says, "If we can't agree I have to eat you." I will learn that he has an anecdote for every occasion. This one may be a warning to a stuck-up Pom, of course.

He points out that a restaurant we pass serves dog. Why not? All meat involves death. Cuddliness is just a distraction. I notice three feral dogs sniffing through garbage. Are they edgy or is that my imagination? Later live skinned dogs are sighted at the market.

"Cha, cha, cha," he says. It is his call sign.

As China rebuilds itself, I had heard that whole districts of *hutong* or traditional districts were coming down. And this is confirmed before my eyes. There is noisy, dusty construction everywhere and acre-wide gaps in the street-frontage. So much building. But it does not seem that they are knocking down buildings of any age to make space; nothing looks to have been built earlier than the 1960s.

The architects I am with are used to thinking big.

"They use pretty poor material," says Irving, in his unique East-West accent. I am not sure whether the singular "material" is poetic or a tick deriving from the very different Chinese approach to plurals. He uses the word *like* as punctuation but then so do my children. Irving is, like most of the Western names of the Chinese, a name he chose for himself. The inspiration could be Irving Berlin for all I know. He moved to Australia in his teens. Who is he really? Like all around him, he slurps and sucks as he eats. He remains very Chinese. I am wary of him not least because I am not entirely sure what that means.

Wuhan is very Chinese too. There is noise everywhere. People sell high-tech software for pence from tables on the pavement. Again there is no way that intellectual property has been respected. As we pass from the shanty area around the campus to the smarter shopping downtown, there are dozens of shops selling phones, computers, scanners, game consoles. They make these things here of course.

Later, back at the University, there is an introductory reception. I discover that the backbone of our party, all here to study hardcore feng shui, is Northern European: Polish and German. And me I suppose. There are also South Americans, three ladies of a certain age from the US, a Slovak, some Swiss. I gravitate again to the laughing Italians. They dismiss the pasta slander with snorts.

If pasta had been Chinese, Mario says, they would surely have developed the fork. He is the author of a respected book on feng shui in Italian and this is a good joke.

I retire quite late to my room. It is perhaps 1am and my body thinks it's lunchtime. I'm not hungry but I'm not sleepy either. I text

Sheila at home; it's surprising how close these letters on the screen bring us. She has been busy – three kids, two businesses, extended family. Our daughter-in-law Tracey, an ex-actress who teaches drama and is to blame for the family epidemic of thespian aspiration, delivered a stillbirth last year and is still fragile. I think there can be little that deserves the term horror more than watching your son and daughter-in-law bathe their dead baby.

Should not a feng shui man have been able to prevent this? I don't want to go there. Every route is festooned with pointing fingers. I gave warnings but we have to live our own lives. If it's not my fault is it someone else's? I don't think so. No one is to blame. The notion is nonsense. Things happen the way they are supposed to. We are all innocent and we are all responsible.

I can nonetheless point out the Imperial Heaven Star to which it relates.

I think of Joey; he and I are joined across the 12,000 miles because we have agreed each of us will read *Cider with Rosie* while I am away. We are both drawn to the gentle poetry of this account of a small boy brought up in a house full of women. I look forward to talking with him; meanwhile we have text and email. He wants a parallel languages edition of Sun Tze's *Art of War.* In so far as a father can deny such a thing, it is nothing to do with me.

Henni wants movies. She is studying Chinese cinema for A level but she would anyway.

As I go to sleep the long curtains seem to wave. There is no wind. The room in the dark takes on the character of a mausoleum with winding sheets and whispers.

Sunday 9 October
Malaria tablets taken: 7
Dim sum **eaten: well into double figures**
Huazhong Normal University, Wuhan

We visit Ting Tao East Scenery Lake: a lakeside prospect that is not unlike Lucerne or Geneva, even Chicago, if you close your eyes and feel the chi. Or Windermere. There is something so hopeful about open bodies of water. The trees are old enough but the centrepiece is a reproduction temple and it is at the top of a flight of steps that rivals Montmartre. The wood is ugly and the plaster flaking.

While I puff the architects tut. These are very smart people who have incorporated feng shui into their practices for a variety of spiritual and practical reasons. They are not keen on concrete.

"Nasty but low maintenance," Wilhelm, who is trim and logical, says. Gertrude, Irving's German partner who gave a dense paper on the semiotics of architecture at the symposium, agrees. Wilhelm has a very informed but linear take on feng shui and indeed his own country's politics. As we speak, a hung parliament means there is no German government. He tells me that Germany can no longer afford its welfare system. Twenty years or so on from similar debates, I tell him, we in the UK are faced with retirement some time after 70 as well as a desperate transport system and I suspect this has as much to do with the rapid enrichment of several thousand fat cats at everyone else's expense during the privatization frenzy of the Thatcher years as economic principles. That surely is what lies over the German horizon. Wilhelm is a good man with a sharp mind and a surprising gentleness. He was, he tells me, brought up by his mother after his father died young. His sadness is not masked with bravado. I imagine these facts are connected.

I think of Joey at home reading *Cider with Rosie*.

Wilhelm listens carefully. I am suggesting that the Blair-Thatcher Project may not be 100% miracle. Emulate with caution. And he is right about the concrete.

Wherever I go, the people are warm and accommodating. We take a bus and I call home on my mobile phone; a young girl behind me goodnaturedly mimics my speech. I am a living language lesson. All these kids learn English from primary level but few have seen more than a handful of Caucasians. Two or three miles from the campus, we are now rare enough to attract stares.

I had expected thousands of bicycles. Ten years ago, urban China was bicycles as far as the eye could see. Now there are none. But there are thousands of cars. No car in consequence is much more than ten years old. Apparently tens of thousands of secondhand ones were bought in bulk from Japan. They are, I remark to Carole, a sassy Italian-American from New York, in better condition than the ones in Manhattan. This rapid sea change is an astounding feat of macro-management. There are side-effects though. On the drive from the airport we witnessed two minor accidents. If they have gone from cars to bikes in ten years no one presumably has more than that amount of driving experience. There is accordingly little etiquette and copious u-turns. Traffic lights are more of a suggestion than an obligation. Pedestrians take their lives in their hands at zebra crossings even when the lights are with them, wading across the streets lane by lane looking both ways.

There is an arcade at the foot of the steps to the ersatz temple. It is staffed by smiling teenage girls. Here they sell all sorts of knick-knacks; medallions of the year animals, red good luck tassels, jadeite jewellery. There are several booths full of Maoabilia: little red books, stern-looking busts and DVDs. On TVs endless crowds cheer the Great Helmsman. There are no snow globes.

Looking at the bombastic brass busts, I think of Alfred Huang and of Tiananmen Square and of Jung Chang and of the "One People Two Systems" principle. Daddy knows best. Despite the veneer of Communism, I suddenly see exactly how Confucian this country is.

 Monday 10 October
Malaria tablets taken: 8
Huazhong Normal University, Wuhan

Dou the Northern Ladle is one of the 28 *Mansions of the Moon* which divide up the Chinese sky much as our Zodiac does. The South East Asian sky is very different. For Europeans *Dou* is part of Sagittarius. Its shape is central to feng shui as it is the source of the pattern of energies known as the *Flying Stars*. This concept of a ladle in the sky is at least 4000 years old.

In all these millennia the idea of the celestial ladle does not seem to have evolved into the serving spoon. Consequently almost all Chinese food other than rice is presented in communal dishes which the individual attacks with chopsticks. These chopsticks will have been in and out of their users' mouths several times by the time the last dish is served. Tables at most restaurants including the refectory at the student hotel we are in, are circular with a revolving glass centre which can be rotated to bring food closer.

Meal by meal, as I watch ever-more slobbery dishes revolving clockwise and then anti-clockwise – in *yin* and then *yang* motion –

I am unsurprised as cold sores, mouth ulcers and sniffles pass around our party. By the time we are ready to return, almost everybody will have suffered.

In the Confucian family, like any other, communal eating must have developed from breast feeding. In time the family would all hold antibodies in common and shared cutlery would be no problem. A tour party consisting of students from all over the world is probably not what Confucius had in mind.

At this, our first meal together inhouse, Julian eats heartily. Valerie, an Australian vegetarian, folds her arms and appears to hold her breath until the egg dishes arrive. She looks in need of love. Carole is visibly squeamish. Most of the party are more adept with chopsticks than I am. But that frankly is not hard.

Formal lectures start today.

We meet Professor Leung who is the head of the Faculty. He is teaching us apparently as a personal favour to Irving. He is 60ish, with the bookish squint of the academic, conveying authority without being punitive. He starts by discussing the history of feng shui. We see slides of an archaeological dig which shows a Bronze Age settlement close to 6000 years old displaying every sign of feng shui thinking. It backs on to high ground and has water in front. It is separated from the dwellings by open space and low hills to either side. It is on a North-South axis. Furthermore there is a deep hole at the front which has yielded a ceramic dish decorated with a fish design. This clearly is a xue or *qi well*. Fish designs of course are still in use today as symbols of wealth.

Feng shui ideas were not committed to writing, he explains, until the 1st Millennium BC and the term itself not until the Warring States period – roughly between 500 and 200 BC.

That night we – me and the Italians – find a bar that claims to serve Irish coffee. We try the two Chinese wines: *Great Wall* and *Dynasty*. One is unbearably sweet but the other isn't too bad. Then the Irish coffee arrives: "Hubei Single Malt aged 20 minutes," we conclude. Hubei – the Province we are in – even sounds Irish: Hough Bay, possibly a little fishing port on the Donegal coast.

"On the other hand," I add, "If the Chinese decided to take winemaking seriously they'd hire a few Italians and lead the world in a decade." There is already unrest in the EU because the Chinese produce better textiles cheaper.

Mario takes a call on his mobile phone. His father has had to go into hospital for a heart operation. I look at Mario's energy from several angles. There is a strength about this man. He is not about to be bereaved. On the other hand when he talks about his family it is clear that there is more to discuss than he is sharing. We talk about his ex-wife who is struggling. I suggest that her failure is his revenge. It was she who walked. He sees this right away. But there is more to it than this.

Daniela, a beautiful young Portugese architect, joins us. She sits on the periphery listening. And then Soon Yi, who is from Korea by way of Austria, joins. She is exquisitely beautiful and talks enthusiastically about her children – four small girls, the oldest thirteen – and about her studies. She is or at least has been, a philologist. Then for no visible reason her energy darkens and her face clouds.

"Where have you gone?" I ask. She speaks good English and French, fair Italian and impeccable German but she is very oriental. Korea is the answer. I can feel a separation between her throat and her gut; between her speech and her feelings. She is like a

Neapolitan ice cream: deeply sensitive on top of desensitized, on top of sensitive. As if there were a wall across her diaphragm dividing North from South. Like Korea.

I tell her so. Which brings a waterfall of volunteered information: about her mother with whom she has had difficulties, her father for whom she has a very Korean respect, her children and the competition between her now husband and her then boyfriend. I am unsure the competition is over.

Daniela asks me to draft a ba zi for her daughter. At first I refuse but she asks me again and I see how important this is to her. I tell her it will take a while. There is about six hours drafting involved which is not likely to be easy to pull from a schedule of six to nine hours a day of formal lectures and field trips, seven days a week. These Chinese academics are not messing.

Mario has been to Wudang Shan before. A one-time experience, he says. At the summit he was approached by a monk with what appeared to be a personal message. There are shrines all over the mountain, Mario says, and red prayer sashes on the mulberry trees. While he was there he prayed for his father, his wife and his ex-wife and was overwhelmed by the contradictions, contradictions that melted as he tied the sash to a branch and watched it flutter over the precipice. Mulberry thorns are quite sharp, he reminds us.

We walk home, seven or eight of us. Julian has adopted a scruffy bar. He is sitting outside in the heat, staring across the road. We greet him and he invites us to join him for a Tsingtao (pronounced *Jingdow* – Tsingtao is an early German transliteration). Tsingtao is a beer costing 1 yuan a pint: less than a tenth of one Euro. You can get plastered for under a quid. He has charmed the many serving-girls who wait on him hand and foot. I note that a linguist has to be this charming. How else do you become fluent? I drink three pints which makes the rest of the walk home a little wavy.

Is it possible there is a feral dog missing?

Cha cha cha.

 Tuesday 11 October
Malaria tablets taken: 9
Huazhong Normal University, Wuhan

There are three major spiritual traditions in China: the Tao, Confucianism and Buddhism. I refer to "the Tao" rather than Taoism because they are different and also because there is something faintly fatuous about an –ism based on the Tao.

The Tao is the flow which underlies everything. It precedes all things and is within all things. Tao means the "way." It is the path itself. This is an elusive idea. Its most famous proponent, Lao Tze, wrote in the *Tao te Ching* that "The Tao that can be spoken of is not the Tao."

There is nothing right or wrong in the Tao. It is what it is. It is going where it goes.

Confucianism, on the other hand, is a special case of the Tao based on a belief that certain things are desirable and certain are not. Confucius derived rules for living that would foster an ordered society. These rules are less spiritual than social. They emphasize respect for parents and the elderly.

Confucius and Lao Tze were virtual contemporaries. It seems clear however that Confucian thought is a hijacking of the Tao. Recent research indicates that this is historically correct. And this relationship seems to reflect something bigger. As I write there is a tension both in China and in the world between control and trust.

The Tao cannot be controlled. It does not matter where we think it ought to be going, it goes where it goes. And in truth, there is little in life over which we truly have much control: not weather, wind, war nor water.

But Confucius with his emphasis on an ordered state, attempts to set up as a principle that the Tao is going a particular way. He attempts to house train it. It won't lie down and Chinese history is basically the story of this tension. But so is the history of the rest of the world. We can control almost nothing but we keep trying. We will not trust.

The joke is that Confucius was Mao's sworn enemy. He identified Confucianism as everything that was wrong with China. The people had accepted the order of society too long. Land was to be returned to the peasants. And so on. The great father figure railed for seven decades against paternalism starting – interestingly – with his own father. And his legacy has been ruled by generations of geriatric gangsters who in their turn cannot be questioned and will not admit they are wrong. The *one nation two systems* lash-up is essentially a way of taking a u-turn without admitting the vehicle was headed in the wrong direction. Like every revolutionary Mao became what he fought.

After the morning lectures, I walk into Wuhan in search of a LAN card for my computer. The university is very modern in this regard. There are plugs in every wall to link to the internet but I have second guessed them and brought one that requires a 'hot spot'. No problem: there is more cheap technology per square foot here than anywhere else on earth.

I need some milk. Every meal includes green tea but I have

brought a few precious English Breakfast teabags with me and I can't drink them black. I try to ask in Mandarin but my accent is so poor the thirtyish lady behind the corner of the small shop laughs. Hearing this, her husband, mother and small child appear from somewhere. The little girl's laugh seems wrong all by itself. When I hear one child laugh I expect several. I remember that no family is allowed by law to have more than one child. It is part of the economic miracle. I do an impression of a cow with my fingers to my temple as horns.

Mario is passing. We become a pantomime ensemble. The family are all laughing together now. The husband reaches into a shelf and produces a carton of milk. I pay and try to say thank you. They don't understand that either.

Mario claps me on the back. What kind of Englishman is this?

All but the mother return to the back of the shop. This I guess is hutong, flimsy buildings, part residential part trade. I have paid around 20p for the milk.

One nation, two systems. Which of the two systems is this?

We bump into Zdenka who is from Slovakia. She is statuesque and aggressive and speaks rapid well-accented English. She lives in Berlin but pines for Bratislava. Who would not? When I ask her to elaborate, her reasons in favour of Berlin appear all to be fiscal and for Bratislava to do with her feelings. For me there would be no contest but what do I know? The heart has its reasons.

My room is again a busy place tonight. It seems white in the half light, from ceiling to floor. The curtains flap and the flapping seems not only to be at the windows but all around me. I hear whisperings and can almost distinguish individual voices. There is a resigned misery here. The voices do not even have the energy of moans.

They are more like hums. I know that whatever may or may not be in this room wants love just like you or me. It hangs in the air like a marionette and I breathe into it. This is frightening but less frightening than not doing it.

I remember Sheila and Joe and Jess and Hen at home. It becomes easy to give love and I fall asleep easily.

Wednesday 12 October
Malaria tablets taken: 10
The Tomb of Prince Zhao, Longquan

Chinese characters can be transliterated two ways. One, *Wade Giles,* a 19th century British imposition, turns up approximations like "Peking" for a city whose name is actually much more like the *pin yin* Beijing. *Pin yin* was conceived under Mao after consultation with Albanian philologists and is the official non-imperialist form. Understanding *pin yin* is vital as it allows us to refer to words consistently without mastering Chinese characters. The Albanian connection may explain why the letter "q" is pronounced "ch" and "r" is pronounced "j" which to the (Western) European may seem perverse. Thus *qi* is pronounced "chi" and "ren" (people) "jen." Not ideal but a really useful middle ground. The fact, for instance, that the Albanian dictator Enver Hoxha's name is pronounced "Hoja" is an indication that Mao was not plugging into the philological mainstream.

Long Shan, that is Longquan, means "Dragon mountain". The name relates to the hills behind the tomb we are to visit, which are in the classic "Dragon vein" formation. One range peters out onto a level plain at the edge of which another range starts. The ranges are the dragons and the "vein" contains the "blood" of the land; the chi. The space where the ranges meet is where the "pearl" is found. This treasure is the location of the perfect chi. In front of and beyond it the job of the feng shui man is to place a ming tang or bright hall, a space for the chi to be cherished. The essence of feng shui is to gather the chi at the water (shui) and protect it from the dispersing wind (feng).

One way to explain this idea is to look at a physical map. China is mountainous in the North West and it is here, about as high up as you can ascend on Earth, that the two major rivers, the Yellow River and the Yangtse, have their source from whence they tip South and East towards the Pacific. The power of a Dragon vein is related to the height and extent of a range. What more logical conclusion than that the life-giving chi should come down from the mountains?

At Longquan is the tomb of a Prince; Zhao the 6th son of the first Ming Emperor Zhu Yuanzhang, was despatched here as local ruler. Typically his father trusted no one. Chinese history vindicates this mistrust. It was a rare Emperor who died in his bed. Zhao apparently found the site himself while out riding. As sites of such perfection are not common, there and then, thirty-odd years before his death, he started planning his burial. The site was complete well before he took possession.

It is not aligned due North-South which is ideal but closer to North West-South East. I know the North-South orientation is reserved for Emperors and Professor Wang confirms that even the son of an Emperor would not have dared encroach on this. Wilhelm measures it carefully with a laser-compass and he is able to calculate that the Flying Stars at the date of death on this alignment are fantastically fortunate. Irving talks of such feng shui "meeting psychological needs" while remarking on the fact that twenty-three generations later Zhao's descendants still visit. These remarks don't seem to belong in the same belief system.

Julian tells me that the road along which we have driven is actually the bed of a dried-up river, extinguished by damming to the West. The tomb now lacks the water that Zhao planned for it. There is something sad as well as humbling about this, I think. The place is neglected. It is grubby and uncared for. Julian explains how damming protects people and crops from flooding. The Chinese have to find food and water for a vast population while huge numbers abandon the land for the city. It has never been done before. Only 11% of China is arable and some of this will have to give in the race to industrialize. China already manufactures half-a-billion euros worth of designer trainers every year. This figure and the demands for manufacturing space can only grow.

The maths are compelling but the lack of respect for heritage saddens me.

I look around beyond the litter that is everywhere.

The entrance arch to Zhao's burial complex is neglected and damaged. Beyond it is ming tang, open space with a couple of hundred metres of paved road leading straight to a humpback bridge, up a small flight of steps. This is the Jade Belt which slows up the chi as it is gathered beyond the bright hall. Past this is a ruined courtyard – the inner ming tang. Here columns have been flattened, walls removed, stone flooring vandalized. The guidebook says that extensive damage was done at the turn of the Ming and Qing Dynasties (around 1644) but the stones lying about show the lichen growth of decades rather than centuries and the fence across the ming tang is steel. Cultural Revolution, I figure, why not say so?

I have given up counting how many artefacts are described in the guidebooks as "repeatedly rebuilt." Successive dynasties destroy what their predecessors leave behind. The colour each dynasty adopts is that which in the *cycle of destruction* destroys its predecessor. It's a sort of tradition. But Mao seems to have taken it a bit far. Time and again the evidence is that the major damage was done in the 60s and this is a good example.

Beneath the bridge the water is sluggish. Nasty energy. The Jade belt has been seriously weakened. Beyond it is the mausoleum proper which is like a small temple, 3 metres high up a steep flight of steps. The tomb itself is underneath in a basement crypt. The roofs are green, indicating both that Zhao was privileged – or he would have had to settle for black – and not an Emperor, who is entitled to yellow.

Above and behind the mausoleum are two hills; the claws of the dragon. The mausoleum is oriented to the nearer but the peak of the further is topped with a pagoda. The near one is clearly the pearl that the dragons are playing with.

As we stand there sudden waves of schoolchildren appear. "Hellowhatisyourname?" they ask singsong fashion, one after another. I'm not sure they want or understand the reply. They are cheerful and noisy like reception-class kids anywhere. One wave after another – there must be hundreds of them – climb to the top of the mausoleum and descend into the crypt. And then the inevitable happens: the groups returning downwards meet the groups entering upwards face-on. There is a moment of panic and it sorts itself out. In the confusion I see that one small boy has lost his group. I am concerned as he climbs up and then down, with and against the tide, but eventually he merges into the swell. I watch him melt into a sea of uniforms. Professor Leung has given up trying to lecture over the hubbub.

We climb the hill. I am with the Italians. Mario is fit and so is Guido. Carla complains entertainingly. It is steep and there is no clear path. There are brambles as well and like tourist sites all over the world, coke-cans and ring-pulls.

It is exhilarating to arrive at the summit. Everybody makes it; for the single ladies, Helen, Anne and Carole, it has been a cakewalk, Hilde, a German lady who is taller then me, is puffing but exultant and frankly I am not Mr Fitness myself. But here we are.

Hilde was born in East Berlin. Her parents escaped when she was three, she tells me. They had to leave behind her grandmother who lived with them. She remembers her grandmother's encouragement and the tears. For years they could not drive along the Transit highway between West Berlin and the rest of West Germany for fear of the checkpoints at any one of which they might have been detained. She has grown up with fear and contempt for state control.

"Interesting place to visit, China, then," I say.

She shivers. She has a degree in Muslim Studies which is an interesting choice too.

As we admire the detritus underfoot I remark to Helen, a teacher from Connecticut, that I have read that when Osama bin Laden was resident in the Sudan in the 90s he bought a major interest in the state-controlled gum arabic industry. Gum arabic, virtually a Sudanese monopoly, is used for keeping fizzy drinks fizzy. This may mean that whenever a can of Coke is sold, Osama gets a percentage. I am no fan of psychopaths of any persuasion but I love this idea. It appears to tickle her funnybone too.

Looking down and Southish from the mountain the xue or chi well is over to the East. There is a small building there which we don't get to. The sheer scale is remarkable; to mark the burial place of one man this is a vast piece of real estate. Which is both more and less than the truth.

The Prince apparently died aged 61; there is a stern portrait of him above the crypt. Across the threshold is a portrait of his fourth concubine who was buried with him, along with five others. I look at Irving and pass the edge of my hand across my throat.

"No, no," he says, "She die of grief."

Hilde never saw her grandmother again. She still halts over the words.

At a scruffy stall I buy a local map. There are posters of the mighty indomitable Father of the Country but the snow globes are feeble things and none features the Great Helmsman.

Beyond the site, on the other side of the dried-up river is a tree that is reputed to be older than the site: the *Nine Dragons Tree.* I watch as Chinese and Europeans alike set off fire crackers.

Now I am beginning to understand what is meant by superstition, I think.

Thursday 13 October
Malaria tablets taken: 11
Fire Crackers set off: just a couple
Huazhong Normal University, Wuhan

Professor Leung is already in the classroom when I arrive. As his English is so slight I ask Julian to enquire if he is up for a question. He is. So I ask him about the elemental values he had added without pause for thought to the lines of the Hexagrams yesterday. I doubt that anyone else noticed how remarkable this was. Impassively, he says something in Mandarin; from the tone it is neither punitive nor encouraging. One of his young assistants preempts Julian:

"He says that it would take a week to explain."

I know that already. Checking his calculation has involved me in a close look at the smallest characters on my luopan followed by 10 or 15 minutes of analysis.

I imagine that in a room full of architects and interior designers I am the only one who spotted what he did. Alone among them I think, I have studied with a Chinese master. With a shock I realize something: this is no theorctical study for him. He is familiar enough with the *Xun* Hexagram (Number 57 in the Yi) and its application in feng shui that he either knows by heart all 64 Hexagram patterns or can work each out in a flash. Professor may be his day job but he has the hands-on skills of a professional feng shui man. I am pretty sure this is a feng shui master. I can only guess at why he would conceal the fact.

Body massage this evening. It was only my feet that signed up but I end up being pummelled all over; what Julian calls the *Full Metal Jacket*. Cyrus, a likeable but batty Polish architecture don, has joined us in express pursuit of this. Carla prefers that to him being in pursuit of her.

The massage parlour is on three small floors. There are dozens of young masseuses sporting badges with identifying numbers. You can ask for number 23 or whatever. I find this a little depersonalizing.

The three Italians have been laughing themselves hoarse about a domestic Italian scandal. It seems a macho playboy, scion of the House of Fiat, has been caught redhanded (if that's the correct extremity) with a transvestite prostitute. He/She is a balding 50-year old with the nom-de-perversion of Patricia. Carla keeps breathing huskily "Prend mi Patricia" and giggling. Carole who as a New York Sicilian, has some claim to it, and I, are voted honorary Italians.

Later in a bar I find myself the only non-Catholic. Beata who has joined us is a blonde blue-eyed Pole with a little boy at home whom she misses. We talk church. Carole rails against it and I see the Sicilian in her. Mario is diplomatic while Beata roots for Rome.

It turns out that Beata is a quarter Jewish. Like me, as it happens. I suggest that Poland sorely misses its Jewishness. She does not like this idea. I state my sympathy for the Poles, citing Cosciusko, Mickiewicz and Borowksi, and summarizing as best I can 200 years of Polish history. My purpose is to reassure her and to explain that I think I understand how a nation that has held onto its identity despite a millennium as buffer between Russia and the Germans has a right to be attached to what defines it. *Polak i Katolik*, they say. Her people have been independent less than 50 of the last 250 years. My point is that now it may be time for the Poles to take the brave step of loosening their self-definition. My son Jaime fell in love with the Poles and one Pole in particular and it is because of him I have the material to explain myself. She relaxes a bit. I guess my knowledge is flattering. I hope so. But she is fragile. My purpose as always is to heal but some people hurt too much to help. There is pain here and I would like to help relieve it but I think she is too fragile. I apologise for distressing her and blame the combination I was born with of Jewish mind and Irish heart. There is red wine:

Dynasty or Great Wall, Great Wall or Dynasty.

Then Carole and Mario begin to express awe at the charisma of the late Pope and then of the Dalai Lama. I am not interested in charisma. I have done cult. The cuddly old *Papa's* medieval stance on contraception condemned millions of Africans to death from AIDS. Show me charisma; I'll show you a psychopath.

Carole now rechristened *Carolina,* is nonetheless violent in her distaste for the corruption and hypocrisy of the faith she was born to. These facts are connected.

I suggest the enemy is not Catholicism but –isms. Today we spent the day watching Irving thrash about trying to pin down the Tao. Which is impossible but especially impossible for a man whose self-respect depends on it. Is "thrash" unfair? He is a very gifted man and I am not sure whether the occasional solecisms express who he is or the party line.

The Tao calls for letting go of the ego which means that it obviously cannot be pursued to serve the ego. The recasting of the Tao in the time of Chuang Tze as Taoism is itself, I suggest, an absurdity. Chuang and indeed Lao Tze would be aghast at the crassness perpetrated in their name. But then so would Jesus, I expect. One of the first things I remember watching a feng shui master do was tear down a Taoist charm stuck to a wall behind the scenes at a Chinese restaurant while berating the owner.

"Bloody superstition," he spat.

There is no limit to the capacity of human beings for turning liberating ideas into bollocks. A group that defines itself by a set of beliefs is not a spiritual but a political gathering. The Chinese want to turn everything – the Tao, Communism, Commerce – into Confucianism. And as far as I can tell they all believe the opposite.

We drink Irish coffee with whiskey from Hough Bay and walk back past Julian's *local* where he is on his third Tsingtao.

The waitress brings us too much change. We were recommended to this bar by Mr Ho, our tour guide. She has been charging us the rates he said she could get away with. She is embarrassed. She is giving the money back. I guess that will come out of his end.

No more heroes any more, I say.

Cha cha cha.

I retire to my comfortable if spooky little room, relieved to be alone. I text home. Jessie has a casting, Hen an essay, Joe a new download. Life goes on. Sheila and I talk at length but she is busy and it is hard for her to contain the several held-up tasks on her mind.

Today was my late father's birthday. He was a difficult and complicated man, full of charisma and contradiction. His father was a cotton mill worker in Salford who never earned more than a fiver a week in his life. My father volunteered for the Navy in 1941 as soon as he was old enough and by observing the confident young officers, became middle class. At one point he was the youngest sublieutenant in the Navy. His Northern vowels disappeared, short 'a's becoming long and so on. Owning a big house in the South East of England did not stop him being a fervent defender of all things Northern or eating tripe and pig's trotters, but he never *sounded* Northern again.

The truth is that when he died I was relieved that I no longer had his opinions to consider. Not that I wished him any ill. I am sad not so much that he is dead but that this was the truth. I still talk with him and he is clearly happier where he is. But my reality is that communication can transform anything and he died with our relationship still unsatisfactory. I know everything is as it is supposed to but if there is failure I failed here.

Friday 14 October
Malaria tablets taken: 12
Huazhong Normal University, Wuhan

Professor Wu lectures us on the Tao and Taoism. This difference is important. He is younger than Professor Leung, less grave and equally courteous.

"Taoists are real laid back," Irving says.

And so it has proven. One lesson has consisted entirely of linguistic debate between the two of them. The Tao, of course, defies translation in the sense that it says what it says and that's it. Somebody once said that poetry is what is lost in translation. So it is with the Tao. It is fluid like a metaphor. And like the metaphor, it loses rather than gains meaning by explanation.

The students respond unconsciously: Professor Wu's lessons leap into life ten or so minutes after the advertised hour, by which time a critical mass of students are present. This is in some contrast to the punctuality that sheer respect grants Professor Leung.

Irving is generally late for both.

Using an hour here and an hour there I have drawn up the ba zi for Daniela's daughter.

It is clear this is a child who has gone from pillar to post. Yik ma, the character that means "upheaval" is all over the place. And mou yuk, which is literally the washing of dirty linen in public. Difficult birth, parental separation; not cordial. Guilty mother. A familiar dynamic.

We agree to skip lunch and find a Chinese latte. Even were my middle-class British sensibilities not threatened by the hygiene issue, I would still be bored by tofu and rice with braised pak choi. I am a vegetarian with views about brute global organizations but McDonalds is looking more and more attractive all the time.

We sit and order coffee. Daniela is now known by the Italian honorific "Danielita." She enjoys this.

I look her in the eye and tell her that that the keynote of this ba zi is a guilty mother and tears form in her eyes.

"Bullet points," I say. The body recaps before the mind catches up. "Take a deep breath."

She did indeed split from her husband when Paula was small. She did leave the baby girl with her parents while she sorted her life out. And she is indeed still beating herself up.

We talk a little about the dynamics of guilt. There are three broad components:

Feeling guilty is a way to punish ourselves because no one else is prepared to.

Leaving a husband involves a mutual separation for which both sides are responsible whoever appears to have done the walking.

What's done is done; regret is a waste of time. It worked out fine and nobody died.

The mou yuk suggests likely poor choices with men.

Like all of us, Paula was presented at birth with a series of apparent choices. The first is Mummy or Daddy and the second is yes or no. Then it all gets tricky. This is a yes-Mummy child.

"She is more likely than most to be run by her mother's example."

"And be like me?"

"Or not like you. Which is a different stop on the same bus route."

"So what do I do?"

"Let yourself off the hook. There is no good or bad, just consequences. And learn your own lessons so she doesn't have to."

More tears. This is hard stuff.

I look out across the street. The air is always a little grey in Wuhan. Down there are average Chinese people with average concerns who like Daniela, love their children and wish the best for them. The streetlight changes and unlike Europe the rhythm does not, half the traffic and most of the pedestrians have been going against the red light and now the other half does.

My father who was among the first Europeans allowed into China on business in the 70s said that the Chinese were the least likely Communists he had ever encountered.

 Saturday 15 October
Malaria Tablets taken: 13
Huazhong Normal University, Wuhan

David Ho is our Guide. His real name is Cai Lin although he is known as Mr David or Mr Ho. He is youngish and livelyish with strong opinions. One he reveals tonight at dinner is about football.

"Chinese footballers are useless," he says with contempt. "All millionaires and still no good."

No change there then.

He tells us the Chinese don't differentiate between weekdays and weekends. A decadent Western distinction, I suppose, and a bit arbitrary when most of us are no longer churchgoers. He tells me the Chinese work in shifts; five days on and two off as I understand it. He concedes however that many banks are closed on Sundays. I don't know about all that but when I walked downtown that afternoon, the pavements were thick with students blowing off steam like students do on a Saturday afternoon all over the world.

He bemoans his lack of free time. He and his wife both work and they juggle a baby boy between their schedules and his mother-in-law. It's not much different to England. I sympathize. Then thinking of the schoolchildren at Longquan, I express admiration for the way China is educating her people. I ask him to translate this for Professor Leung who is at our table with his daughter. It is a relatively subtle idea and David is not a subtle man. The Professor's daughter helps me and the Professor smiles cautiously. Who might be taking notes?

I suggest more daringly that China's experience with the rejection by each dynasty of its predecessor has prepared the Chinese for the current leap forward but this flummoxes him altogether. For reasons I can't follow David seems to think I am suggesting the Japanese invasion of 1936 was a good idea. A bridge too far, I guess. Time to shut my mouth. Professor Leung and his daughter are still smiling. Is this because they are more tolerant or because they have not understood a word?

Professor Leung is in his 60s I guess. That would make him in his 20s during the Cultural Revolution. What compromises would a man of his education have had to make? He has devoted his life to the culture that was reduced to rubble in those terrible times. How safe is he today when aid workers and protesters alike can disappear overnight?

What I do know is that every Chinese looks over his shoulder.

No one ever knows who is informing on whom. It is reasonable to suppose that every unguarded word is vulnerable. I have no idea what deals Irving must have done to get us here.

Football is a safe topic the world over. We return to it.

"So much money, no goals," David says.

When I log in to my computer I find an icon telling me I am being monitored. There are two new messages, on the face of it from admirers asking to be included in my web mailing list. Both names are in the same format: European first name, Chinese family name, @ Yahoo. It is very unusual for anybody Chinese to contact me in relation to feng shui and I know Yahoo has been advising the Chinese Government on how to prevent their people getting the most from the latest technology. I email them both with a non-committal welcome, explaining where I am and how impressed I am with China's commercial progress.

Perhaps I am paranoid but I am in most senses all alone here in Central China. So much of this is alien. Perhaps the very efficient European toilet in my room is so to speak, window dressing. Such small fears concern me as I fall asleep wondering who Mr Ho's chosen European name honours. Presumably not David Beckham.

Sunday 16 October
Malaria tablets taken: 14
Huazhong Normal University, Wuhan

Lectures seven days a week. Sometimes I forget and confuse this with a holiday but these hours are not leisurely. Today History of Chinese Philosophy.

Mario's father is still in hospital, Carla cannot get hold of her husband on her mobile phone. Carole misses her family and Helen is concerned about her daughter.

Mr Ho has announced that we can only keep our rooms when we go overnight to view the walled city of Jingzhou if we pay the university 200 yuan which he will collect. I am happy to do this rather than up sticks. Others prefer not to pay.

Mario and I moot a little sweepstake:

100-1 everybody who vacates their room gets the same one back.

20-1 exactly the same block of rooms is available.

In other words the purpose of the upheaval is to get payments that will never go anywhere near the university bursar. I know a scam when I see one.

No one takes up the challenge. This makes Mario laugh but many things do. He is a wag for an architect, with his goatee and his designer clothes.

Before we leave we get teeshirts made. Just outside the university precincts there is a small shop that makes custom shirts. It is run by smiling young men who chainsmoke. I speak desperate Mandarin of course but Mario has bought a digital translating machine. They find its Chinese almost as incomprehensible as mine. It does not stop them smiling though. Or smoking. After confusions between the thousands of Chinese words that sound the same to us, we make some sense to them. The design wants the words feng shui and a little tag. At first they think we want a quotation from Moh Tzu under an image of Britney Spears in profile. Interesting misunderstandings. Chinese is in its way the opposite of English; they can say lots of things with the same words, we can say the same thing dozens of different ways.

We agree a price. We plan to tell our co-students to come here and buy their own. We suggest a facsimile sellotaped inside the shop window but the guys can't or won't get the idea. We put this lack of enterprise down to the Confucian disease; it is a consistent contradiction that this most industrious and enterprising of peoples appear to a man terrified to step out of line. I will observe something similar when we return to check the prototype; they are out of blank teeshirts and cannot trade. They do not meanwhile update their accounts, harangue the suppliers or make promotional phone calls, they play computer games in a mushroom cloud of tobacco smoke.

After a gamut of handshakes, we leave them still smiling, still smoking.

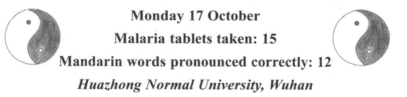

Monday 17 October
Malaria tablets taken: 15
Mandarin words pronounced correctly: 12
Huazhong Normal University, Wuhan

The Italians smell espresso. They have a genetic ability to locate a coffee bean over several miles. In this case they have tracked the aroma to a store on the other side of town. It is a brisk walk through the shanties, past the construction sites and the bootleg hightech on wallpaper tables: CDs, DVDs, software and computer games for small change. I pluck from a cardboard box a handful of Chinese movies to take home for Henrietta. Less than a fiver the lot. I can't work out who is trading here. Is this private enterprise or are these people working for some corporation or is there some uniquely Chinese third alternative? It's all a bit grubby and there are several children here. If this is an example of *one nation: two systems* the further we travel from the campus, the more capitalist things appear. Stores gradually become smarter, Chinese chains pretending to be foreign heave into view but no actual Western stores. The trellis tables are some sort of nomansland, I guess; by day these people are traders, by night they return to squalor in one direction or glamour in the other.

There are many newspaper stands. All the news appears to be sport or show business. No politics. Lots of flesh showing. We were warned not to bring certain types of printed material into China with us. One was pornography. I had taken this for a moral position. It turns out, I see, simply to be protection of the local product. Hong Kong was the same; lots of words little information.

We, Mario, Guido, Carla and myself, are heading, past McDonalds, towards the glamour. Chicony is a big store by any standards and its prices high also. Back at the gates of the campus, bread is a fraction of a yuan, the teeshirts were a couple of quid all in. Here there are serious consumer goods, even something like designer clothes. They are not actually designer clothes, that is to say that few of the labels are familar but I think if I knew one cut from another I'd recognize couturiers. Alexander would know.

Pure ginseng is on sale at daft prices and the coffee is very expensive. The pretty young shop girl whose job I think is actually demonstrating the coffee-maker, offers us a bag of beans for about £10. We demur with our different species of native charm. Mario smiles and fusses over her. We get another cup free.

Italians.

There is a huge facsimile of a Hollywood star whose name I can't remember, towering over the cosmetics department. Its incongruous familiarity comforts and jars.

Tuesday 18 October
Malaria tablets taken: 16
Cups of espresso drunk: 2
Jingzhou.

We drive West by coach for 4½ hours. We have taken on additional guides who do not speak English and have no obvious skills; presumably they are from the Party. David does all the announcing. The others restrict themselves to whispers and note-taking. I imagine they know the countryside.

This is agricultural country. The combined flood plains of the Yangtse and Yellow Rivers are folded between mountains to the North and West and desert to the North. The Chinese economic gamble involves building much of this up while continuing to feed over a billion people.

On the other hand, that a nation this large has chosen to attempt world domination by commerce is reassuring. It beats hell out of war. They are unlikely to bomb their customers, I would have thought. This is what Fukiyama termed "the end of history" the final victory of capitalism. No country that has a stake in trade is going to foul up the system. And when you consider that the Chinese mainland population has grown from 1.2 billion to 1.27 billion in the first five years of this century you start to get a sense of scale: .07 of a billion is 70 million or a nation slightly larger than Britain. And that's just the increase.

When I left there were still thousands of bales of Chinese cloth awaiting release into the EU. European competitors cry foul but manufacturing has been moving East for decades. The consuming beast seeks workers willing to do jobs we won't do at wages we would not accept. It can't last forever but this is the status quo. Surely if we trade royalties on intellectual property for access to our markets everyone will gain? They pay the Eagles and Microsoft, we get cheap shoes.

Either side of the road are ponds of brownleaved lotus plants as well as cotton and rice.

Elise is restive. She is a tall Swiss-German lady, in her early forties. She has, she tells me, just broken up with her lover. It is obviously painful. There is something like a wince in her voice as she tells me. She is dark with an aquiline nose and her energy is sweet and injured. I listen closely without comment which appears to be what she needs. I hear someone who does not feel valued.

The roads are flattish but mostly two lanes. There is a lot of hooting and overtaking. The driver has to be especially wary because there is oncoming traffic to consider on the left as well as pedestrians, bicycles, three-wheelers and broken-down vehicles to the right. We pass what looks like quite a serious accident: a bus has hit a car head-on. The bodies have been disposed of and I guess the injured taken to hospital. I offer up a brief prayer.

I think of Thom as I usually do when I pray. He can turn out a polished song in any style you request inside minutes. He is a wizard with light and sound mixers and can identify five-digit prime numbers in seconds. And he is the father of my only grandson Gabriel and of Ruby, a dead baby. You can't save your children from pain by feeling it for them but there are times I wish I could. There is no mending him.

"Nothing is ever quite right," he said to me shortly before I left,

"Even the best stuff is just a bit crap."

The pain I feel is Elise's and less demanding but his seems to reach across the globe to amplify hers.

Elise looks out of the window into the distance.

The papers are full of the succesful Chinese Space Mission. It has been all over the TV too, Mario tells me. In the newspaper photograph one of the Generals in charge has risked a grin. This is a country where lightheartedness is not considered adult and every television announcer is straightfaced.

Resources spent on space exploration may have military payoffs but to provoke the US to compete is surely healthy for everybody. The sci-fi movies of the 60s foresaw air bubbles on the moon and colonies on Mars by now. Although they also predicted one-piece spandex suits and pills for meals, these are risks worth taking, I think.

We stop at the least attractive toilet I have ever seen. If you were to consider the toilets on the final day of a rock festival, subtract paper, water, soap, flush systems and towels and multiply by eight, you might approach its horror.

"The real China," someone says. Or was it "the real china?" There was something ceramic under there somewhere.

Across the road is a heap of raw cotton. Some of us take a closer look. You can't smell the toilet across the road.

We drive on. The skies are clearer out in the country.

The Chinese get a bad press for ecological irresponsibility. Few people realize the rock and hard place they are between: they have precious little oil and lots of coal. This is why the Wuhan skies are grey and why China is the ozone-layer villain of the world. But what do you do? On this trip I have seen many trucks loaded with cardboard boxes folded flat and several lorries laden with used tyres. Many times I have seen bins with individual apertures for glass, organic and other waste. There is an effort being made. And frankly we've had our CFC-spewing fridges and our gas guzzlers for decades. Why should they miss the fun just because they are late for the party?

More roadside shops, vast irrigated fields, tombs packed into the hillsides like overdecorated garden sheds and we drive into Jingzhou through the city gate. Although the walled city dates from the Han Dynasty (roughly contemporary with the height of the Roman Empire, that is the centuries either side of Christ) the wall has been 'repaired' under successive dynasties. In this sense as in others, the Communists may be best considered as just another dynasty; or perhaps two, one before and one after the Cultural Revolution. The latest rebuilding was in 1988. There are remains nearby of settlements up to 4000 years older; indeed this city is the ancestral home of the Zhou dynasty who reigned somewhat before the Han and whose gift to the world the *Book of Changes*, is invariably referrred to in China as the *Zhou Yi* or Zhou (pronounced "chew") *Book of Changes*. In such ways the powers-that-be distance themselves from 'superstition'. Like so much of China, the settlement of Jingzhou is ancient and the architecture new.

This dismissal of their own artefacts is typical of the Chinese. They – if you can generalize about 1.27 billion individuals – appear to lack sentiment altogether. What else can you conclude of a people who skin animals alive for the fur trade? There are normal decent people here, I know because I keep meeting them, but this is a bruised culture, numb from centuries of abuse from above.While we are here the BBC will film toe-curling cruelty to animals at Wuhan railway station.

There are only seven walled cities left in China, of which Beijing is the largest and best-preserved. A little less than half is left of Jingzhou's perimeter. A feature of these walls is the hollow bastions that protrude into dead-end corridors called "hidden archer holes" which is pretty much self-descriptive. These are early Ming, that is 14th century, which makes them contemporary with similar features in London Wall. The only original stretch of London Wall is about three yards in a cellar under the Barbican, as I recall.

The rebuilt wall here is pretty tacky. The materials are noticeably poor; there is shrinkage, flaky plaster and careless brickwork.

We are staying in the Jingbao Guest House, the sort of slightly shabby provincial establishment you might well find in England or France. There are differences: there are piles of things in odd places, the swimming pool for instance is full of furniture. The service is the usual smiling "Xie xie," (pronounced "shu-shu" and meaning "thank you.") Julian charms the four ladies behind the reception counter with a reference in Mandarin to a folk tale concerning four legendary beauties. He is equal-opportunities affable: two of them are neither young nor in any conventional sense beautiful.

In my room the bed faces a mirror; a feng shui no-no. The toilet makes the unlikely claim that it is "pasteurised." Outside it is very noisy.

 Wednesday 19 October
Malaria tablets taken: 17
Public Toilets visited in Jingzhou: 0
Jingzhou

Morning. It is drizzling and I am wearing my one and only

Bermuda shirt.

We visit Jingzhou Provincial Museum where we see turtle shells, swords, lacquer mirrors and some impressive Terracotta Phalluses. There are silk robes from the Warring States Period – that is the half-millennium before the Romans arrived in Britain. They look as if they'd be good as new after a swift visit to the drycleaners. The embroidery is exquisite, the tiny stitches still almost invisible.

The chief exhibit here is the 2000-year old corpse of a local baron. In other galleries there are models of early townships. The first, showing settlements four to six thousand years old, demonstrates proto-feng shui. It is oriented North-South with the fields in front forming the ming tang and a watercourse further forward again. Even in this timescale there is, just as there is within the city wall reconstructed by the Qing in 1646, a separate enclosure for Royalty: Zhou presumably, this being their home town.

The Zhou ruled central China for the last thousand years BCE. There's not much about that in the museum study material which divides the people of historic China neatly into peasants and parasites.This explains a good deal.

Irving talks about Maslow's hierarchy of values: first people need shelter and safety, then food then reproduction. Only after these are assured do they pursue higher values.

The prehistoric city is on the plain and so lacks a Black Tortoise which may, we have discovered, more properly be translated as *Mysterious Warrior.* Either way the missing piece is the protection at the back which is a primary consideration in Classical feng shui. They must have felt pretty safe to settle where the tilling was good so far from the protective mountains. The city was sacked around 0 AD which emphasizes the daring of the choice. The mummified chieftain whose postcard is the money shot here, died at this time and was buried along with the 25 wives and concubines who handily died simultaneously.

On one wall we notice a proto-luopan with a handle. The characters are archaic. The position of a character that resembles that for "West" and one that is like ren (or yang water) that belongs slightly North of West imply that North could be at the top. This could be a breakthrough for the maverick Australian school of thought that insists all feng shui measurements are reversed for the Southern Hemisphere where the seasons and shade patterns are the other way round. The genesis of luopans from sundial-like instruments supports this but I don't think so. Feng shui is about a lot more than seasons. It concerns space as well as time and incorporates metaphor that would be hopelessly confused by inversion. Call me simple-minded but the way I see it is that the most unmissable example of fire, the sun, is always above.

Mario points out that a character that looks like an early shen (the Monkey character) sits in its appropriate position only if South is at the top. It's a score draw: Australians One, Rest of the World One.

We see a bronze short sword; not ceremonial. It is about the size of the Roman semispatha, designed for close combat. It is still sharp. Modern technology apparently can not replicate this. Mr David makes the point that it was these swords which kept the Zhou in power. Whether it is spaceships, CDs, air-conditioning, coca-cola or sharp swords, technological superiority makes for power. What did Mao say: "Political power grows out of the barrel of a gun?"

Soon Yi is studying some silk work.

"You do needle point?"

"Jah," she says. "But not like that."

Soon Yi calls her children every day.

"Do you miss them?"

"Today," she says mischievously, "I have been gone so long I even miss my *husband*."

The corpse is hideous, the limbs obscenely flexible. The walls are, in the unsentimental Chinese way, full of pictures of the autopsy. For some reason I think of the restaurant we ate at last night. Tanks had, much as in Europe, been stocked with fish that customers could point to and pick. Unlike Europe there were turtles as well. One appeared to have a damaged shoulder which did not seem entirely fair play and another seemed to be waving its fins across each other as if to inform us that a mistake had been made.

The corpse's mouth is an outraged rictus. It is in extraordinary condition. Is this attributable to the consistent humidity of the grave, the mummifiers' skill, the fluid in which he was buried, or something else?

Soon Yi shudders: "They should not do this," she says.

I'm not so keen on corpses myself; they all remind me of the same beautiful small one.

The baron, I read, was buried with 26 female servants. Grief, I suppose.

At dinner that night we celebrate Sylvie's birthday. She is a strapping Polish girl with a pleasant face. The birthday cake that has been bought turns out to be a foam dud. Language problems.

We sing Happy Birthday and Zdenka from Bratislava adds a loud harmony.

Valerie seems to have a terrible time with the food. Although I don't eat meat this is not a moral issue for me and I'm happy not only with bean curd but with fish and eggs just as long as there is a ladle or I can get there first with clean chopsticks. Actually I like meat; it's just that I feel sad when I eat it. Don't ask me to explain or produce a consistent argument for this preference. I haven't got one. When I think I'm morally superior it's time for a Big Mac. For Valerie however, only the vegetarian products appear to be alright. And since there is a two-thousand-year-old Buddhist tradition of vegetarianism this should not be a tall order. Time and again she has a long face while all around are filling theirs.

The coach is driven round to the baker's and as one man, the tourists file out to remonstrate. As one man, except me. I'm not a big man for mobs. Julian speaks with the baker. They return with genuine cake.

I have seen no Mao snow globes in this one-wall town. Time is getting tight.

Thursday 20 October
Malaria tablets taken: 18
Preserved corpses viewed: Just the one,
thank you
Jingzhou

After breakfast I join Julian for a walk. He walks every morning after breakfast. He tells me about a symposium he has chaired about what is and is not scientific. He walks briskly, I have to accelerate to keep up but we seem to see eye to eye. He does not explain but it seems to me he walks not because he has been told it is good for his health or in response to some idea but just because he *does*. This brilliant man is just responding to his nature. He walks because he walks.

Cha cha cha.

A street fortune teller is drafting ba zi's for a couple of yuan. Andre a cheerful thickset young German I suspect of hidden depth, is game. His friend Sallust looks on.

Sallust is less extrovert. He has a friendly sort of face but his energy is just a little bit staccato, he is quite uncomfortable to be with. He says things that may or may not be jokes which hang in the air while people decide whether or not to be insulted. Last night in a club, a Chinese girl threatened him with a bottle. It is healthy to take such things as reflections. Violence attracts violence. Both he and Andre appear to treat feng shui as a crusade, which is a sweet way to look at it. He is young and means well.

They may seem young to me but I notice with a start that the street fortune teller has written ding wei as Andre's year pillar. This makes him 38. Ding wei is a resolute pillar.

Andre and the elderly Chinese man have very little language in common. Irving steps in. With a broad smile on his face he questions the man. His excited "ah" as he listens, suggests sensational revelations. But he sounds just like this in class – which can be very encouraging by the way – and the man is only offering platitudes. I drift off and sit on one of the medieval steps dating from 1988, to write my journal outside a shop loaded with the usual complaisant busts but no snow globes.

Elise walks up. She sees me writing and makes to go away.

"Please stay," I say, "I'll be more sociable in a moment." I complete the thought I was recording and look up at her still standing. I breathe in deeply. How she hurts. I cannot feel another's pain unless it impinges on my own and I pause to own this. I think again for a moment of Tracey back at home where she has been nursing a gap where a baby ought to have been. Now she is pregnant again. No one wants to jump to conclusions.

When Ruby had been two or three months in the womb, Tracey asked me what gender the baby was.

"I can't see Thom with a little girl yet," I said. I wish I had not. I so wish I had not.

"Richard," Elise asks, sitting next to me on the repro step, "How do I let go of control?"

This is a tall and humbling order. Just as the Tao that can be named is not the Tao, so claiming to have answers takes daring, some might say arrogance. Still I rush in where angels fear to tread. It's what I do.

"When you consider how little control we truly have, it becomes easier," I say carefully, measuring each word. "The earth could open, the bus could crash."

"I see," she says. She is a bright woman. As is always the case, I could not deliver this stuff if she did not already know it. I look in her eyes and breathe in deeply to feel how it feels.

"Still painful," I say which hardly qualifies me for the Order of Merit but is clearly true. "The problem with pain is trying not to have it."

"You mean fearing de fear?" she asks. We have firm *f* sounds in common with German but the *r* comes with something like a *t* attached and *th* tends to turn out *d*. This is an Englishman, with just a semi-smattering of French and an academic grasp of Latin making these judgements deep in South East Asia, by the way.

"Absolutely. Or being angry about anger. When we feel it, it's no longer pain. As far as I can tell the human condition seems to involve lessons which come attached to feelings.

Some of these are what we call unpleasant. But each one appears to be finite."

"Finite? I do not know dis word."

"Measurable. Limited. Pain does not go on forever. What we tend to do is try not to feel the unpleasant stuff. We smoke, we drink, we eat, we get busy but it is still there waiting to be felt. So feel it. And it is no longer pain."

Elise, Hilde and I find a Taoist teagarden. The teenage waitresses – there appears to be no other kind in China – giggle as we arrive and giggle even more as one sizes us up and quotes about six times the going rate for a pot of green tea. It is probably enough to keep her extended family for a fortnight. But they are good-humoured and it is a lovely spot and and the er hu music tugs at the heartstrings like a kite on a windy day.

Hilde has been uneasy on the bus with the Party supernumaries. She feels watched.

"Is it the Wall?" I joke.

"Don't," she says but smiles and relaxes.

Elise's brow is still furrowed.

"So to feel pain is to not feel pain?"

"Think of it this way," I say to her, "The sooner you feel through this, the sooner you start again. As you feel through the crap, get ready to feel good. Choose the crap. Embrace the crap. Welcome it. Volunteer for it. Think of it as motivation."

"I like that," Elise says.

We visit a tacky repro Taoist temple. It's gold; they can't even get the colours right. Circa 1988, I guess. And there is a yin (even) number of ceramic beasts on the roof. This is wrong: yin numbers of beasts are used only on tombs. Like so many public projects and the overstaffed shops, its construction probably had as much to do with keeping people busy as anything. Few people are hungry in China any more but meaning does not seem to be a central concern. And regard for spiritual practice even less so.

There are Taoist 'priests' playing cards and smoking in the doorway.

Irving propounds the difference between spirituality and religion. The one he says, is an essentially lone pursuit, the other a social behaviour. He is right of course this strange, big hearted, passionate man. But still his ego swishes like a horse's tail ensuring I keep my distance.

Zdenka tells me she had hoped to find spiritual guidance here. Rashly I complement her on her harmony singing which encourages her to enlist me into two-part versions of songs from the shows. I leave when her back is turned during the solo middle eight of "I know him so well."

On the coach I react pedantically to Daniela feeding me the same position on the German economy as Wilhelm. She is a German resident also. I tell her that it is not as the politicians tell them, that the country cannot *afford* proper infrastructure but that no party that makes public the intention to collect the taxes the maths dictate will ever be elected.

Wealth is not work, I suggest, and Labour, as Mrs Thatcher's winning election posters pointed out in 1979, is not working. Even poets need paying, I say, pushing the boat out. Carolina says she objects to paying for people who don't make the effort to work. I know she has a good heart but I've been out of work and I've been about as broke as it is possible to be in a civilized country and I am wary of knee jerk judgements. It's just too easy.

Irving holds a tutorial on the Flying Stars on the bus.

Mario and Carla have heard that there is an article in the Italian press about the censuring of Nanjing University for offering a course similar to the one we are on. I am reminded that an opinion can be a life choice here in the People's Republic.

One of the guides comes up the aisle sniffing around the tutorial. I meet his eye and tell him firmly and untruthfully we are talking politics and he scuttles away like a wounded turtle.

Andre and Sallust leave tomorrow.

Set in every hillock like beehives, I watch the graves go by. Then there are miles of lotus plants in the lower ground. Lotus plants, graves, lotus plants, graves, high, low, high low.

Cha cha cha.

 Friday 21 October
Malaria tablets taken: 19
Medieval walled cities viewed: one
Huahzong Normal University, Wuhan

A *normal* university is one that produces teachers.

Those who did not pay the bung and indeed those who did, have their rooms back.

More classes today; the history of the Tao: Mo tze, Lao tze, Chuang tze.

Irving is late again.

He is red in the face; as he clenches and unclenches his fists he looks explosive. I am reminded that he is a teacher of martial arts. I would not want to be on the wrong end of the anger of this man.

"Hands up," he says, "All those who care whether they get a certificate for this course of study."

The *likes* and forgotten plurals are gone.

About half the hands go up. Not mine, what is another piece of paper?

Now, having committed the group to positions on the issue, he gives us some information on which to base them. The rumour about Nanjing is true. The university authorities have been seriously criticized. The verb "to criticize" means something very different in China, carrying implications that range from a career black mark to long-term detention. I think of the 15 year jail term of Alfred Huang whose crime was respect for the classics. In the Cultural Revolution when all purposeful thought was suspect, people who wore glasses could be censured for the implied crime of straining their eyes with reading and there are several recorded cases of pupils killing, cooking and eating teachers. It makes torturing dogs look like a prank. At least they cooked the teachers before eating them.

This was only a generation ago. It is also, if my maths are right, just when Irving left mainland China for Oz. It is hard to relate to such alien violence.

"Will it embarrass Professor Leung?" I ask.

"The University may come under pressure," he almost answers. Aha.

"Hands up again, who seriously wants this certificate?"

More hands, not mine. I don't want to put anybody under pressure. He glares across the room at Gertrude.

"There, you see. So many of them. We work so hard for this. This is the first time ever – the first certificate for Feng Shui in

China. And you," he adds pummelling a desk, "You say it don't matter."

Gertrude mutters something about not making private disputes public.

Later that day Professor Leung lectures us. He is as ever calm, concise and authoritative. Julian translates, Irving adds the occasional comment. Feng shui I learn, can be included in university studies under the title "Ecological Studies."

We examine the way that li xi pai – micro feng shui – has descended and diverged from kan yu, which concerns itself with mountain formations and rivers. It is clear that Irving, who is an architect by vocation, does not consider the first a serious discipline. He says that he can't understand people who prescribe 'cures'. It is not clear that Professor Leung, who has been tutoring Irving for over a decade, shares this view. But I know his secret identity now.

Professor Leung uses the university campus as an example for study and shows how the Kun Lun Mountains to the North West feed the chi down to the Yangtse, how the large-scale twists of the river mimic the mountain range. He shows how the university is in the protective crook of the river as is the most prosperous part of Wuhan. We are sitting in the xue or pearl. This is kan yu.

It figures then that the campus turns out to be on a huge graveyard. What constitutes good positioning for a grave is equally good for the living. Good chi is good chi. I am unsurprised to learn that Professor Wang advised the authorities on the use of the land at the time. Several thousand tombs were turfed out; many more were too deep to access. So thousands of corpses remain under the university. It is classic yin-yang thinking. A burial place which is as yin as things get, can be balanced by lots of young, vigorous yang energy. It seems to work; this is among the most successful seats of learning in China.

And it makes sense of my visions of white winding sheets.

Afterwards the Italians and myself make for Chicony for espresso. Many in our group have stuck with the bars recommended by Mr David. We have found it cheaper not to.

On our way back from the hustle downtown we (the Italians and I) pass what looks like a Pizza house. *Gianno's*. Can this be? Is this some sort of gingerbread house? There is margherita on the menu outside. Guido licks his lips.

"We try eet," says Carla. It is a statement not a question

It turns out the proprietor who calls herself Chang, is a Chinese who has lived in the Bronx. In New York she had observed the way the Italians rolled the pastry, cooked it once filled and once again unfilled. She had clocked the wide ovens and the skill and love involved in choosing the correct cheeses and flour. Her aim is to make *Gianno's* a real pizzeria and she is tickled that these are real Italians. The décor, which is sort of ranch house, is not inappropriate. There are rafia mats and portraits of the *Azurri* (the Italian football team) on one wall. On another, Italian *tricolore* flags.

The restaurant is very quiet even at 8pm. The Chinese eat early and the Italians eat late but at 8pm everybody is eating. Why is it so quiet?

It appears that all the construction work has moved the main drag across town. The xue has crossed the river. She is now part of the shanty-town rather than the shopper's paradise. *One people, two systems.*

I do a little subtle li xi pai. I am narrowing in on a paradox. Good feng shui works whether we believe in it or not, whether we even know it is there. But some works only if there is powerful engagement between practitioner and client. The more *interior* feng shui is, the more engagement is required. The mighty forces of river and mountain take some diverting. While we are here the Chinese are completing the world's largest water feature: the Three Gorges Dam, a few hundred kilometres to the west. The diverted water from this shoddy wonder may change the world. I have read that it it may actually alter the earth's axis. I am trying to make differences with fractions of an angle.

I test the pasta origin slur on Chang who dismisses it with an exaggerated exhale.

To me the margheritas taste wonderful but I bow to the natives' judgement.

"Bella," says Carlo.

We tell Chang that we will get a party along here before we leave for Wudang Shan. She asks if we will write her a recommendation to put in her window. Gildo, Priscilla and Carlo all take the felt pen in turns. I demur.

"Not qualified," I say.

There is Dynasty *rosso* (or Great Wall) and passable espresso but something is still not right. It is the music which is western – John Denver, Abba, Paul McCartney – but not pizza music. I ask Chang if I can look at her CD collection.

"Sure," she says.

In the CD drawer there is an Andrea Boccelli. I put it on and his yearning tenor fills the room. *Canto della Terra.*

"Fantastico," says Guido conducting and we all clink glasses of

Hough Bay whiskey (aged 20 minutes).

Saturday 22 October
Malaria tablets taken: 20
Hubei whiskey consumed: a little too much
Huahzong Normal University, Wuhan

Morning – the alarm on my mobile phone goes again. 6.40am. Another malaria tablet. The disinfectant wipes and face-masks are beginning to look a bit self-conscious up there on the counter unused. Even malaria tablets seem insulting to this well-ordered place with its maid service on every floor. On the other hand they may prove important up-country. The Holy Mountain may not be so commodious.

Actually there is another wing to this student residence. It consists of bare dormitories for the students we meet in the lifts who are poor Chinese or from the Third World: Madagascar, Bangladesh, even Ukraine. Some of these kids tell me they have to translate English first into Mandarin and then into their native tongue so as to keep up with their studies.

One people, two systems.

I had texted Sheila last night that I would text again at 7am my time, midnight hers, so that she could call me back after her busy day. As well as everything else, she is running an audition workshop this week. I wait till 7.30, showering, brushing my teeth, collating my notes, always with an eye on the phone. Not a Bo Peep.

It seems a long way from home.

I check my email. There is a panicky message from Sheila; it's all a bit much. Well she's only used to doing the work of three or four women (that's six to eight men). No wonder she is tired. We speak finally on the phone. I reassure her; it's fine. What's important will fall into place. Trusting can be hard. All this is easy for me to say gallivanting half a world away.

Joey is enjoying *Cider with Rosie*.

"While you are away, it's as if I haven't got a Daddy. Just like Laurie."

A pang.

"Perhaps that's what opened him up to writing so poetically."

He considers this.

"You can have both, can't you?"

"Course you can."

Henni tells me about the films she is appraising for Film Studies A-Level. She can get a bit obsessive. Last night she stayed up till the small hours checking out Polanski shorts from the early 60s. Jessie is tense; she says she is unsure she will ever get the film part she wants. I calm her. She knows better but the waiting is so painful.

Today we leave for Changsha, Mao's home city and Zhou Rong Ji's too. This is no coincidence. The national hierarchy of the Party tends to follow a pecking order. High-ups will often have been Mayor of Beijing or Mayor of Changsha first.

Zhou Rong Ji is one of the chief architects of China's progress into the black. I marked his card when I read an interview in the early 90s. His ideas about the repossession of Hong Kong seemed unusually practical. I had expected the usual ideology and was agreeably surprised to learn that progress could be a higher priority. And by progress he meant creating wealth and feeding people.

There is an important museum in Changsha and it is only half-an-hour from Mao's birthplace at Shaoshan which we will also be visiting.

Chang sha means "long sands" and derives from the long narrow islet midriver. This word sha is a feng shui technical term meaning something like "terrain" but is often confused with its homophone sha meaning "poison". As feng shui has been diluted on its journey west many simplifications have been introduced. Few have served authenticity. The confusion between shas only appears if you ignore the very different Chinese characters. Unlike Western tongues, similarity of sound in Chinese implies nothing at all about meaning. The syllable sha has a hundred different meanings and that's before you add in the tones that multiply this by five. I'm not going to settle all these issues on a single trip.

We arrive in Changsha. There are long wide roads into the centre which imply a lot of hutong demolition. This big city is about half shanty and half gleaming spires. There are many big stores with glamorous shiny windows, even some Western outfits: Kappa, Kentucky Fried Chicken, McDonalds. There must be so much money to be made here.

Even deep in central China far from the tourist-beaten path of the East coast, many of the shop names are in English.

There are now four supernumeraries on the coach including one beautiful young woman, Sharon, who unusually for a courier on this trip, has a courier's skills and speaks excellent English. Another stubby 30-ish man speaks no English but addresses the group in German.

I lean over to Hilde eager to learn what he has said.

"No idea," she says.

Liliana, a trim serious-minded lady from Berlin confirms the man's German is very poor but I notice Hilde still has her MP3 player on. The deeper we get into the country, the less she likes it. We are only a day from Mao's birthplace.

That night Mario, Carolina and I and some others wander through the hutong. On the way we notice in the shadows David and the guide who doesn't know that he doesn't speak German. Can they really be keeping tabs on us? We greet them loudly; they respond and disappear.

The hutong is what China looks like in the movies: terraces of uncared-for brick with corrugated iron roofs. The streets are narrow and adults are playing cards while children play with dogs. The streets give out onto a wide boulevard overlooking the river. It is quite dark. A smiling young man offers to take all seven of us up and down the river in his five-seater. Refusing him we end up in a brand new club at the water's edge which is full of cheerful young Chinese boogying. There is the usual pretend Western music and then a Chinese guy sings Beatle songs to a backing track. We are the only Europeans and when he has finished he approaches us, keen to know if he is pronouncing the words right. Indeed he is; he does a pretty good Paul McCartney and a tolerable Lennon. All the kids here are cheerful and the barman patient with us as we brave both the hubbub and the gulf of tongues. I see none of the posturing I expect at a European club. These kids seem just to be enjoying themselves. None of the guys present themselves as macho. I doubt this club's equivalent in London or Manchester would welcome Chinese as unambiguously.

Carolina boogies with a young Chinese. It suits her.

Sunday 23 **October**
Malaria tablets taken: 21
Changsha Museum, Hunan Province

In the museum are two major archaeological finds; both from Mawangdui. One is the Yi Jing *On Silk*. The other is the preserved corpse of the Marquise of Tai. Both were found in 1971 at the burial site of the Marquise.

Unusually this dowager, the widow of the Marquis Liu Cang, awarded herself a slap-up burial. Her outer coffin carved from a single 1000-year old oak tree, is a cuboid something like 30 feet by 12 by 12 which itself held three further ornate inner coffins. Buried with her were foods, spices, utensils and a whole library of texts on silk. And no retainers.

Local silk remains among the finest in the world. Hunan was one of the destinations on the ancient *Silk Road* trading route from Europe. Who knows how far Hunan silk travelled in the last few centuries BCE; to Greece and Egypt for sure, possibly further North and West. Oriental silk has even been found among Roman remains in Britain.

Some of the pennants and jackets are breathtakingly ornate, the needlework as fine as brushstrokes.

A new guide, a handsome young Chinese with excellent American, explains that as a widow, the Marquise was able to have just as munificent a funeral as she liked.

Carolina, Helen and Anne, who are all of a certain age and travelling alone, sigh comprehension.

"Of course," Carole says, "She had it all."

"Couldn't take it with her," agrees Helen. The daughter she has been concerned about is an actress back in New Jersey, she tells me. She is herself a big noise in television. She doesn't usually volunteer this to people she doesn't know well.

"In case they break into Moon River?"

Several of the younger women, weeks away from their partners in either direction, stay close to the guide.

In the lift I remark to Carole: "I hope the widow Cang had a good time."

"Widows always have fun," says Valerie sharply.

"Takes some planning."

Like the corpse at Jingzhou, the Marquise herself is grisly, mouth open in a mute howl, tongue out. The guide explains that there was oxygen trapped in the preserved body, so the old girl had at some point in the mists of time suffered a minor explosion, damaging eardrums and anus and pushing her tongue out. More than I needed to know. I feel as if I have invaded her boudoir.

As at Jingzhou there are forensic images on the walls. And again the skin apparently (she is in a plastic case) is elastic. It does look like a recent corpse. The double chins and dark wig to disguise her baldness make her very human. I wonder if she had toy boys after Liu Cang's demise? The guide explains that although she died of arterioschlerosis, there are signs of other ailments including lead poisoning. Probably, he adds, from the "immortality" elixirs of the Taoist monks which often included lead and mercury. This may account for her baldness and perhaps a certain eccentricity. Victorian hatters who handled mercury in treating skins for hats were noted for their light grip on reality; Lewis Carroll's Mad Hatter immortalizes this stereotype.

Good on her: a slap-up widowhood and off with a bang. Perhaps bang is not the right word.

The Chou Yi *On Silk* was found with the Marquise among a veritable library of works of philosophy, healthcare and protocol. You have to be able to read classical Chinese though. I find Julian peering through the glass at a 2nd century BCE sex manual.

"Read it out then."

"I prefer to enjoy pornography alone," he replies without missing a beat.

I don't know how standard a procedure it was to leave volumes of learning in the tomb. The possibility that the dead might wake for a bit of a read doesn't chime with the sophistication of the texts buried here. This woman was just going through the motions of ornate burial rather than attempting to sustain eternal life, I think. On the other hand, the Emperor Qinshi Yuang who was buried about 60 years earlier (206 BCE) accompanied by the Terracotta Army, also had retinue slain for company. But he was a bastard and anyway wasn't that Jeffrey Darmer's excuse?

It was Qin who first burned books he considered dangerous. All unauthorized history was wrong even if it was the truth. So it needed to be destroyed. The people needed to believe *his* way.

He united the Chinese, standardized writing, fortified the Great Wall and is in some ways the father of modern China but the philosophy of Legalism that guided him – basically the most inflexible variety of zero tolerance – made him hated. The Legalist statute book was full of hideous disfigurings for minor crimes. He became obsessed with the fear of assassination. When he died campaigning in the South his rotting corpse, the stink in high summer disguised with spices, was brought discretely back to the capital; lest the news should be released unmanaged and the many candidates to overthrow his dynasty be given notice before the succession could be secured. Nonetheless his son Er Shi was a wuss who was deposed and killed inside two years and the Han regime of Liu Ban, a commoner, was noticeably gentler. Some attribute to Liu Ban's* court philosophers the notion of the Mandate of Heaven which states that Heaven appoints the Emperor but that if he is weak enough to be overthrown, then Heaven must have withdrawn it.

The stout, balding Marquise for whom no retinue appears to have been murdered, would have known all this. Did she bury the texts as an insurance policy? The Mawangdui Yi remains the earliest there is and, for reasons which are still debated, places the Hexagrams in a different order to that which has come down to us. It is a rare treasure indeed.

What I do know is that the feng shui master I have known best not only shares the ascetic academic demeanour of Professor Leung but works from a Yi in this order. It is a hands-on type of arrangement putting the Hexagrams with the same lower Trigram together just like my luopan and perhaps this was its purpose.

Until this century many Chinese believed Confucius the author of the Yi or at least that it was a sensible compendium of Confucian homilies with fixed meanings. Some still believe such things. It has suited many different shades of totalitarianism down the years.

I like to think the Marquise intended to preserve the true Yi and the other Classics. Perhaps the recent reign of the only Dowager Empress to rule in her own right gave her a role model that encouraged her humane wilfulness. Perhaps being on the silk route

---

* Others credit the early Zhou.

made the local social climate more liberal. But the Empress Li was as ruthless as Qinshi Huang and a climate of prehistoric girl power doesn't sound likely. I like the idea that she used her fancy send-off as a time capsule in case things got rough again. Maybe I have too much imagination.

 Monday 24 October, Evening
Malaria tablets taken: 22
Preserved corpses viewed: two now
Changsha, Hunan Province

There is weird Chinese muzak on the coach: Western standards recorded sometimes carelessly, sometimes eccentrically. A saxophone plays *Unchained Melody* as if the player has no idea that the song ever had a lyric. There are grace notes in the middle of sentences and strange punctuation. Weird. And then other familiar tunes follow that are by turns rushed and dragged like a soundtrack for pass the parcel.

Mr David tells us there is a show on in Changsha tonight. Actually it's on every night and people pile in from miles around. Interesting. He quotes a price he plainly believes extortionate. Surely even we dim Westerners won't fall for it. We do. There is considerable enthusiasm on the bus for a glimpse of what it is that entertains the Chinese. David is delegated to check availabilities. He's pretty enthusiastic now too.

He returns flushed with success and even higher prices. But they are still pocket money to people used to paying £100+ to see Madonna or The Rolling Stones. He can hardly contain himself. The price goes up again.

It is a huge concert hall, capacity I estimate above 5000, perhaps twice that. And it is packed full. Spirits are high. There is an overture playing as we enter and everyone is clapping and presumably because this hurts after a while, we are handed free plastic clapping hands.

You couldn't make it up.

The music sounds Western but isn't. It is as if a computer were fed a selection of dance hits of the last few decades and told to take them apart and use the pieces to make up new ones without tunes. Just as the music is pretend Western music, so the entertainment is like some sort of a bizarre Vaudeville.

Dancers come on in incongruous outfits: *Cabaret*-style bowlers and hot pants, then boas and big skirts, waltzing and doing the polka to music that sounds familiar but isn't. There are definitely Caucasians in the cast. In fact some of the girls counting in a number, sound as if they come from South London.

"Wahn, toe, fry, fower"

They dance and strike shapes with energy.

Everyone is still clapping.

Then for no reason that will ever be clear, the girls are all in saris and dusky make up and a Nazi on a motorbike crosses the stage followed by two more on foot carrying plastic sabres. They are attacking the defenceless "Indian" girls when a handful of Ninjas appear. A Nazi loses his trousers and is then skewered.

The story appears to concern the liberation of India from Nazis in tights by a pair of Ninjas. This may be the apogee of rewritten history. They are good at this stuff. The rapturous bussed-in audience are loving it. And apparently this hall is filled for these shows every night. 10,000 a night – how many is that in a year?

We leave soon after.

Wilhelm looks at me: "Not a word," he says.

Actually I'd been expecting Bobbies in tutus, I tell him, pursued by rhinos, dancing round an inflatable Stonehenge next.

"Not funny, alright?" he says but this sweet gentle German is obviously more amused than outraged.

The show crystallizes a suspicion. The Chinese don't give a damn whether they attract Western tourists or not. They want the West without Westerners. The shops say the same thing. The vast hall at Changsha was packed. People had travelled hundred of miles to be there. Similar shows in Mexico or Madeira or Mombasa draw on local culture. But this grotesque vaudeville was Western culture remixed for the Chinese. They don't want the original; they want their own. Which is absolutely their right but it's a moment of clarity for me.

I return to my room. The shower curtain rings pull away when I open it. There is a text from Sheila; Tracey, now eight months gone has had to go into hospital. I look at what I know. We're not losing this one. Still a long way and some time from home. Even Wuhan is three hours.

I text Alexander, having not heard from him all month. As he is now firmly in the rag trade he refers to trousers as "a trouser" and fat men as "the larger gentleman." He is doing very well and I am proud of him. Some of the girls in the department store think he is gay. This can be very helpful for a young single heterosexual. I catch him on a cigarette break. Not much time to catch up. He has been outfitting Russian oligarchs.

It is windy outside and my room is very high up. Out of my window I can see the usual urban skyline of cranes and scaffolding.

Some of the scaffolding is made of bamboo.

Tomorrow Mao's birthplace. I have again failed to find Jessie's snow globe. Tomorrow may be my last chance.

Tuesday 25 October
Malaria tablets taken: 23
Local entertainment: one
Shaoshan, Hunan Province

"You have no idea what it is like to be constantly watched," Hilde tells me. "My father" (it comes out "farder") "went to Libya on business in the 80s. This was 10 years after we escaped and he was still being tailed by the East German Secret Police."

"What a waste of taxpayer's money," I say but get no change. She is tough to amuse this morning.

Hilde loves English music and English shows. Actually everyone feels sentimental about Western entertainment after last night's Moulin Rouge on acid. She is nodding to MotÖrhead on her MP3.

As we approach Shaoshan, Mao's birthplace, she becomes visibly more and more uncomfortable, shifting in her seat and muttering. The earnest young tour guide doesn't make it any better by banging on and on about Mao. And on and on. And then another guide. More banging. Then Earnest again. Endless laughable hagiography. Like a tag team in the Boring Olympics.

As I nod off he is saying something like:

"Mao Zedong was born with superstrength and x-ray vision. Able to leap tall buildings at a single bound, by the age of six he was writing his own textbooks and showing his primary teachers the error of their ways…"

Mercifully at the back of the bus, I can only hear snippets but I know myth when I'm force-fed it. And Earnest is only fulfilling his brief because when Irving in all his unmistakeable Chineseness, stands up and says politely but firmly words to the effect "Enough of the Mao stuff already," he carries on from where he has been interrupted. Probably the members of the tag team must report each other if they do not tell enough whoppers.

"Madame Mao was an ugly, manipulative, slimy, ambitious, reactionary enemy of the people with a pointy nose, bad teeth and poor taste in shoes. She and the rest of the Gang of Four plotted to blow up the triumphant (octogenarian) Saviour of the People during his dawn 10-mile run, swim and weight-press but luckily his alarm didn't go off" or something. How do mass-murderers arrange these escapes?

It is four-lane blacktop all the way to Mao's birthplace. I joke; "It's hardly surprising he did so well with a motorway up to his front door."

We visit the village school Mao attended. It faces North with a mountain right behind it, a round, still pond in front and a table mountain beyond. This is excellent form school feng shui. Even if it is not facing South. The schoolhouse sits across a slope which has been built up and levelled underneath. We are several thousand miles West of Beijing and also a thousand or so South of it. The weather is still very hot – in the 30s Celsius. In a subtropical climate, facing North is not such a bad idea. Facing away from the orthodox implies revolution.

Mao's home is oriented very similarly. Here the incline has been compensated for by adding a wing to the side that would be higher had the slope not been levelled.

The house dates from 1887 – the 2 Fate, we agree. Irving draws up a Flying Star chart and we can see it is a "7 Robbery" with the numbers 2, 5 and 8 clustered into triangles. This suggests success that will last generations.

Irving notes that the ming tang was big enough for a family but not for a nation; so the Maos had to move.

Perfect feng shui maybe but the tensest place I've ever been. There is a trace-feeling that intense fear leaves behind in brick – like an imprint. Here there is less of an imprint than a crater. Not in the visual landscape which is a quaint little homestead nestling in the lap of a hill over looking a duck pond, but in the chi. This place is excruciating.

Literally millions of Chinese have passed through this little farmhouse, petrified in case they smile at the wrong moment or make an innocent remark out of turn. How many have disappeared on their return home? And it is in the walls, in the thatch, in the brick, like a sheet that has dried by a smoky fire.

As they photograph each other every Chinese is more po-faced than the last. It is so uptight it hurts. I can barely breathe. I spot a youngish couple with a pretty little girl. They are in what would be their Sunday best if the Chinese observed Sundays. Suit, frocks, shiny shoes. The parents shush the little girl sternly as they enter the farmhouse.

I deliberately inhale deeply when we come to the courtyard, and feel into the flinty heart of this building. I try to track some of the terror as it fans out across China. You cannot imprison men's minds. It's been tried. Drugs and surgery will work for a while but you just can't keep up. Human beings have been given the gift of separating thought from speech for a reason. I see families separated and decent people degraded, tortured, killed. This place feels worse than Auschwitz.

In that original binary choice Mao went in a big way for "No, Daddy." His father was a violent dictatorial man and Mao who grew big young, was having stand-up fights with him before he was a teenager. This gave him the energy to overthrow the landlords and contribute his single worthwhile achievement: restoring the means of feeding themselves to the people. But at what cost?

In the coach park, there is a giant statue of the Great Helmsman, staring infallibly into space.

"Mao seely orse," says Carla.

Beyond the house there is a lot of tacky Mao-crap: medals, triumphant portraits, smug portraits, saturnine portraits, avuncular portraits. In the shops there are videos on a loop, crowds cheering while hysterical commentators make glosses that sound something like; "Our infallible Chairman presides over another bumper beetroot crop."

Still no snow globes.

Up the hill we actually get to see the bath and jumbo bed in the Mao bunker which is carved into mountain. In the event of nuclear attack there may have been no one alive to lead but at least the Chairman would have lived to lead them. This place is total bollocks. On the other hand climbing this mountain leads to Mao's grandfather's grave which is very interesting indeed.

It is a long climb and before that we endure a trip around the Mao bunker. There is a corridor going around the living area which we can view through glass. We see his unswerving bath and his unshakable toilet. The mansion is very cold because it is built into the mountain. But that is not the whole reason. There is coldness at the heart of this monument to self-righteousness.

Madame Mao never came here, probably because she would have been in competition with Mao's copious mistresses. Dictators whether they are Tiberius, Napoleon or Genghis Khan are depressingly similar. They believe there are special rules for them. This is how Mao got his own back on his father at the cost of tens of millions of lives. And still they worship him. There are hushed voices here too but as it has been open less and is harder to get to, it is not as painful as the homestead. Those are the hushed voices of worship. Human beings have such a huge capacity for giving away their power to bullies.

In the West right now the opportunists and dynasts seem to have stolen the initiative from hapless electorates who are happy to be duped into suicide as long as they are led there by someone with charm. The Chinese prefer stern to charming but it's the same thing.

The American Constitution may be the single most important product of the human mind. The idea of a nation run by and for the people remains unique. It is a mind-blowing idea; one to which all democracies should and do aspire. But on current evidence democracy is valued as little by democracies as Chinese history is by the Chinese. In the war between control and everything that actually matters to human beings, control appears to have the upper hand.

After a long climb we arrive at the tomb of Mao's grandfather. The theory goes that it is this placing which was successfully hidden from Chiang Kai Shek and the Kuomintang during the Civil War, that is the magic behind Mao's extraordinary rise to power. We are on a shallow plateau near the top of the mountain. The view, which is flawless, is across a long tight valley. Several ranges meet here. It is called the "Butterfly" formation though there are some who see multiple Tigers. This is form school feng shui, the most powerful and the hardest. A pointy mountain, for instance, is called a t'ang lung or Hungry Wolf; there are over seventy variations of this shape alone and they all mean different things.

The grave faces South East and off in that direction is Mao's grandmother, also kept concealed from Mao's opponents in the difficult years between the Long March of 1936 and the Revolutionary Victory of 1949. The grandfather's coffin faces another way again but we can't see that as it is sealed off.

There was a delay of several years between death and burial. Part of this may have been to locate the site but I am inclined to suspect that it derives from a dispute between feng shui masters as to when the Fate Periods changed. The difference between a burial in the 2 Fate and the 3 Fate is crucial and opinions as to when this change took place vary by several years. One feng shui master when I suggested that this may have been the most successful piece of feng shui placement in history dismissed it saying: "They got it wrong. It lasted just the one generation. It should have lasted three. Mao died without heirs." Pretty good go though.

I walk down the mountain with Mario and Carolina. Mario is anxious; affairs of the heart are troubling him. Nonetheless he knows what really matters: as we trudge past the connurbations of Mao shops stocked with the usual nonsense, he lets outs a sudden cry and disappears into a tent that holds a dozen or so trading stalls. I follow him. He is at a stall negotiating. In his hand he holds the only true genuine kosher honest-to-goodness Mao globe we have seen in all of China.

Rosebud.

I call home on my mobile phone at a cost of about thirty pounds. I hear a cheer at the other end.

We stop at a restaurant on the way to Changsha that evening. The hat is passed for Earnest, our toothsome young guide. Then we are asked to complete questionaires. How did we rate the hotel? The food? The bus? The guiding?

Hilde goes white.

"A little less Mao," someone says.

"I wanted more," I say deadpan,"Perhaps a selection of his favourite recipes. Or say, songs he sang behind his revolutionary shower curtain."

Gitte, a soignee Berliner of a certain age, steps in: "I appreciate your dry English humour," she says "But I think we must say something."

Of course we do.

Back in the coach after dinner, Hilde is curled, almost foetal.

"You must find China a demanding place," I say to her.

"Yes. I am finding that."

"You know something," I say, "The Berlin Wall is down, there are no secret police in Western Europe and even China is reaching out. Things can only get better."

She is not too sure.

"Have you seen Jessie's snow globe?"

She smiles at last. I imagine it's what her grandmother would have wanted.

Wednesday 26 October
Malaria tablets taken: 24
Huazhong Normal University, Wuhan

We have the same rooms back again. This time however no choice was offered other than packing everything up over and above what was sufficient for the trip. All our stuff is in a communal room from which it needs to be ferried up. I am tired. It is heavy. I will have to do this again in two days and then again in a week. I am close to ready to go home but there is still Wudang Shan ahead.

Before we leave there is a passing-out ceremony and gala dinner. We are invited to prepare entertainments which will be judged by the Professors. The prize is one of Irving's proprietary luo pans.

Mario suggests a truly smutty diversion. I'm a public schoolboy brought up on toilet humour so I'm a sucker for it. And I like Mario and Guido and Carla. People will ask me next month how much Mandarin I learned. Well plenty but almost as much Italian.

The judges sit impassively through some touching traditional Korean song from Soon Yi, some very sexy *Fado* from Danialita and some glissandos and trills from Zdenka, gratuitous nastiness from Cyrus and an engagingly off-the-wall piece from the Poles. Oh and us.

They sit barely able to contain themselves as we go through this smutty routine; farting noises and sexual references so blatant they cannot be graced with the description innuendo. The academics love the smut, virtually punching the walls as we perform.

And they award us the prize.

Then we are presented with the contentious certificates. They have spelled many names wrong but we all know enough now to value these. Irving shamelessly pilfers some teeshirts from us for the Judges.

Next morning Cyrus upstages us all with a case of chronic diarrhea that keeps him in Wuhan while we set out for the Holy Mountain.

Julian is not coming. I thank him for all he has done. This would have been a very different trip without him. Joey and I have agreed that I should give him my copy of *Cider with Rosie* which I have just finished. But I don't, fearing he might feel patronized. Silly me. I hope I will see him again.

Cha cha cha.

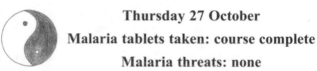

Thursday 27 October
Malaria tablets taken: course complete
Malaria threats: none
Local entertainment: nil, Toilet humour: one
The train to Wudang Shan

Down the aisle comes a little bloke selling gyroscopes. Another blows rubber gloves into improbable shapes. These are also for sale. The tradespeople wear paramilitary uniforms so we know they are tradespeople.

We have new guides: Mr David plus two more as well as the one with the ersatz German.

It's raining and it's been a long journey. The Chinese are just as companionable and bored as any other people on a long train journey. Children snuffle and complain. People queue for the toilet. We play cards and a middle-aged Chinese lady joins Daniela, Mario and myself for a few hands. She speaks no English but there is no confusion over rules. This is the international language of cards. She plays well and smiles a lot.

On Wudang Shan the monks, Mario tells me, practise the traditional mortification of the flesh. They walk barefoot in sub-zero conditions and contort their bodies. I say I respect the discipline but it reminds me too much of Sai Baba and his Rolexes. Snake oil. These sorts of demonstration are impressive but they don't matter much do they? We discuss Gurdjeff who was the first modern thinker to see that spiritual connection was not necessarily very spectacular.

When he first came here, Mario says for the second time, he felt a sense of recognition. It was as if he had arrived at last in the right place. Before the monk gave him his own prayer to float, he beckoned Mario down a long dark corridor which opened into a room where the monk had fished out of an ancient chest the prayer pre-written. Then he had handed it over without explanation. As if to welcome him home.

Mario is a sweet man. His powerful hunger for the spiritual hangs on his sleeve. His father is on the mend he tells me. Told you so.

I am unsettled but I sleep on the train. If you can call it sleep. And at one point I hear Jessie cry out in distress: "Henni's gone," as if her sister were dead and the distress had travelled 12,000 miles in an instant. It is a deep hopeless feeling I think it is what Tracey felt when she knew the baby within her was dead. I have been away too long. I can't get a signal to send a text.

When Tracey felt the baby die inside her, she called me and I drove her to the hospital, just the two of us. She knew as only a mother can that what had been growing was no longer growing.

"What do I do?" she asked, with a calmness that was beyond frantic.

"You have to make it okay," I said, wishing this were not so.

"You mean accept that she is dead."

There is a paradox here. To accept the unacceptable is the only way to change it but we cannot do it *in order* to change it. This is not a trade.

We talked at soul level where there is no pretence and personality does not get in the way. For some minutes we allowed ourselves to doubt that the life of the baby was actually gone. Then we got to the hospital and Tracey was taken into a booth and a nurse came out to tell me the facts.

They have special rooms for these events.

There followed a rapid delivery and then Thom washed her and we all held Ruby as she grew stiffer and colder. She looked much like Hen with beautiful blue eyes. In-laws, siblings, doctors, nurses all wept. And as they cracked Tracey and Thom comforted them.

Back on the train, heavy-handed transport police bundle a miscreant down the aisle, cuffing him as they go. The ghost of Legalism walks.

Joey loves to read the list of penalties from the Legalist statute book. It is mostly amputations, starting with the feet and working up so to speak. The astronomer-historian Sima Qian was condemned to death for defending the actions of the innocent general Li Ling who had displeased the Emperor Wu Di and then because his work was essential to the imperium, had his sentence commuted to the more *severe* penalty of castration. Shang Yang, the first great Legalist who laid the foundation for the Qin administration, had this to say: "In an ordered society there are many penalties and few rewards." All this was long ago but the harshness remains. These people have been brutalized forever. I have seen enterprise, good humour and affection but almost no *thing* that is more than a decade or two old. I still cannot make up my mind what this means.

Several of our party are in the dining car when the prisoner arrives there and is seriously roughed up. This is a mistake; the Europeans are not supposed to see.

We arrive at the station. It is cooler here and the air is clear. I can smell mountain.

David admonishes us to "Move!" His tone is impolite. I doubt this is intentional. The tones of Chinese speech have commandeered the tonal space in which Europeans express unspoken meaning. We can convey urgency with tone. Sometimes all the Chinese have left is volume. But he may be showing off for his new friend, the guide who thinks he speaks German who appears also to think we should do what he says because he says so. He treats questions as an impertinence. I cannot be bothered with his fatuous warnings against lions, wolves and indeed tigers. I think this is actually an entomological nonsense as lions and tigers occupy exactly the same slot in the food chain. So, by the way, do koalas and giraffes, I remember Joey informing me.

I have no plans to wander the precipices after dark. This is because I don't want to fall over one.

But like some oriental Laurel and Hardy, the two of them, one bilingual in Mandarin and gibberish and the other incorrigibly on the make, insist. I am tempted to enquire about whales. As we debate whether we will walk up the mountain tomorrow or take the cable car, it becomes clear neither guide has been here before or has any idea of the local conditions. There is no one whose position is as fixed as someone who has no idea what he is talking about.

Mario, who has been here before, says if there is rain or it freezes, the steps can be dangerous. There are 5000 and most of us want to walk to fully experience the place. His recommendation is to take the cable car up and walk down if the weather is inclement. Irving, who has also climbed Wudang before, agrees.

There may be opportunities in the next few days for a rare closeness to God.

Later, sitting on my bed I make contact with Tracey's not-yet born baby boy. There is a lot of healing for him to bring. He is up to it. I can feel his warm young optimism. What I felt across the 10,000 miles was from him, I think. He is recapping. He is asking the ancestors for help. That's me, I guess. There is so much hope in him.

I am reading Chung and Lu: *The Tao of Immortality*. They warn against the snake oil of Taoist excesses. This is not the point, they say. Part of this text is two and a half thousand years old, the rest twelve hundred. In that very Chinese way, half brazen half poetic, they are referred to on the cover as 'collaborators'. The physical stuff does not do it, they say.

There is still a coach journey to our lodge up and around the ever-rising peaks. We ascend to meet the fresh chi.

A Wu Li master wheels on the coach's TV screen. The local guide is droning on but no one is listening. The view of the mountains is just amazing, peaks nestling together as if embroidered in place. Like an imaginary perfect landscape. Miles of ferns cover the spaces like a fleece between the huge conifers. There are high cultivated terraces flecked with orange plants, planted on the northern ridge to face the sun.

At a checkpoint the bus is boarded by a grave-looking guard. So serious. No wonder toilet humour tickles them.

I read the local guide book; spectacular pictures, beautifully reproduced. The English text is so ambitious it's incomprehensible. There is beauty in its ambition as well as comedy. It speaks of local guards 'on petrol', obviously intending 'on patrol' but I enjoy the image of freelance solvent abuse. The guide books big up Wudang as where *Crouching Tiger, Hidden Dragon* was filmed. Actually I find out later, it is not where the filming took place at all but only where the script places the last scene.

Today visits, tomorrow the climb. This makes life hard for Anne and Helen, the New Yorkers, who return home in twenty-four hours. It is unlikely climbing the mountain on foot will now fit their schedule.

I think about snake oil. Both feng shui and the *self-cultivation* of the Taoist monks risk this pitfall. It is a paradox: we as well as Madonna live in a material world but none of it is real.

Anja who is of the Mexican persuasion joins me to look at the Purple Dragon Temple, which is one ridge up from the Lodge. At the front are yin and yang stone Tigers: to the Dragon Side (left as you look out) the male clutching a pearl, to the Tiger side the female with a cub. The wings of the Temple are complementary but not identical. They rise high up, level by level into the terraces of the mountain, the shining green tiles outlined against the sky. There is water spanned by a small bridge at the approach. In front of this is open space – the ming tang – and a pool inscribed with the ba gua, eight huge Trigrams on the inner perimeter just above the water line. It is well-maintained and the tiles the same green as the temple. The orientation is hard to figure but it is something close to North-South.

As we enter, more levels become visible. The Father-Mother Temple is at the rear, the son at the front; a model of filial piety. There are mythical beasts set in the gutters and their numbers are correct: odd, that is yang, numbers meaning in the service of the living. The numbers of steps are correct too.

The temple is wrapped into the mountain which protects it from the North Wind. In front past the pool there is a small hill but it is overgrown. We figure this as the margin of the outer ming tang which actually is on a roundabout where buses are parked. At the rear of the temple higher up, there are springs that feed the pool. To the South we can see from the heights, is a single peak which forms the Dragon mouth. Legend has it that a house built there against expert advice once caused the bells of the temple to cease to sound. There has been shelter here for 4000 years.

Looking for short cuts we find a recent tomb behind the temple. It faces a small wall and is cramped into a terrace. It feels horrible. A careless recent addition, this is the portakabin of tombs.

"Not a good man," I say, breathing in. "Someone who demanded information from the unwilling. And didn't get enough. He was not revered but feared. This will not last."

Anja thanks the spirit for allowing us there and blesses it. I join in the blessing but I think this man had something to do with the destruction I expect to see soon. We will see broken stones but I am thinking of broken people.

Chung and Lu are clear that no physical exertion or deprivation guarantees awakening. This man believed no such thing.

Anja is young and certain. She has interesting ideas about the uses of the lo shu for prediction. They are very interesting. She is obviously gifted.

Friday 28 October
Buildings Destroyed in the Cultural
Revolution: several hundred
Buildings Fully Restored: None
Wudang Shan The Holy Mountain

Next day we make the easy (South) ascent. There is a lot of rebuilding going on; Mario and I pass labourers carrying loads that must exceed 60 kilos of rubble and bricks balanced in buckets between sticks. There is a lot to rebuild. Shrine after shrine has been levelled. Few have roofs, some not even pillars. Many times my eye meets the eye of a man carrying such a load and I am at a loss as to how to acknowledge. Money? I feel like applause.

There are stalls everywhere. I ask at one where *Crouching Tiger* was filmed and we are shown a view down into the valley that is magnificent but does not seem correct. The pool with the ba gua was more familiar. We climb higher along wide then narrow paths and finally covered passages at the cliff edge. There are towers and a temple above us.

In the temple, monks are offering divination to the passing punters. It is true, they do draft ba zi's and divine from the Yi.

Helen receives a Yi reading from two monks in a uniform of grubby white satin jackets. They charge 300 renminbi (about £25) which is very expensive. At first they take no risks, their findings are mostly vague and generic. They get inners on issues, outers on timing but no bullseyes. They draw up a rough ba gua shaped ba zi.

The ordering is odd to me but I can follow.

Mary wants to know the future of her feng shui practice.

The Hexagram she draws is Number 7: ☷ *Shi The Army*, Earth over Water, which is about organization and getting things done and quite adversarial. The changing line is the 1st so when it is changed it yields Number 19 ☷ in *Approaching*, Earth over Lake. This suggests a reasonable outcome. The monk suggests she has had a hard time recently which is not far off the mark. I conclude he has drawn this from Shi. He predicts from Lin a positive outcome and that it will be within a few months. He reads time scale from the ba zi.

I have learned volumes.

We walk on.

We are shown a spirelike peak where an emperor whose name I do not learn gave up on self-cultivation and leapt only to be scooped up by four Dragons. The Gods had recognized in his despairing act the humility called for to achieve immortality. There are six varieties of Immortality according to Chung and Lu.

From the top the view down to the lake is devastating; like Cumbria in wide vision. But in most directions there are ruins. The Temple's earliest portions date from the late Song (12th century) but most of the damage is from the Cultural Revolution. I think of the guy in the cramped tomb. Who told him that dreadful folded-up position was good feng shui?

The Cultural Revolution will I suspect, in time be looked upon as the high water mark of Confucianism.

Here's the scenario: China realizes that it has been eclipsed by the West. Despite or because of Mao, its arrogant isolationism has made it a Third World nation. So it decides to act. Not in the form of embracing the Western culture that make it by contrast so backward. Nor in embracing and updating its own. No, having murdered several tens of millions of his own people by way of the neo-Confucianism of the Command Economy and unprepared to accept a Western Heritage, he smashes his own. So all over China *superstition* is crushed: temples, monasteries, places of contemplation, irreplaceable jewels of design and philosophy are destroyed. Up here extraordinary devotional work that has taken centuries to erect is destroyed in hours by rabbles with hammers. A moral panic China will live to regret but does not actually regret. Yet. A vast dummy spit.

And now here up on this ridge, they're rebuilding these near-inaccessible gems with Western help. It is an ironic fact that the special concrete comes from the US.

I place a prayer sash – red cotton with white characters – on the branch of a stout tree, hanging over the abyss. I place it with intention, summoning my family, children, grandson, unborn grandson, stillborn granddaughter, sons, daughters, Sheila. I know that things happen just the way they are supposed to. I know also that sometimes it does not feel like that. And then we have to identify the Tao and the gap between it and our preference.

The higher path is easy for the man with no preference.

But there is no high or low, no better no worse, just what is. This is the Tao.

I make to pay for the sash and am told it is xu – free. I ask for the grace to say yes to whatever comes down the pike.

Zdenka strides past; she has placed her sash banzhai style round her temple. Wrong end of the stick, I think.

At the highest point there is, set back from the passage, a confessional-type booth dedicated to a deity to whom one may pray on behalf of one's children. The monk uses sign language to explain that he must not touch the prayer and then does his best to explain what else to do without touching it. I follow his instructions. I invoke whatever powers there may be on behalf of all those I care for, for many that I do not, for the oceans and the rainforests and the theatres of war. And it is as if I have placed both Tracey's lost baby girl and the boy that is still to be born into a single red sash and I feel as if something has lifted from me.

It must be close to 1000 feet down to the lake below. I think of the Emperor reaching that point at which he knows he can progress no further without help. I feel his honest attempt to be all that he can be. I see his mistakes. I see him asking for help and not receiving it and I think of him leaping in despair. I see in my mind the Dragons catching him in their teeth. And then he changes to a small bundle wrapped in a red sash and the red sash opens like a parachute ensuring that the bundle comes to no harm.

Perhaps during the Cultural Revolution, Mao himself looked down from this height upon the destruction he had ordered and saw that it was good. He'd have had to climb but that would have been no challenge to a larger gentleman of his powers. Seely orse.

 Saturday 29 October
The Golden Temple, Wudang Shan
The Holy Mountain

3600 feet up, the Northern face, the harder ascent, all on foot. They say there are 5000 steps. I took each flight as 25, skipped a few, allowed some big ones to count double, left out landings and the initial downward steps and made it 3000 odd. I append this not to challenge the official count but to let you in on how I occupied my mind against the discomfort of the climb.

The mountain is named for the deity Shen Wu.

Mario and I climb together. He is fit. I am dogged. Every now and then I am grateful that he stops to take photographs and I can catch up. Three-quarters of the way up we stop at a place that sells water and green tea. It is a blazing hot day and dehydration is a real danger. We started out with Guido and Carla but they have dropped behind. Now they catch up. We are offered eggs boiled in aniseed by an elderly Chinese with black teeth. Thanks but no thanks. Mario christens the three tressle tables and a bench "Carlo's."

On this last lap, panting, I see specks above on parapets. They appear to be hanging out of the sky. At the summit there is a whole complex: monastery, terraces, shrines, a small city just below the clouds. Every stone of every building was brought here by hand. It's been a three-hour climb. That probably equates to a marathon time of seven or eight hours but when the chips were down it proved too far for the hotheads with chain saws.

Thousands of emerald-coloured tiles gleam in the sunshine. There are stretches of tall shining wall just like the Forbidden City, its twin, also reconstructed between 1406 and 1421 by the Ming Emperor Yongle. Estimates of the number of workers required then vary between 100,000 and 300,000. I imagine that number of people climbing up and down the mountain.

Here is the Golden Temple which one way or another has been here a lot longer than six centuries.

The cable approach dates only from the 90s. Before that everyone had to climb. I watch the cars appear and disappear like wasps. There are mythical creatures built into the layers of roofs. A stroppy-looking brown deity looks as if he will punish unfilial behaviour by casting the impious over the edge. Every staircase is steep.

Unfilial behaviour. Lord knows the Chinese could have used a bit more of that over the years. A small deity riding an elephant that is itself mounted on a cloud looks out over the fluttering pennants and prayer sashes and at the lower mountains that overlap each other a dozen miles away. The sky is the blue of a calm sea.

The lung mei or dragon vein is strong here where five ranges meet. The Golden Temple is built on the 'Pillar from Heaven', the highest mountain in the range, so-called because it is vertical. All the other mountains are said to face it in obeisance. There are 72 of them. Originally the Golden Temple was open only to the Emperor as such height is exclusive to him and the Gods. In time the Southern gate was opened but meanwhile the many buildings outside were built to contain the excluded common people. Whether they are ruled by Emperors or Great Helmsmen, the common people seem always to be putting up with something.

The feng shui men sent by Yongle ensured that a wall around the Temple *assembled* the chi. Although it is windy the chi does not fly away.

There are firecrackers and a furnace and the old, the portly, mothers carrying not-so-young children, what looks like the terminally ill, queue to cast prayers into the flame. A bald Texan with a shaven head and an ache in his gait, steps forward.

I am greeted by a young Chinese who says he likes my smile.

This is so typical; either a sweet openness or some sort of chicanery. No one would greet you that way walking down the Mile End Road. He asks me what I'm doing here. I tell him and he says I should register with Nanjing University. I tell him I had heard they had been 'criticized' but he is adamant they will go ahead. Is it possible he knows who I am and is tracking me?

The sky looks close enough to touch and wispy clouds drift by like hovercraft. The air is full of the smell of incense. People bustle everywhere. And there at the gates of the Golden Temple, seated at a table that hangs over land 3000 feet below, Mario and I sit down with Carlina and Wilhelm. I may not see these people again and I feel great warmth for them. We eat pot noodle and look out over the valley.

22.
SOLAR FORTNIGHT BEGINNING:
MONDAY 7 NOVEMBER 2005 15.54

Lap Dung: *Winter Begins*
Month: ding hai **the Fire Pig**

Hour	Day	Month	Year
wood	wood	fire	wood
chia	yi	ding	yi
shen	may	hai	yuw
monkey	sheep	pig	rooster

An easy heading to translate this one: lap *beginning*, dung *winter*. Just as well, my Classical Chinese being as slight as it is.

To Market, to Market, to buy a fire Pig

Oh for a Pig of Fire! Was that Shakespeare?

Early dwellings in China housed pigs under the residential floor as a sort of proto-central heating; not as sophisticated as the Roman hypocaust but at least as reliable. So the Pig stands for the comforts of home.

Elementally it is water. And belonging to winter and the North, it prefers the cool. So the fire Pig is an uneasy sort of porker. This combination is sometimes termed "Roofing Slate," protective but not robust.

Unsurprisingly there are some tricky implications in the month's Periodic or *Dial Plate* characters: November 2005 houses the infamous 5 Yellow Star, generally thought of as forecasting illness, as well Tin Sat and Tin Koon which together suggest literally 'threats from the sky'. This sounds like bird flu. The other characters are largely about wealth so ill-gotten gains may be involved. Here in the UK perhaps the harsh frosts will discourage these particular microbes.

This slightly neurotic Pig rules not only over this month but over the whole of 2007. So November 2005 may prove to be some sort of prefiguring of 2007. Similarly the month just passed, October 2005 (fire Dog) was ruled by the same combination as 2006.

How was last month for you? It may well have been a taster of next year.

It will be instructive to stay awake to what November may now be telling you about 2007.

Stand by Your Man

Almost as soon as I am back from China Fay calls. She is nervous about an improvement to one of the houses she owns. I have told her to replace a metal fence with a wooden one and paint a door green. She is tempted to let a debtor off £1000. Is this wise? She has little chance of collecting it but won't she appear weak?

Fay was not always a ruthless entrepreneur although she was always ruthless. She lives in the North West. I surveyed her house some years ago, not long after I relinquished my secret identity. As I often don't, I did not ask her what was wrong or what she wanted before I surveyed but halfway through realized that I was customising her home to keep her boyfriend there.

I can do it but the question was whether I should. There was an ethical dilemma. As I was already halfway through I decided to continue. There were gaps in her fence at the South which needed plugging as this is where Qian the Father resides in the garden and a suspect tree at the North West where he resides indoors. She is a hard woman. I interpreted her priorities with the proviso that it was for the greater good of all. She wanted me to make changes so as to hang onto the relationship and also make her independently wealthy.

Five years on he's still there and she owns half-a-dozen houses.

What I didn't then know was that Fay had a very realistic arrangement with her lover. A single mother, she had advertised for a millionaire. The deal was he paid for her and her daughter's upkeep in return for exclusive access.

Recently, she told me, business partners had been letting her down left right and centre. This tends to happen to ruthless people. The metal fence I had condemned was in a wood location which is a particularly merciless place to put it. Metal can be aggressive and wood is what it attacks. They were "witches" she told me.

But the bottom line was that she was tempted to show mercy by letting someone off a debt.

"You're learning," I said.

"I'll have you up again to look at the ones I'm hanging onto," she said.

Last time, she had presented me with a reinspection of her home as well as three rented-out houses in a single visit. This is the sort of demand a ruthless person may make.

"Try to allow half a day per house if you want a decent job and me to live through it."

Divine Mission

This week I have been working on predictions for next year. The starting point is the moment that the year changes or dung gee, set out as above. If you read this a particular way you can derive Hexagrams, elemental balance and much more. Which themselves yield symbols. The skill is to sort through and make sense of the huge number of symbols.

This ancient form of divination for 2004 produced such results as:

US troops to be re-engaged by September
New trouble in the south of the old USSR
George W Bush to be re-elected in a climate in which it is
    virtual treason to vote against him
By the late summer house prices may have levelled out in areas
    where recent booms have taken place
Sofia Coppola's *Lost in Translation* to win at least one Oscar

The earliest Chinese divination consisted of burning the shells of turtles and examining the holes in the distorted shell. I have seen these shells.The turtle was evicted before the divination began but nonetheless the Chinese river variety was actually driven to extinction. Which perhaps explains why they took to using also the shoulder bones of domestic animals. This is called *scapulomancy* from *scapula*, a shoulder bone. Some of the records of this method form the earliest text of the *Book of Changes* and of feng shui. I have seen some in China. The earliest document in feng shui – the ho tu *river map* is itself said to have been delivered by a turtle.

And today one word for the rear of the house is still the *Tortoise*. This back boundary should be higher than the front and always kept secure by the way.

Every year I aim to get my predictions more specific. They will be available via my website before the New Year. I may even send them with that edition of the diary. And let me continue to emphasize that we can always choose how we experience anything. And we are always able to choose from any situation an outcome which we might judge 'good' as opposed to an outcome we might judge 'bad'.

A client recently accused me of 'malapropism'. I guess it's these sorts of pronouncements that draw that sort of comment. Ho hum.

Also, this week a lady whose flat I had been engaged to get sold, accepted an offer on it. I had recommended in September that a huge and critically positioned mirror come down. The offer came less than a week after I finally moved it for her myself early one morning – with the help of a hunky young man who had conveniently stayed the night.

Why the mirror? Briefly (there was a lot more to it than this) the client's ba zi showed that her father was an unduly powerful influence in her life. This of course is not unusual. Nor is there anything inherently wrong with it. But in this case there was a track record of dicing with danger in order to compete with him. The mirror was in the North West which is traditionally the area of the father, so everything she did was metaphorically overseen by him. By removing the mirror we reduced the power of the competition.

So what's wrong with a bit of healthy competition? Again, nothing, except that the extent to which we are doing things in order to make points is the extent to which we must fail. This idea may by the way, seem radical. Don't agree with me. Play with it a bit and see if it makes sense for you. And reject it with my blessing if it doesn't.

23.
SOLAR FORTNIGHT BEGINNING:
MONDAY 22 NOVEMBER 2005 13.09

Siu Shuut: *Slight Snow*

Month: ding hai the Fire Pig

Hour	Day	Month	Year
metal	metal	fire	wood
xin	geng	ding	yi
wei	xu	hai	yuw
sheep	dog	pig	rooster

Time on her Hands

Back to Sue in Scotland. I fly into Edinburgh airport first thing – this involves rising at 4am – and she greets me at the baggage check. She looks downcast and a little crumpled. Her eyes are dull.

She is absolutely clear she is going to do what it takes to find Mr Right. She is fed up with life alone and not about to lower her standards. The ba zi (personal feng shui) work we did in July revealed that her *Big Fate* started at age five.

The *Big Fate* is the point at which a child 'arrives', often but not always, accompanied by trauma. This can, on the Chinese model, happen anytime between birth and 10. Very early starts indicate difficult birth, very late ones a sheltered upbringing. A Big Fate opening at five is very common in Europe because it tends to coincide with starting school.

In July Sue had denied any drama but had since called me to own up to the fact that her mother had suffered a nervous breakdown just as she, the fifth of five children, entered school.

And now arriving back from a long break in Australia she finds herself deeply depressed. Task one is to move through this.

As there is no need to be at her house for the ba zi work, I get her to stop at Starbucks where we discuss over lattès what it must have been like for her mother after raising five children, to finally bundle the fifth safely off to school.

"Freedom at last!" Sue says.

"Exactly," I say, "Except that it was too much freedom."

Faced with time on her hands, her mother had just crumpled; not that unusual; a sort of temporal agoraphobia. How many people retire at 65 and die at 66? Enough to make pensions a source of huge profit to insurance companies but that's another story. Sometimes the hardest thing in the world is to deal with our dreams coming true. I tell Sue of my own mother whose funeral address I had given in June: hidden away in a remote part of Cornwall, no roots, no transport, no family support, husband away for months at a time and five children under seven. She deserved a medal for keeping us alive! Sometimes the best material to share comes from our own lessons.

There were reasons for Sue's mother's breakdown – if you believe in causality – to do with Sue's father and both sets of grandparents but the heart of the matter was that her mother had been in pain. For the doctors it fitted the criteria of a nervous breakdown. There followed years of distress shared around a family which is even now fractured.

"So you arrive back from Australia, expecting your life to take off and then it doesn't," I say. "Sound familiar?"

"You mean I imitated my mother? Why would I do that?"

One of the most useful things about the Chinese metaphysic is that it is binary. Everything is made up of yin and yang; everything is made up of a series of yes/no choices. More complex just means more choices. Oh and of course on the most profound level this is all illusion. Which makes this model even more useful.

"I see. And how does that help?"

"Once you notice your choices you can change them. It's not gravity or a court order. It's choice."

"Going a bit fast," she says.

"Okay. Rewind. You're born. You're faced with a choice right away: Mummy or Daddy?"

"Okay. And then?"

"Yes or No. A little girl is likely to choose Mummy as model in answer to the first question and if her mother suffers some huge upset during her formative years, she's likely to go for a no to the second."

"So I decided not to become my Mummy. Why choose the pain?"

"As not-Mummy you decided to be single, childless, independent and strong. When you decided not to be single you thought you had to take on the rest. Including all the pain."

"And?"

"You didn't have to."

There was more to it than that but broadly, having seen this, she could choose the useful parts of the decision instead of all of it: she could find Mr Right but stay strong. She could have children and examine the value of independence. The ba zi had located the where and when of the problem.

In Hong Kong an elderly Temple diviner had said to me that everything starts with destiny. By this I took her to mean that the ba zi will tell us what's going on and feng shui gives us a chance to do something about it.

Sue and I discuss as we have before, that feng shui will not always of itself do the job. The choice to call me in will coincide with a choice to change. To affect change with a model like feng shui, we must both know it is a model and respect it as if it were the only solution. This may be the Tao. And it's as true of Chinese Emperors as it is of you and me.

"You need a big heavy Buddha by the front door," I tell her and mark exactly where. "Will you get away with that? The neighbours? You could just have a big stone."

"That'll be fine," she says. Her eyes have changed completely.

24.
SOLAR FORTNIGHT BEGINNING:
MONDAY 7 DECEMBER 2005 08.34

Dai Shuut: *Great Snow*

Month: Wu Chee the Earth Rat

Hour	Day	Month	Year
metal	**wood**	**earth**	**wood**
geng	yi	wu	yi
chen	chow	chee	yuw
dragon	**ox**	**rat**	**rooster**

Earth Rat

This month's animal is the *Rat in the Field*. Best place for him you might say. A woman born in the year ruled by this rat will according to Man Ho Kwok, be "garrulous and annoying." 1948 is that year, by the way and address complaints to him not me.

And we can expect *Great Snow*. I am told the odds are so short at Ladbrokes against a White Christmas that it's not even worth a punt.

Dai Suut is the last fortnight of the solar year which ends at dung gee or Midwinter, the winter solstice. Anyone who thinks this is at odds with celebrating New Year in February is quite right but I've gone into that elsewhere.

Stone Tapes

Liz is a high-flying accountant. Tony is currently unemployed. He is in Surrey. She's in Russia. Not much of a basis for a marriage. And yet. As they say, the physical universe does not lie. Right now she is a success story and he's at a loose end. She doesn't know whether she wants him full-time in Moscow without portfolio and he's not sure he wants to be there. But they're sure they want to be together.

Their house in Surrey was smart and unlived-in. By the front door were the Flying Stars **7:9,** associated with insecurity and in the worst case with mental problems. Without going into detail, I urged them to put a hefty charged crystal there right away: an amethyst or rose-quartz geode. Elementally this forms a safety curtain between the metal of the **7** and the fire of the **9**. And a crystal can be instructed to do a job. The imminent arrival of her mother as catminder made this particularly urgent. The door was in the South West which of course is about mothers generally.

I also prescribed a procedure involving moldavite and rhodochrosite which is to gently bind relationship.

To the tough-minded, this may sound wacky but frankly it's about as linear as I get. There was a play by Nigel Kneale in the 70s called *The Stone Tapes* which suggested that haunted houses are simply recording machines: extremes of emotion are 'recorded' in the crystals of the walls and similar emotions can play them back. Since what is happening when a tape recording is made is that silicone crystals are being agitated in a distinctive way that is duplicated on playback, this idea is not so – if you will – off the wall.

The late TC Lethbridge did pioneering work in this area. In his own books and follow-up work by Colin Wilson, it is revealed that he discovered a 'dowsing calculus' whereby he could identify stones that had been used in battle by the width of the arc described by a dowsing cord and he was able to duplicate his findings time and again. I would not be surprised if in time this became scientifically explicable.

I doubt that this is true of much of feng shui. Which seems to me pretty unimportant; I'm only really interested in whether something works.

The Chinese authorities monitoring my studies in Wuhan insisted that feng shui remain scientific and steer away from *superstition*. But I doubt that there will ever be a linear system that will explain rationally how the placement of a corpse on a North-South axis can influence the wellbeing of the descendants. Which I repeat, is not to say that such a test is important or that such placement does not work. I have seen the tomb of Prince Zhao at Longquan which is still visited by his descendants 23 generations later.

To suggest that the placing of crystals or mirrors or dragons is *superstitious* in the light of this is what *I* would call wacky!

It is relatively unusual for a man like Tony to be on the wrong end of such a domestic arrangement. The question "Do you work or are you a mother?" seemed until recently to have been jettisoned as the Edwardian throwback it was. A woman who provides the context in which a man can be a bigshot is legally entitled to half the assets of the marriage for a reason: there is more to success than turning up at the office. Clearly this also applies to a man. But with our fragile egos men seem to find it that much harder to depend on recognition. This takes grace. Grace which Tony clearly has.

We walked round the house; there was water and fire (kitchen and bathroom) in the North West which – you will recall – would tend to disempower him, and both had their laptops where the chi was weakest and worst.

We spent some time talking about Tony's ba zi which was satisfyingly accurate, revealing among other things regret for his disappoinment as a professional sportsman. I told them where to work and where to sleep and gave him the welcome advice not to cook too much. Love will find a way.

If you want to visit somewhere the stones have clearly taken on powerful emotion you should visit Mao Tse Dong's birthplace at Shaoshan. Here the feng shui is excellent: like Prince Zhao it enjoys a flying star "Robbery" pattern that stretches prosperity into the sixth and seventh generation. But there is more pain in the stones there than almost anywhere I have been. You can feel, if you are sensitive to these things, generations of fear and awkwardness: hundreds of thousands of people who had for political reasons to make this pilgrimage and could never be quite sure who was watching and judging. You can feel the need to be respectful at the right moments and the physical danger of not doing so. It's in the stone.

So What Else is New?

I get an SOS from a lady in a block of flats that's full of restless stuff: hands coming through the wall, semi-clad medieval youths, that sort of thing. She has been keeping this as well as the rest of the world out of the flat and her life for decades. Now in order to get her back into the world we are dealing with both.

The flat is at the top of a block built on a plague pit; tens of thousands of corpses, mostly unshriven, were buried here in a hurry in 1348. My luo pan (Chinese compass) goes haywire. Its readings imply angles that my eyes disagree with. It is not possible for a front door to be 48 away from a door opposite! I don't tend to *see* stuff.

I feel it. This is a disturbed place.

A famous actress rings for a walkround. Her very distinctive ba zi adds to the growing evidence that fame is quite easy to predict.She is, as it turns out, Hollywood thin, sweet and very down to earth. And yes, she has just the same sorts of problems and confusions as everyone else. Interestingly the best spot in her house for spiritual practice is full of her Jimmy Choos.

Two of my clients await approval to adopt this week. I've done my stuff. I advise them to sit in the tai chi and *feel*. This is simple to do. Simple not easy. This is an important distinction. If we feel what is up for us to feel, there is no need for us to create a reality in which we appear to have no other choice.

Rats and Oxen

This is the month of the **Rat**; wet and cold, the approach to dung gee, the death of the old and the birth of the new year. If your birthday is between dung gee, 23 Dec approx and 8 Feb approx, you were probably not born under the animal sign you think you were. Many Western practitioners calculate year animals from lap chun, the beginning of spring. This is wrong: the year is born at the moment of maximum yin, the Winter solstice, dung gee. So, many for instance, who think they are **Rats** born in say January 1961, January 1973 or January 1985 are actually **Oxen**. Not by the way, that your year animal is more than an indication of who you are. A properly drawn-up ba zi (or personal feng shui) will consider the cyclical characters that relate to your hour, day and month of birth also. What is most significant is actually the day and the way its elemental characters relate to the rest.

A ba zi identifies the cycles of our lives and can be

extraordinarily revealing.

The **Rat** is nocturnal. It likes dark places. It is cunning and ingenious as well as deceptively busy. You don't see them but if you have rats you know they are up to something. In Britain apparently, no one is ever more than 10 yards from a rat; a hell of a thought. The **Rat** is known for its scratching noises by night. Perhaps the worst aspect is hearing them scratch, wondering what they are scratching and knowing they won't stop till they're done. Few things are less attractive than finding droppings in your cornflake packet.

In nature this is a time of hibernation but the **Rat** doesn't care. So by extension this is a time of busy-ness; not of productivity particularly but of harder effort. Shops are open later and later with lower prices and bigger offers. People are working longer and longer hours. Here in the commuter belt, the trains to Waterloo fill up by 6.30am. Is anyone gaining as a result?

I am often asked what to do about the experience of busy-ness. How many of us feel constantly rushed?

One remedy is to find the tai chi of the house and simply sit there. The tai chi or *Great Tentpole* is the point where the longest length and the widest width of the house meet, the geometric centre, reputedly 27" in diameter.

What you do is sit, ideally at night – the small hours are perfect if you can't sleep – and deliberately worry. *Choose* to worry. Conjure up all the issues that are bugging you. Take a piece of paper and a pencil if that works for you. Some worries will dissolve with the attention, some will indicate solutions. Some will demand planning, some visualization. A few call for prayer if you're that way inclined. All come attached to certain feelings. These feelings though harmless are generally unwelcome. Breathe deeply and feel them. If you do this diligently you will start to get answers and the pain that kept you restless will start to recede.

Some people can't do much of this at first. Be gentle with yourself: do a few minutes and build it up next time.

I was able to confirm in China that this Taoist procedure was authentic. Medieval European philosophers called it the *Via Negativa*. It is best outlined in a 13th century work called *The Cloud of Unknowing* which was written by an anonymous East Anglian priest. It is available in Penguin. Marvellous.

This has been a demanding year and a year of change. I hope for you it has been full of change that you are, like myself, able to see as invariably positive if we will pay attention.

See you next year.

Post Script:

1. On 22 December 2005, Tracey Ashworth gave birth to a healthy baby boy Levi James.

2. Early in 2006, Jessica Ashworth played Lucy in *Becoming Jane* with Anne Hathaway, James McAvoy, Maggie Smith and Julie Walters.

3. In August 2006, Henrietta Ashworth gained three A level passes at A grade.

O

is a symbol of the world,
of oneness and unity. O Books
explores the many paths of wholeness
and spiritual understanding which
different traditions have developed down
the ages. It aims to bring this knowledge
in accessible form, to a general readership,
providing practical spirituality to today's seekers.

For the full list of over 200 titles covering:

- CHILDREN'S PRAYER, NOVELTY AND GIFT BOOKS
- CHILDREN'S CHRISTIAN AND SPIRITUALITY
- CHRISTMAS AND EASTER
- RELIGION/PHILOSOPHY
- SCHOOL TITLES
- ANGELS/CHANNELLING
- HEALING/MEDITATION
- SELF-HELP/RELATIONSHIPS
- ASTROLOGY/NUMEROLOGY
- SPIRITUAL ENQUIRY
- CHRISTIANITY, EVANGELICAL
  AND LIBERAL/RADICAL
- CURRENT AFFAIRS
- HISTORY/BIOGRAPHY
- INSPIRATIONAL/DEVOTIONAL
- WORLD RELIGIONS/INTERFAITH
- BIOGRAPHY AND FICTION
- BIBLE AND REFERENCE
- SCIENCE/PSYCHOLOGY

Please visit our website,
www.O-books.net

SOME RECENT O BOOKS

Colours of the Soul
Transform your life through colour therapy
June McLeod

A great book, the best I've read on the subject and so inspirational. **Laura,** Helios Centre

1905047258 176pp + 4pp colour insert **£11.99 $21.95**

Crystal Prescriptions
The A-Z guide to over 1,200 symptoms and their healing crystals
Judy Hall

2nd printing

Another potential best-seller from Judy Hall. This handy little book is packed as tight as a pill-bottle with crystal remedies for ailments. It is written in an easy-to-understand style, so if you are not a virtuoso with your Vanadinite, it will guide you. If you love crystals and want to make the best use of them, it is worth investing in this book as a complete reference to their healing qualities. **Vision**
1905047401 176pp 2 colour £7.99 $15.95

Grow Youthful
David Niven Miller

A practical, extensive guide covering everything you can do to avoid ageing.

1846940044 224pp £10.00 $19.95

The Healing Power of Celtic Plants
Healing herbs of the ancient Celts and their Druid medicine men
Angela Paine

Each plant is covered here in depth, explaining its history, myth and symbolism and also how to grow, preserve, prepare and use them. Uniquely, here, their properties are examined together with the scientific evidence that they work.

1905047622 240pp 250/153mm b/w illustrations **£16.99 $29.95**

The Healing Sourcebook
Learn to heal yourself and others
David Vennells

Here is the distilled wisdom of many years practice; a number of complementary therapies which are safe, easy to learn from a book, and combine wonderfully with each other to form a simple but powerful system of healing for body and mind.

1846940052 320pp **£14.99 $22.95**

Healing the Eternal Soul
Insights from past life and spiritual regression
Andy Tomlinson

Written with simple precision and sprinkled with ample case examples this will be an invaluable resource for those who assist others in achieving contact with the eternal part of themselves. It is an invaluable contribution and advancement to the field of Regression Therapy. More so, it is an incredibly interesting read! **Dr. Arthur E. Roffey**, Past Vice-President, Society for Spiritual Regression

190504741X 288pp **£14.99 $29.95**